Rudolf Steiner & Peter Deunov

Anthroposophy and
The White Brotherhood on
The New Man

HARRIE SALMAN

Rudolf Steiner *and* Peter Deunov

⊕

Anthroposophy and
The White Brotherhood on
The New Man

LOGOSOPHIA

First published in English
by LogoSophia, an imprint of
Sophia Perennis 2023
© Harrie Salman 2023

All rights reserved

No part of this book may be reproduced or transmitted,
in any form or by any means, without permission.

For information, address:
Sophia Perennis
64 Prospect St
PO Box 931
Philmont, NY 12565

978-1-59731-186-1 (pbk)
978-1-59731-187-8 (cloth)

Cover design: Michael Schrauzer

TABLE OF CONTENTS

The Dawn of the New Age 1

PART I: TWO BIOGRAPHIES

Introduction 9
1 The Youth of Rudolf Steiner and Peter Deunov 11
2 The Preparation For Their Missions 28
3 The Creation of Their Spiritual Circles 64
4 The Work in Their Spiritual Schools 97
5 Who Are Rudolf Steiner and Peter Deunov? 127

PART II: TWO SPIRITUAL SCHOOLS

Introduction 147
1 The Evolution of the World 150
2 Involution and Evolution 155
3 The Second Coming of Christ 160
4 The Evolution of Consciousness 169
5 The New Culture of Community 175
6 The Connection of Head and Heart 180
7 The Paths of Schooling 190

PART III: THE DESTINY OF THE TWO SCHOOLS

1 The Anthroposophical Movement after 1925 213
2 The School of the White Brotherhood after 1944 219
3 The Significance of Rudolf Steiner and Peter Deunov 224

Conclusion: The Cooperation of Head and Heart 231
Translated Texts and Lectures of Peter Deunov 235

For Marie-José

Motto

The new man, who is now being created, I call the man of light. Wherever he goes, he illuminates things with the light he radiates. With his subtle senses he can feel the internal life of nature and communicate with the intelligent beings that govern it. The new man is sustained only by positive thoughts and feelings. He lives in joy. He is cheerful, generous, and easily overcomes difficulties. The new man is a hero with a generous soul, using everything wisely and needing little to be happy.

The new man is more helpful. He is less selfish and acts in harmony with intelligent life, with all intelligent beings with whom he is one. He is the man of truth and freedom who has found himself. He is also just and wise, with new views on life and new relationships with other people. His consciousness transcends the limits of the family, of the nation, even of humanity. He considers himself a citizen of the boundless universe. The new man and the new world are being born. The future belongs to him.

Peter Deunov

The Dawn of a New Age

At the beginning of the twentieth century, two great spiritual teachers stepped forward into public life in Europe. They were the heralds of a new culture with which everyone who wanted to go through a process of inner transformation could connect: the Austrian Rudolf Steiner (1861–1925), founder of the anthroposophical movement, and the Bulgarian Peter Deunov (1864–1944),[1] founder of the School of the White Brotherhood. They were teachers of man's inner development. Their teachings, based on the universal values of humanity, stood in the tradition of esoteric Christianity: the Christianity of the inner path.

We live in a time when Church Christianity of the exoteric (outer) path is losing its meaning because it no longer corresponds to the consciousness of modern man. In our time, the focus is no longer on institutions, but on giving meaning to one's own life and attending to social life. In the past, the churches have usually allied themselves with the established order and thus ignored the radical call of the Gospel to put into practice the message of love, which is the essence of Christ's life.

The shadows spread by outer Christianity have obscured this essence. After Buddha brought the teachings of compassion and mercy, Christ, as the "Spirit of the Sun," gave to humanity the universal love that rises above the sphere of kinship. Rudolf Steiner and Peter Deunov brought the practical meaning of the liberating message of universal love into the consciousness of millions of people.

Anthroposophy as developed by Steiner is a spiritual science that offers a new perspective on our spiritual life and development as

---

1. His name is pronounced as Dunov (with the *u* as in "must"). The spellings Danov, Dânov, and Dunoff also occur. Prior to his stay in the United States, Peter Deunovski changed his name to Dunoff, which is the French rendering. Deunov is the common English variant.

Rudolf Steiner and Peter Deunov

human beings. Deunov's work has its roots in religion, which he saw as a science of the education and transformation of the human heart. His teaching is a science of love to be applied in daily life. With this we move from a materialistic vision of man and the world (which leads to transhuman people and a totalitarian society) to a vision in which the nurturing of our inner life and our social life, in connection with the forces of our heart, is central.

Rudolf Steiner and Peter Deunov opened the door for the activity of other teachers, such as the Swedish Finn Pekka Ervast (1875–1934), Theosophist and founder of the Ruusu-Risti (Rosicrucian) school, the Danish teacher Martinus Thomsen (1890–1981), the Dutch gnostic Jan Leene (Jan van Rijckenborgh, 1896–1968), founder of the Lectorium Rosicrucianum, the Estonian anthroposophist and Hermetic philosopher Valentin Tomberg (1900–1973), the Bulgarian teacher Michael Ivanov (Omraam Mikhaël Aïvanhov, 1900–1986), who founded the Universal White Brotherhood in France, and the Greek Cypriot teacher Stylianos Atteshlis (Daskalos, 1912–1995). Their work represents aspects of the path leading to a spiritual renewal of man and society.

The spiritual being we call Christ (which in Greek means the "anointed one") was known in different aspects to the initiates of many ancient cultures. We can think of Krishna, Ahura Mazdao, Osiris, Apollo, and the sun gods of other peoples. Also in our time, the solar being Christ is active as a carrier of the impulse of love outside the world of Christianity. Spiritual teachers from schools in non-Christian cultures, such as Islam, Hinduism, and Buddhism, can therefore also show a path to this solar being. We can, for example, think here of Sri Aurobindo (1872–1950).

With the arrival of the spiritual teachers mentioned above, the time has come to transform the one-sidedly intellectual and materialistic culture of our time into one that connects the intellectual and the spiritual aspects of life. Steiner and Deunov brought inspirations for a future global culture of love and brotherhood—the center of which, in their vision, will be in Russia. The preparation of this culture began with their work in the 20th century. The expectation of the Age of Aquarius in the 1960s was also an expression of this. In the following years, many people discovered Steiner's Anthroposophy, the School of the White Brotherhood, and other entrances to esoteric Christianity.

In 1970, I first read about Rudolf Steiner and his clairvoyant abilities in the Dutch magazine *Bres*. In September 1971, I studied his book *Christianity as Mystical Fact and the Mysteries of Antiquity*, which I had discovered in an antiquarian bookshop just before beginning my studies at Leiden University. I then joined a group of students interested in Anthroposophy and studied this book together with them. In this way, a more than 50-year connection with Rudolf Steiner and Anthroposophy began.

Also in the magazine *Bres*, I read an article about Peter Deunov in 1978. In 1991 I read several articles about his teachings in the German journal *Novalis*, and in 1997 I met members of the School of the White Brotherhood in Bulgaria. I joined their circles several times a year between 1999 and 2011, especially at the summer camp in the Rila Mountains (about 100 km south of the capital Sofia). This resulted in a lasting connection with Peter Deunov and the people inspired by him. I read and speak Bulgarian, and for 25 years I have enjoyed dancing the sacred circle dance "paneurythmy" (developed by Deunov) and singing the songs composed by him.

In 2007, I was asked by the Brotherhood's publishing company in Sofia to transcribe Deunov's thesis, which he had written for the theological faculty at Boston University in 1893. It was a handwritten text, and many words on each page were no longer legible. By immersing myself into his way of writing, I was able to reconstruct the illegible pieces of text. I also wrote an introduction to this thesis.[2] In 2014, I translated from Bulgarian into English the message Deunov had received from the archangel of the Bulgarian people in 1898. This message was published in a bilingual book by the White Brotherhood and Sofia University.[3]

In the fall of 2021, I started writing this book. Many books have been written about Rudolf Steiner,[4] but only a few about Peter

---

2. Peter Dunoff, *The Migration of the Teutonic Tribes and their Conversion to Christianity*, Sofia, 2007.
3. *Peter Deunov, Prophet of the New Age*, Sofia, 2014.
4. Steiner wrote the unfinished autobiography, *The Story of My Life*.

Rudolf Steiner and Peter Deunov

Deunov and his teachings.[5] He is the unknown colleague and "brother in spirit" of Steiner. His life and work deserve to be known more widely. Their very different life journeys have fascinating similarities, which we can also find in the teachings they developed. The paths of inner development they offer do not contradict each other at any point. Rather, they complement each other and are ultimately aimed at the same goal: the preparation of a new spiritual culture that overcomes the one-sidedness of modern materialism and is built on an inspiring vision of man, nature, and society.

Rudolf Steiner and Peter Deunov each delivered more than 4,000 lectures, which have been stenographed and published. Steiner's lectures have been translated into many languages; Deunov's are known only to a small extent beyond Bulgaria's borders. Projects are underway, however, to translate Deunov's texts and lectures from the time between 1895 and 1944, mainly into German, English, and French.[6] Steiner's books and lectures have content that requires deep reflection. They treat aspects of spiritual science in a systematic manner. Deunov's lectures appeal more to the heart; they are instructive, practical, and poetic. They appeal to readers to change their lives, to live more healthily, thoughtfully, and with greater awareness of their own behavior. They can be compared to Old Testament wisdom literature, and show how wisdom can be connected to the power of love and to a life in truth.[7]

Anthroposophists and people from the School of the White Brotherhood can learn much from each other. Rudolf Steiner offers us deep insights into man and the world, calling us to cooperate

---

5. Milka Kraleva, *The Master Peter Deunov: His Life and Teaching*, Sofia 2001; Eva Kovacheva, *Die Weisse Bruderschaft des Peter Danov* [The White Brotherhood of Peter Deunov], Marburg 2011 (http://de-petardanov.com/pdf/Binder2.pdf); Omraam Mikhaël Aïvanhov, *Life with the Master Peter Deunov*, Fréjus 2014; David Lorimer (ed.), *Prophet for Our Times*, London, 2015; Vlad Pashov, (https://ia800703.us.archive.org/3/items/PeterDeunov/The_Extraordinary_Life_of_the_Master_Beinsa_Douno_Pashov_Vlad.pdf).

6. English translations on https://powerandlife.com/txt_en/.

7. Peter Deunov dictated nearly 1,800 meditative thoughts that can be read for meditation and are collected in the book Beinsa Douno, *Sacred Words of the Master*, Sofia 2004, on https://ia800703.us.archive.org/3/items/PeterDeunov/Sacr ed%20wor ds%20of%20the%20Master/Sacred%20words%20of%20the%20Master.pdf.

with the spiritual beings who want to inspire us. From Peter Deunov we learn to sing, to perform sacred dance, to pray, to connect with nature, to live healthily and lovingly with one another—to live in a new culture. Also, readers unfamiliar with the lives and teachings of these two spiritual leaders can discover that the paths of inner development opened by Steiner and Deunov a century ago are accessible for everyone. People from both movements, which have the same source, can cooperate with each other for the sake of humanity's potential development into the future.

The first part of this book describes and compares the life paths of Rudolf Steiner and Peter Deunov. The second part is devoted to a description and comparison of their teachings. What happened to their spiritual schools after their deaths, as well as their significance for the future, are themes explored in the concluding third part. In 2022 and 2023, these schools celebrate the 100th anniversary of their spiritual mission. May this book contribute to a reflection on that common mission!

The translations from Peter Deunov's work are my own. I received advice from Svetoslav Costoff and Darina Lazarova. I want to express my gratitude to my publisher James Wetmore for the careful editing of this book and to its proofreader Richard Bloedon for his substantial efforts to create a well-readable text.

Harrie Salman, January 2023

with the spiritual beings who want to inspire us. From Peter Deunov we learn to sing, to perform sacred dance, to pray, to connect with nature, to live healthily and lovingly with one another—to live in a new culture. Also, readers unfamiliar with the lives and teachings of these two spiritual leaders can discover that the paths of inner development opened by Steiner and Deunov a century ago are accessible for everyone. People from both movements, which have the same source, can cooperate with each other for the sake of humanity's potential development into the future.

The first part of this book describes and compares the life paths of Rudolf Steiner and Peter Deunov. The second part is devoted to a description and comparison of their teachings. What happened to their spiritual schools after their deaths, as well as their significance for the future, are themes explored in the concluding third part. In 2022 and 2023, these schools celebrate the 100th anniversary of their spiritual mission. May this book contribute to a reflection on that common mission!

The translations from Peter Deunov's work are my own. I received advice from Svetoslav Costoff and Darina Lazarova. I want to express my gratitude to my publisher James Wetmore for the careful editing of this book and to its proofreader Richard Bloedon for his substantial efforts to create a well-readable text.

Harrie Salman, January 2023

PART I

Two Biographies

I want to build on the force that allows me to bring spiritual pupils into the orbit of their development.

—Rudolf Steiner in a letter dated August 16, 1902 to Wilhelm Hübbe-Schleiden

I am a messenger of the spiritual world, sent to proclaim Love and to bring its power into life.

—Peter Deunov, on his mission

Introduction

On the basis of their spiritual research, both Rudolf Steiner and Peter Deunov regarded the year 1879 as the beginning of the age of the archangel Michael. Already around 1508, the German abbot Trithemius of Sponheim had written in his book on the seven planetary intelligences that humanity undergoes spiritual influences from our planetary system during successive periods of about 354 years. The archangels operating from the sun, moon, and the planets (Mercury, Venus, Mars, Jupiter, and Saturn) alternate as "time spirits" of these periods. According to Steiner, the solar archangel Michael was the custodian of the so-called cosmic intelligence, which he placed in the custody of humanity at the end of the Middle Ages. As a result, intelligence became gradually an earthly intelligence, losing contact with the spiritual world, as we see in the rise of materialistic thinking.

During the 19th century, materialism became dominant in science. To reopen for humanity a new connection with the world of spirit, the archangel Michael waged a battle between 1841 and 1879 against the spiritual beings inspiring materialism. In 1879, these beings were cast to earth. Steiner called this the "fall of the spirits of darkness." These fallen angels gained direct access to man's soul and social life. They inspire materialistic science and technology, along with a view that denies the spiritual dimensions of life. Their activities can spur us on to develop spiritually.

Around the middle of the 19th century, a new awareness of the reality of the spiritual world had already appeared as a result of the fascination at this time with spiritism, or contact with spirits (which, according to Steiner, was an experiment by initiates to reopen awareness of the spiritual dimensions of existence). Spiritistic séances took place in many countries. This experiment was a failure because there was no real contact with the spiritual world in this way. The initiates then sought out a gifted medium who could pass on spiritual insights from the spiritual world. This was the German-Russian occultist Helena Blavatsky (1831–1891), one of the founders of the Theosophical Society in 1875.

Blavatsky wrote *Isis Unveiled* in 1877, which Steiner said was inspired by Christian Rosenkreutz—a great initiate who incarnates in the course of every century as a teacher of esoteric Christianity, but works also from the spiritual world. Steiner worked within the Theosophical Society for 10 years before founding the Anthroposophical Society in 1912/13. Deunov was asked to give lectures for the Bulgarian Theosophists in the late 19th century, but declined.

Steiner and Deunov went their own ways in the development of esoteric Christianity. This first part describes their life paths. First, the period until around the age of 21, which was concluded with important spiritual experiences. Then the second period, in which they prepared themselves for their particular spiritual tasks. During this time, they had new spiritual experiences, which in a third period enabled their activity in their own spiritual circles—from which, around their 60th year of life, the new Anthroposophical Society and the School of the White Brotherhood emerged. Steiner's activity in the Anthroposophical Society lasted only a few years (until the age of 64). Deunov worked within his school until the age of 80. At the end of this section, the question of how these two teachers saw each other and who they were is raised.

1

The Youth of Rudolf Steiner and Peter Deunov

Rudolf Joseph Lorenz Steiner was born Feb. 27, 1861, in Kraljevec (pronounced Kralyevets), a village in present-day Croatia, close to the border with Hungary. It was then part of the Austrian empire. Steiner died on March 30, 1925, in Dornach, Switzerland, near Basel, at the age of 64. Peter Deunov was born on June 29 (in the modern calendar, July 11) 1864, in the village of Hadurcha (now called Nikolaevka), which is near the Bulgarian city of Varna.[1] This city lies on the Black Sea. He died in Sofia on December 27, 1944, at the age of 80. Both were born in a Slavic environment. In this chapter we will describe their childhoods and some of their early spiritual experiences. We will follow their life courses until they were about 20 years old.

Rudolf Steiner's parents were from northern Austria. Before his marriage to Franziska Blie (1834–1910), Johann Steiner (1829–1910) was a hunter and woodsman in the service of a count. The latter did not consent to his hunter's marriage, so Johann Steiner left his native region and took a job with the Austrian railroads. While he worked for a short period as a telegraph operator at the station in Kraljevec, his eldest son Rudolf was born. Two more children followed: Leopoldine (1864–1927), who later earned a living as a seamstress, and the deaf-mute Gustav (1866–1941). Mother Franziska was

---

1. The Bulgarian dates in this book are in the old, Julian calendar until March 31, 1916. From that day on, the modern calendar came into use. The old calendar lagged 12 days in the 19th century, then 13 days until 1916.

a quiet woman who lovingly cared for her children. Father Johann was a freethinker. Their children had to be baptized Catholic for the registration of their birth, as there was no civil registry at that time, but they did not receive a Christian upbringing. There was no prayer at home. As a child, Rudolf Steiner was for a short time an altar boy.

The parents of Rudolf Steiner

Until the age of ten, he had a deep connection to Catholic worship.

Thanks to a large number of documents, we are well informed about Rudolf Steiner's life. Between December 1923 and March 1925, in 70 weekly installments, Steiner wrote the unfinished story of his life, which later appeared in his autobiography *The Story of my Life*. Thus we know that he grew up in poor conditions. The family moved several times to other small stations in eastern Austria, where father Steiner was stationmaster. At these stations, young Rudi daily expe-

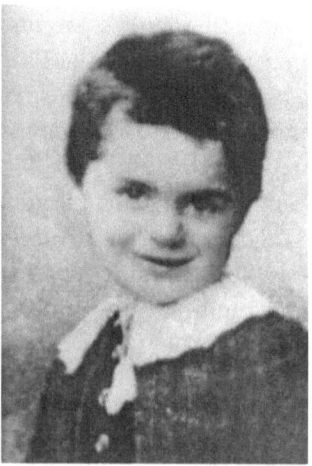

Rudolf Steiner in 1867, 6 years old

rienced the new world of technology. As a child he was taciturn and strongly connected to nature. His health was weak.

Steiner later described that, in the waiting room of the railway station in the village of Pottschach, he had observed the spirit of an aunt who had just committed suicide. He was seven years old at that time. She approached him, asking for help. Swiss researcher Thomas Meyer pointed out that this was a total experience in which sensory, imaginative, inspirative, and intuitive knowledge were connected. This was the germ of Steiner's later spiritual research.[2] After this experience, he also had clairvoyant experiences of nature beings and of those who had died, which he could not share with anyone. He was able to follow the path of the deceased in the spiritual world. In his autobiography he wrote about the two currents that ran side by side in his life: "One I pursued as a solitary wanderer, and the other I spent in lively conviviality with people dear to me."

A few years later, during his elementary school days in Neudörfl, the young Steiner discovered geometry, which gave him the experience that, *beyond* the visible world of material objects, there is an invisible world of mathematical relationships. This was for him a happy experience, as he describes in his autobiography. Later he wrote that a particular feature of his school days was that, until the age of fourteen to fifteen, he made the most foolish mistakes in the German language in his school assignments. He struggled to connect completely with physical life. The spiritual world was then as real to him as the earthly world.

From 1872 to 1879, Steiner attended high school in Wiener Neustadt. In 1924, he remarked that it was only by a hair's breadth that he had not entered the *Gymnasium* (classics school)[3]—where Cistercian fathers taught. "Then I would have become a priest in the Cistercian order," he said.[4] In his classes he was introduced to the materialistic worldview of his time. During this period, he also read

---

2. Thomas Meyer, *Wegmarken im Leben Rudolf Steiners und in der Entwicklung der Anthroposophie*, Basel, 2012, 17–21. (*Milestones in the Life of Rudolf Steiner and in the Development of Anthroposophy*, London, 2015, 10–11.)

3. Students went either to a classical, "liberal arts" school (*Gymnasium*) or a more technically oriented school (*Realschule*). Steiner attended the latter.

4. R. Steiner, lecture of July 18, 1924, in *Karmic Relationships*, vol. 6 (CW 240).

his first philosophical books, including those by the German philosophers Kant, Fichte, and Schelling. A good student, he was able to tutor fellow pupils in high school. In doing so, he eased the family's financial burden. After high school, Steiner received a scholarship for the Institute of Technology in Vienna, where from 1879 to 1883 he studied mathematics, physics, chemistry, botany, zoology, and mineralogy, while simultaneously taking courses in literature and philosophy at the University of Vienna. The family moved in 1879 to Oberlaa near Inzersdorf station, which was closer to Vienna.

Rudolf Steiner in 1879, 18 years old

The Youth of Rudolf Steiner and Peter Deunov

In October 1879, Steiner passed through his first lunar node.[5] Spiritually, the time around a lunar node may bring an awareness of our birth impulses. In November 1879, moreover, the activity of the Archangel Michael as a *Zeitgeist* (or, time-spirit) began. As the archangel of the sun, Michael emanates an effect that inspires people to overcome materialism and to connect with each other worldwide.

At the beginning of his studies in Vienna, Steiner met two people who were of great significance for his development. In the late fall of 1879, he met the herbalist and healer Felix Koguzki (1833–1909), who sold his herbs every Friday in Vienna. Koguzki was a person with

Felix Koguzki

5. A lunar node is an astronomical event that repeats itself every 18 years, 7 months and 9 days, when the orbits of the moon and sun cross at the same point in the zodiac as at birth.

the clairvoyant nature consciousness that was still present in many people in earlier centuries. Steiner helped him collect herbs several times and learned from his knowledge of nature. With him, he could talk about his own clairvoyant experiences.

The young Steiner struck up a second friendship with Professor Karl Julius Schröer (1825–1900), who taught German literature at the Institute of Technology where Steiner was studying. Schröer was a Goethe specialist and the discoverer of the German-language mystery plays at Oberufer near Bratislava. In 1882, he recommended his student Steiner as a collaborator on a new edition of Goethe's works.

The meeting with Felix Koguzki led to another meeting that took place around 1880 with an unknown person from whom Steiner

Karl Julius Schröer

The Youth of Rudolf Steiner and Peter Deunov

received for some time instructions for his inner development. In September 1907, Steiner gave three autobiographical sketches to the French Theosophist and writer Édouard Schuré, in which he called Koguzki an "emissary of the unknown master." Based on conversations with Steiner, Schuré described in 1908 in a biographical sketch how Steiner's "spontaneous initiation" occurred. This sketch should be read with some reserve, however, because it contains errors and is stylistically embellished.[6]

Who this unknown master was, Steiner did not disclose to Édouard Schuré. In a conversation with Friedrich Rittelmeyer, who wanted to write a life sketch of Steiner, he is said to have revealed this information in the presence of his (Steiner's) wife. On July 9, 1924, Rittelmeyer informed Walter Johannes Stein, regarding Steiner, that "He had two initiators: Christian Rosenkreutz and Master Jesus (Zarathustra). The latter pointed him to Fichte, the former worked through Felix Balde [Felix Koguzki]."[7] Christian Rosenkreutz is associated with the initiatory path of the Rosicrucians, which leads to the spiritual dimensions of the world around us; and Master Jesus is associated with a mystical initiatory path, which leads to our inner world.

If this is correctly rendered by Stein, in addition to a meeting with Christian Rosenkreutz, Steiner also met Master Jesus, which possibly took place on the spiritual plane—i.e., not in a physical form. As already noted, the latter pointed out to him the importance of Fichte's philosophy, in which Steiner had been immersing himself since the summer of 1879. Fichte's work is based on the connection with the higher I of man.

According to Édouard Schuré, Steiner faced on his inner path the question of how to deal with the dragon of modern materialism and

---

6. Steiner's three biographical sketches and Schuré's sketch are included in: Rudolf Steiner and Marie Steiner-von Sivers, *Letters and Documents 1901–1925* (CW 262), Forest Row, 2020. On February 4, 1913, Steiner gave a lecture during the first general meetings of the new Anthroposophical Society, in which he spoke about his life. In *Beiträge zur Gesamtausgabe 83–84* [Contributions to the Collected Works of Rudolf Steiner, vols. 83–84], Dornach, 1984, 2–30.

7. Friedrich Rittelmeyer, *Meine Gespräche mit Rudolf Steiner* [My Conversations With Rudolf Steiner], Stuttgart 2017, 31.

the bull of public opinion. To this question he was given (probably by Christian Rosenkreutz), in Schuré's words, the following answer:

> If you want to fight the enemy, you must first understand him. You can defeat the dragon only if you put on his skin. The bull you must take by the horns. In the greatest adversity, you find your weapons and your comrades-in-arms. I have shown you who you are; now go—and stay true to yourself![8]

Another element of the education Rudolf Steiner received from his initiators was a deepening of his understanding of the nature of time. According to him, there are two streams of time—namely, the time that flows from the past into the present and the time that comes into the present from the future. For Steiner, this schooling led to a connection with his higher Self, which comes from the future. He could now consciously develop his inner life and deal with spiritual forces. This can be called a first step on the path of his initiation. Steiner had thus reached a state of consciousness in which he could discover "the truth in the essence of things," as he wrote in his autobiography. This was not based on an obscure mystical feeling, but on a spiritual activity schooled by the mathematical and natural scientific thinking he had mastered.

Christian Rosenkreutz is the name of a high initiate who lived from 1378 to about 1484. He founded the brotherhood of the Rosicrucians, who traveled from Germany throughout various countries as physicians and alchemists to spread a spiritual vision of nature and human development. According to Rudolf Steiner, Christian Rosenkreutz was a reincarnation of Lazarus. In an even earlier incarnation, he had been Hiram Abiff, the master builder of the Temple of Solomon in Jerusalem. In a later incarnation, he was known as the Count of Saint-Germain (1696-1784). He is considered one of the two masters of the Western spiritual schools who can also manifest themselves from the spiritual world into the physical world.[9]

---

8. *Beiträge zur Gesamtausgabe 42* [Contributions to the Collected Works], Dornach, 1973, 10.

9. Researcher Richard Cloud believes that German mystic Alois Mailänder (1843–1905) would have been the incarnation of Christian Rosenkreutz at that time. His Rosicrucian group included the prominent theosophists and occultists Friedrich

The Youth of Rudolf Steiner and Peter Deunov

Master Jesus, Steiner's other master, was incarnated in the late Middle Ages as the *Gottesfreund* (Friend of God) from the Oberland (c. 1300–c. 1382), the leader of a group of mystics who met every year in the Swiss mountains. He was an incarnation of the Jesus child of the Gospel of Matthew, who was in turn the reincarnated spiritual teacher Zarathustra. According to Steiner, the I of this child (the I of Zarathustra) passed into the Jesus child of the Gospel of Luke "in the temple" when the latter was twelve years old. The Jesus child of Matthew's Gospel died shortly thereafter, but his etheric body was preserved. At the baptism in the Jordan, the I of Zarathustra left the Jesus child of Luke's Gospel so that this child could receive the Christ being (more on this later). The I of Zarathustra then connected with his preserved ether body and incarnated in every century thereafter as Master Jesus, the teacher of the path of inner development in the spiritual schools of the West. By contrast, Steiner's other master, Christian Rosenkreutz, who also incarnated in every century, teaches the spiritual study of nature.

Steiner's reading of the German philosophers Fichte and Schelling led to an important experience. On the night of January 10–11, 1881, the nearly 20-year-old Steiner passed a sleepless night, about which he wrote in a letter to his childhood friend Josef Köck. It was the night of the birth of his I. He experienced forces from a prebirth life in the spiritual world, forces from past lives, as he later described in a lecture.[10] With this deep experience of his I-consciousness we can conclude the description of Steiner's youth.

Peter Deunov

Peter Konstantinov Deunov was born on July 11, 1864 (modern calendar) in Hadurcha, which is near Varna. Since this was the feast day of St. Peter, he was named after him. Bulgaria was then part of the Ottoman Empire. Peter Deunov's father, Konstantin Deunovski (1830–1918), was a priest of the Bulgarian Orthodox Church. His

---

Eckstein, Franz Hartmann, Wilhelm Hübbe-Schleiden, Gustav Meyrink, and Karl Weinfurter. See https://pansophers.com/dem-m-revealed/(2017).

10. Hella Wiesberger, "Rudolf Steiners Lebenswerk in seiner Wirklichkeit ist sein Lebensgang," in *Beiträge zur Gesamtausgabe 49/50*, Dornach, 1975, 19.

mother, Dobra Atanasova (c. 1836–c. 1884), was a daughter of Atanas Georgiev, mayor of Hadurcha, who in 1847 opened the first school in the region with education in Bulgarian. In the same year, 17-year-old Konstantin Deunovsky became a teacher of this school.

Peter Deunov's Parents with Maria and Atanas

However, Konstantin's mother had made a vow that her son would become a monk or priest. And so, he set out in 1854 with three companions to the holy Mount Athos in northern Greece to become a monk in the Bulgarian monastery on Athos. On the way, on Good Friday in Thessaloniki, Konstantin met an old priest who, on the following day, gave him a precious relic: an *antimensium* (a conse-

The Youth of Rudolf Steiner and Peter Deunov

crated silk or linen cloth depicting the burial of Jesus, which could be used as an altar). Since 1747, Bulgarian priests had prayed over this cloth for Bulgaria's independence and the unity of the Church.

Konstantin Deunovski, who wrote about this journey in 1905, was advised by this old priest to return to the place divine providence had determined for him, because this place was and would be the threshold of miraculous changes in the world. He returned and in 1857 married Dobra, the daughter of Atanas Georgiev. In the same year, he was ordained a priest. From this marriage three children were born: Maria (1858–1940), Atanas (c. 1862–1912), and Peter. Maria was associated with her brother Peter's spiritual school until her death. Atanas, who probably died at the front in the First World War, was a specialist in building water mills. Deunovski saw in the birth of his son Peter (in 1864) the fulfillment of the priest's promise from Thessaloniki. His wife Dobra died c. 1883/84.

Konstantin Deunovski was the first priest in Varna to hold worship in the Bulgarian language (instead of Greek) and to teach in Bulgarian. He established in a school the Archangel Michael Church, which was consecrated in 1865. From 1876, he also performed the priestly duties in the chapel of the Russian consulate in Varna. Because of this connection with Russia, he was imprisoned by the Turkish government at the beginning of the Russo-Turkish War (1877–1878). Due to the intervention of the Dutch consul, who had a Russian wife, he escaped death by hanging. He was released from prison after seven months, when Russian troops captured Varna.[11] Priest Deunovsky was known for his expertise in Church Slavonic singing. He passed the last years of his life in a hermit cell in the Archangel Michael Church in Varna, where he died in 1918.

Rudolf Steiner pointed out that certain individualities bring their parents together and create the conditions necessary for their birth. He emphasized, for example, that he was himself born, not in his parents' region, but outside Austria, in Slavic territory. We can also imagine that Peter Deunov brought his parents together in a

---

11. Georgi Christov (ed.), *Mladiyat Peter Deunov* [The Young Peter Deunov], Burgas, 2012, 9.

constellation in which his father and maternal grandfather were actively involved in the movement for the national revival of Bulgarian culture, and for ecclesiastical and political independence.

Peter Deunov spent his early childhood in Hadurcha. According to his sister Maria's recollections, Peter was very weak in health and thin as a child. She remembered him as a gentle, quiet, and very sensitive child who respected his parents and listened to them. It worried his parents that he did not speak until he was three (others said it was not until he was six). But when he suddenly did speak, his words were clear. As a child, he had clairvoyant abilities and could predict what would happen in the future. It has been said that he once predicted a storm when wheat was being harvested. His mother took the warning seriously, brought in the harvest, and after an hour the storm did indeed break. Later, he told his sister Maria, who was worried because of an arranged marriage to a man she did not love, that the marriage would not take place. In his younger years, Deunov lived in the world of observation. His biographer Milka Kraleva wrote: "He was impressed by everything he saw or heard. He listened to the songs of birds and stood bent over streams, fascinated by everything new and unfamiliar to him."

In 1872, 8-year-old Deunov entered elementary school in Hadurcha. The school had been closed during the Russo-Turkish War (1877-1878), which led to the autonomy of the northern part of Bulgaria. Bulgaria's ecclesiastical independence from the Greek patriarchate had already been established in 1870. In late 1879, 15-year-old Peter was sent to the high school in Varna (founded that year) for a four-year education, where he had to repeat the first year. He lived in Varna with his sister Maria, who was married to the preacher Peter Stamov, a weaver and tailor. They were Methodists, and in their home the local Methodist congregation gathered to pray. (Methodism originated in the Anglican Church in England in the 18th century.) During these years, Peter took violin lessons. His first teacher taught him technique; but only with his second teacher, who was from the Czech lands, did his love of music blossom. This love was expressed until the end of his life in his virtuosic violin playing and his many musical compositions.

In a letter to Penyu Kirov dated September 16, 1900, Deunov

The Youth of Rudolf Steiner and Peter Deunov

wrote of his youth: "The long sufferings and sorrows of my life, which I had to endure from my infancy, taught me one thing: my weakness. And in the midst of this hopelessness I said in my soul, 'Lord, You are my hope, salvation and strength!'"[12] In early 1884, in his last year of school, he became seriously ill at the age of nineteen. This was possibly related to the death of his mother, who was still alive in 1882/83. In the registry of pupils, his name is missing from February to June 1884. During this period his life took a spiritual turn, about which he wrote in 1886:

> There are two reasons that led me to my conversion. The first reason was reading religious books; and the second reason, my illness—which helped me devote my life entirely to Christ. When I was still young, I felt a force working in me, leading me to some purpose that I could not understand at the time. My father had books that he read to me. I felt very miserable, but I did not follow the truth. My father sent me to high school in Varna. During the five years I spent there, I constantly felt in my soul a struggle between good and evil. Often I went to someone from the Faithful Brethren [the Methodists] to speak to him about the truth, but my hardened heart did not follow Christ. I was then in a very miserable condition, but Christ helped me. I was afflicted by an illness that took me almost to the threshold of death. Feeling so helpless and thinking that I would soon appear before God, I decided to follow Christ—and with tears in my eyes, I prayed for forgiveness of my sins. Soon after, my health recovered. It is my desire to be Christ's forever and to testify for him.[13]

Reading this candid account of his conversion, we witness some experience of his initiation. Since both Rudolf Steiner and Peter Deunov went through initiations, it makes sense to explain here the process of initiation. Steiner described in his book *How to Know Higher Worlds* that occult schooling consists of three stages: prepara-

---

12. Peter Deunov—Penyu Kirov, *Epistolarni dialozi* [Dialogues in Letters], vol. 1, Sofia, 2010, 220.
13. Report by Peter Deunov from 1886 to the director of the Methodist school. In Velichka G. Draganova and Ludmila T. Dimitrova, *Nachaloto na putya* [The Beginning of the Path], in *Bratski zhivot* [Brother's Life], nr. 39, July 2009, 4.

tion, enlightenment, and initiation. Initiation is the awakening of the soul to a higher state of consciousness. It opens conscious intercourse with higher spiritual beings.

The stage of preparation includes the cleansing of the astral body (the soul), which takes place through the development of new qualities and through exercises, meditation, concentration, and contemplation. During this process of cleansing, we work in our astral and spiritual bodies to develop new organs of clairvoyant perception. These are known as chakras or lotus flowers.

In the second stage, that of enlightenment, it can help when we undertake to focus our perceptive faculty. For example, in order to work further on these organs, we can observe beautifully shaped stones, plants, and animals in meditative exercises. Thoughts and feelings must now be brought under control; courage and morality must be developed. As Steiner warned, whoever wants to take one step on the path to occult knowledge must take three steps in perfecting his character. Those who wish to develop themselves in this way must also meet certain conditions. The changes in our organs of perception that occur through these exercises in the astral body must then be imprinted into our etheric body (the life-force body). This happened in ancient times during a so-called initiation sleep of three and a half days. After the resurrection of Christ, however, new methods for this became possible. In this phase, at some point, light phenomena are observed that indicate which of our new organs of clairvoyance are beginning to open.

In the third stage—initiation—tests must be passed: the fire test, the water test, and the air test. This involves having sufficient self-confidence, courage, self-control, judgment, and presence of mind. At initiation, a person consciously crosses the threshold of the spiritual world. Now he can further master the use of his clairvoyant organs to conduct spiritual research on the imaginative, inspirative, and intuitive levels of higher consciousness.

During occult schooling, numerous new experiences occur. One of these is the encounter with the "lesser guardian of the threshold," who mirrors to us an image of the state of our soul and thus leads us to self-knowledge and to work on ourselves. Peter Deunov called this "looking into the frightful mirror." Then, an encounter with the

The Youth of Rudolf Steiner and Peter Deunov

"greater guardian of the threshold"—who asks us what we want to do for *others*—can lead to a turn in our lives.

In two lectures given in May 1908, Rudolf Steiner gave additional explanations of the process of initiation.[14] He compared the ancient yoga initiation, which works primarily with contemplation of thoughts, with the Christian path of initiation from the Middle Ages (which was based on feeling experiences) and with the initiation of the Rosicrucians (in which feeling and will were addressed). On the Christian path of initiation, the Passion of Christ was taken as the starting point for achieving enlightenment. This was done by evoking the feelings associated with the foot washing, the scourging, the crowning of thorns, the crucifixion, the mystical death and descent into hell, the entombment and resurrection, and the ascension of Christ (i.e., his complete assumption into the spiritual world). The intense experience of these feelings furthered the development of the chakras and their imprinting in the etheric body. This led to enlightenment. Steiner pointed out that continuous meditation on especially the first fourteen sentences of John's gospel, but more generally on the whole gospel, could lead to purification, enlightenment, and initiation.

In Christian esotericism, the purified astral body is called the "pure, chaste, wise Lady Sophia." At enlightenment, this is irradiated by the Holy Spirit, who descends into the soul as the cosmic or universal World-I, which—in a long process—individualizes in the soul as the higher self of man.

The initiatory path of the Rosicrucians worked with symbolic, imaginative images. In Anthroposophy, this path has been adapted to the development of modern man's consciousness. According to Steiner, the study of his book *Philosophy of Freedom* can itself lead to a high degree of purification, as can the study of his lectures. Undertaking the exercises from the book *How to Know Higher Worlds* and later texts can lead to enlightenment. In his esoteric school, Steiner wanted to guide his students toward initiation.

During his illness, Peter Deunov went through the phase of puri-

---

14. Rudolf Steiner, lectures of May 30 and 31, 1908, in: *The Gospel of John* (CW 103).

fication. Included in this, we can assume, was his encounter with the lesser guardian of the threshold; and behind his desire to witness for Christ is quite possibly his encounter with the greater guardian of the threshold. He did not write about his enlightenment in his 1886 account of his conversion quoted above; but in Izgrev (Sofia) in the 1930s, after a former classmate from Nikolaevka addressed him as "Peter," Deunov remarked: "He thinks here is Peter Deunov, but Peter Deunov died at the age of 19." He pointed to his chest with his index finger and said, "Since then, the Spirit of Truth has lived here."[15] Spirit of Truth is a title of the Holy Spirit. The death of his ego allowed the Holy Spirit to descend into him and enlighten him. Thereby he had become an initiate. Later on, his initiation continued.

Deunov must have made the decision at the end of his illness to become a pastor. His path led to the seminary of the Methodist Church in Svishtov in northern Bulgaria, where he finished high school and was trained as a pastor. For his father, the Orthodox priest Konstantin Deunovsky, this must not have come entirely as a surprise. After all, he already had a son-in-law who was a Methodist preacher. He also knew that the priest from Thessaloniki had given him a special prophecy in 1854 that was about to be realized in his son Peter. In confidence, therefore, he gave him the freedom to go his own way.

Methodism has its origins in the work of John Wesley (1703–1791), an Anglican preacher and theologian. Wesley promoted the idea of "Christian perfection," which he saw as the holiness of heart and life. The "methods" for developing this perfection included receiving communion regularly, fasting, living a humble life, supporting one another in the church—as well as visiting the poor and sick, and prisoners. Wesley and his friends had a great sense of social justice. As itinerant preachers, they had a strong missionary zeal. To them, the Methodist Church owes a tradition of enthusiastic hymn singing in congregations.

In 1857, two Methodist missionaries toured northern Bulgaria.

---

15. "Reminiscences of Galilei Velichkov," in Vergili Krustev (ed.), *Izgrevut na Bialoto Bratstvo* [From the White Brotherhood], vol. 1, Sofia, 1993, 31.

The Youth of Rudolf Steiner and Peter Deunov

Shumen became their first mission post. In 1880, they opened two schools, one for girls and one for boys. In 1883, the boys' school, officially called the "American Scientific Theological School," moved to Svishtov. In early 1885, 20-year-old Deunov came to Svishtov, where until June 1887 he attended the theological training to become a pastor. Normally this training lasted five years, but for him it was abbreviated because he had already completed more than three years of high school.

Retrospective

It is notable that, at the age of 19, both Rudolf Steiner and Peter Deunov underwent an important spiritual experience that was of decisive significance on their inner paths. For Steiner, after meeting his two initiates in early 1881, the way to self-knowledge opened up in the experience of his eternal Self. The three years younger Deunov experienced his first initiation in 1884, after his conversion to God, and thus his spiritual path of development began for him as well.

In the following chapters we will follow Rudolf Steiner and Peter Deunov on their paths of inner development. In his professional life, Steiner went to work as a publisher of Goethe's natural science writings at the age of 21 (in 1882). Deunov began his training as a preacher at the age of 21 (in 1885). Thus began the preparation for their later missions.

2

The Preparation For Their Missions

Three periods of about seven years can be distinguished in Rudolf Steiner's life between the commencement of his activities as publisher of Goethe's natural scientific work in 1882 and the beginning of his work for the Theosophical Society in 1902. These septenary periods coincide with his time in Vienna (until 1890), Weimar (1890–1897), and Berlin (from 1897).

During his years as a student and young Goethe specialist, Rudolf Steiner lived with his parents in Brunn am Gebirge (near Vienna) from 1882 to 1886/87, before living independently in Vienna. Through Professor Karl Julius Schröer, he met a large number of people in the cultural life of Vienna. From about 1885, he could often be found in the famous Viennese café Griensteidl, where he was able to write in a warm room. From 1886, he attended an intellectual and artistic circle, whose central personality was the poetess Maria delle Grazie (1864–1931). In this Catholic milieu he met the Cistercian priest and professor Wilhelm Neumann (1837–1919), with whom he often had conversations after the Saturday soirées on his way home.

Rudolf Steiner in 1882, 21 years old

The Preparation For Their Missions

Steiner took on the editing of the *Deutsche Wochenschrift* (a German weekly magazine) for six months, beginning in early 1888, writing political editorials and overviews of weekly events. This brought him into contact with the social and political realities of his time. Beginning in 1887, another circle he regularly visited was the group of young poets around Fritz Lemmermayer (1857–1932). With Lemmermayer's help, he was able to meet the 60-year-old poet Johann Fercher von Steinwand in June 1888. This important meeting led to Steiner's "vague impressions" regarding the question of reincarnation condensing into "concrete insights." In Fercher he met a wise man whose personality fascinated him and in whose soul, upon deeper reflection, he detected the afterglow of early Christian times.

On November 9, 1888, Steiner gave a lecture on Goethe as the father of a new aesthetics. Fr. Neumann was present at this event and afterwards remarked to Steiner that the seeds of this lecture could already be found with the medieval theologian and philosopher Thomas Aquinas.[1] In a later conversation with Friedrich Rittelmeyer, Steiner said that this remark made it dawn on him who he had been in his previous incarnation, namely Thomas Aquinas (c.1225–1274). Furthermore, in a lecture on September 12, 1924, he said that Neumann's 1888 remark contained a memory of his (Neumann's) connection with him in a previous life.[2] This meeting with Fr. Neumann took place seven years after the first deep experience of his I in 1881. His karma research now became more concrete, focusing first on the individuality of Crown Prince Rudolf of Habsburg, who committed suicide in 1889.

During this time, Steiner learned about Theosophy. He read A.P. Sinnett's 1883 book *Esoteric Buddhism*, which explained the basic ideas of Theosophy, including the doctrine of rebirth. In his autobiography, he noted that Sinnett's book had not impressed him. With Friedrich Eckstein (1861–1939), who had founded the Vienna Theosophical Lodge in 1887, Steiner often discussed in (1889 and 1890) esoteric questions and the symbolism in Goethe's work. Through Eckstein, he came into contact with the mystical-theosophical circle

---

1. Lecture of May 24, 1920, *The Philosophy of Thomas Aquinas* (CW 74).
2. Lecture of Sept. 12, 1924, *Karmic Relationships*, vol. 4 (CW 238), 65.

around Marie Lang (1858–1934); and through her, with the painter and writer Rosa Mayreder (1858–1938), with whom he was able to discuss his philosophical ideas.

He found an entirely different milieu in the Jewish Specht family, where, on Schröer's recommendation, he was house teacher to the four children from July 1884 until his departure for Weimar in 1890. He tutored three of them and supervised the fourth, Otto, who could not learn normally because he suffered from hydrocephelus. Steiner developed a special curriculum for Otto that enabled him to complete his primary and secondary schooling and even to study medicine successfully. The income Steiner earned from this made tutoring others unnecessary. In his autobiography Steiner wrote that with Otto's mother, Pauline Specht, he could discuss anything that was on his mind.

Karl Julius Schröer cared about the destiny of his young, gifted student Steiner, who was 36 years his junior. Schröer had been asked to publish the works of German poet and natural philosopher Goethe as part of a major critical edition of classics of German national literature. This series was published under the direction of Joseph Kürschner between 1882 and 1899. Schröer limited himself to publishing Goethe's literary-dramatic works, and in 1882 recommended the 21-year-old Steiner as publisher of Goethe's natural science writings. Steiner, who had not completed his studies by then, had already studied these works of Goethe intensively. He accepted the challenge and wrote introductions to Goethe's virtually unknown scientific work in the four volumes that appeared between 1884 and 1896. Steiner formulated as the goal for his work that he wanted to enable an unimpeded "open view" of Goethe's natural scientific intentions and of the entire scope of his work. Schröer assisted him, and wrote a comprehensive preface in which he pointed out that, through Steiner's introductions, Goethe's scientific work had appeared to him in a new light, and its connection with Goethe's whole being had become clearer. This work consisted not only of his *Color Theory* and his vision of the *Metamorphosis of Plants*, but also of a large number of nature studies.

Goethe, Steiner noted, had an artistic access to nature and was therefore able to perceive nature's creative principles. Goethe pos-

The Preparation For Their Missions

sessed a "contemplative power of judgment" that enabled him to perceive forms that were both sensory and spiritual (supersensory). Thus, in the plant kingdom, the "primordial plant" appeared before his inner eye, shaping the development of *all* plants in various metamorphoses. Goethe, however, had never worked out his method of research, and so Steiner faced the task of establishing this method of knowledge for the organic world. In Anthroposophy, this method is called "Goethean phenomenology." As a first step, that which we perceive (the phenomenon) is observed as purely and objectively as possible, without emotion, prejudice, interpretation, or theory. This perception is then taken into our inner being and brought into experience. And finally, we try to receive what speaks from the phenomenon: the message it carries.

In 1886 Steiner elaborated this method in his book *Goethe's Theory of Knowledge* (CW 2), arguing that reality is not yet given in sense perception, but comes into being only when thought is added to it. In thinking, we must therefore detach ourselves from the sense perceptible so that we are able to form concepts and behold ideas in a creative process. We then become one in our thinking with the objective spiritual reality of being. In 1887, Steiner formulated this experience thus: "The sensing of the idea in reality is the true communion of man." In this way, *in the process of knowing*, the path to the world of spirit is opened.

Steiner believed that the publishing of Goethe's natural scientific work had actually belonged to the task of Schröer. However, the latter was unable to engage in the intellectualism of science. Steiner regarded taking over this karmic task for Schröer as a profound experience of freedom, which formed the basis of his later book *Philosophy of Freedom*. He thereby made a sacrifice based on an understanding of what was necessary, temporarily setting aside his own karmic duties. In his autobiography, he explained that our destiny is formed by what emanates from ourselves (in this case, the exploration of the spiritual) and what comes to us from the outside world (the task Schröer left to him).

In a conversation with Walter Johannes Stein, which took place in The Hague in 1920, Steiner explained to him that the experience of freedom has several layers. Behind the freedom in thought and will

Rudolf Steiner and Peter Deunov

lies the moral imagination that makes visible what we decide to do. Then comes inspiration, with the inner voice saying "Do this!" And the experience becomes complete only when a real intuition arises of a *new* destiny in which we place ourselves with conscious actions.³

Through karma research, Steiner discovered that Schröer had been the Greek philosopher Plato in an earlier life and that it had been his karmic task to give Goethe's legacy a place in the scientific culture of his time. If Schröer had further developed his intellectual thinking and connected it with the spirituality of Plato, then, according to Steiner, Anthroposophy would have come therewith. If Schröer had developed "Goetheanism" (the scientific method of Goethe), then through him the whole teaching of imagination, inspiration, and intuition, as well as the architectural forms of the First Goetheanum in Dornach would have appeared. Steiner could then have devoted himself to his proper task. According to what he said in 1920, this task was the teaching of reincarnation and karma, and looking for solutions to problems of social life.⁴

In the summer of 1886, the 25-year-old Steiner received an invitation, as a specialist on Goethe's natural scientific work, to collaborate on a new edition of Goethe's complete works in the Goethe and Schiller Archives in Weimar. Goethe's literary estate had become available then. Only three years later, Steiner made a short trip to Weimar to inspect this estate. He was expected to write a dissertation in the near future in order to obtain an academic degree.

He repeatedly postponed his move to Weimar because he found it difficult to leave Vienna. With pain in his heart, he said goodbye to his many friends. His work on the Kürschner edition was not yet finished (it was not completed until 1896). Finally, on September 29, 1890, the 29-year-old Steiner left Vienna. Thus began his years in Weimar (1890–1896). These were again years of relative poverty, for his income was meager and barely enough to live on. As in Vienna,

---

3. W.J. Stein, "Das Haager Gespräch" [The Conversation in The Hague], in *W.J. Stein/Rudolf Steiner, Dokumentation eines wegweisenden Zusammenwirkens* [W.J. Stein/Rudolf Steiner, Documentation of a Pioneering Collaboration], Dornach, 1985, 293–300.

4. Hans Peter van Manen, *Twin Roads to the New Millennium*, 1988, Forest Row, chap. 14.

The Preparation For Their Missions

he had to earn money on the side. He reviewed theater performances and wrote book reviews and commentaries on current events.

Compared to Vienna, Weimar was a provincial town, but it had a rich cultural life. In this milieu Steiner found many new friends. He also came into contact with spiritualists. He did not like the harsh weather in Weimar and often caught a cold. His working conditions were disappointing to him, so in a letter to Rosa Mayreder he called his stay in Weimar an "exile." He felt lonely in his soul and not understood spiritually. In his work in the archives he wanted to make Goethe's intentions visible, to illuminate his research of nature and his method, but that was not the intention of the project leader Bernhard Suphan. In order to publish Goethe's entire legacy, much philological work had to be done and manuscripts and texts had to be compared.

Rudolf Steiner in 1888/89, about 27 years old

Steiner hoped that after his work in Weimar he could secure a position teaching philosophy at the University of Jena, or possibly in Vienna. This required a doctoral degree. He completed his dissertation in July 1891 and received his doctorate in philosophy on Oct. 23, 1891, in Rostock with a dissertation on the foundations of epistemology, in which he built on the research from his Viennese days. An adaptation of this dissertation appeared in 1892 as *Truth and Science* (CW 3).

Since 1890, Steiner had rented a room in Weimar. He led a rather chaotic life, in which he saw his friends regularly, smoked a lot and sometimes had little to eat. On February 8, 1892, he filled out a questionnaire that circulated as a parlor game at this time. As his motto, he wrote above the list, "In God's place the free man!!!" He would have liked to be the philosopher Friedrich Nietzsche (before

Rudolf Steiner and Peter Deunov

Nietzsche became mentally disturbed), if not Rudolf Steiner. His favorite writers were the philosophers Nietzsche, Hartmann, and Hegel. His favorite composer was Beethoven; his favorite food and drink were Frankfurter sausage, cognac, and hot coffee; his temperament was changeability.

Living alone did not suit him. In the summer of 1892 he was able to move in as a tenant with Anna Eunike (1853–1911), a widow eight years his senior, with whom two of her five children still lived in the house. He was now well taken care of and could lead an orderly life as a valued member of this family. A friendly relationship developed between the two that became a kind of partnership. Steiner had spiritual perceptions of her late husband. When it was clear in 1896 that he would leave Weimar, Anna Eunike sold her house, lived elsewhere for a short time, and then followed Steiner to Berlin in May 1897.

In Anna's home in Weimar, Steiner found the peace to complete his main philosophical work, *The Philosophy of Freedom* (CW 4). The book was published in November 1893, when he was 32 years old. In it he was able to put into words the experience of freedom that had already become manifest eleven years earlier in taking over Schröer's karma. As he wrote in his autobiography, these were thoughts which the spiritual world had given him. As early as 1880, he planned to write a philosophy of freedom.

With his book, Steiner wanted to reach people who, out of their sense of individuality, longed for freedom. From his own experience, he wanted to show the way to this freedom, which is based on insight into the world and into ourselves. Then we become individuals who determine ourselves. The first part of the book, called "The Knowledge of Freedom," deals with acting from insight that arises when we connect our perceptions with our intuition, which provides us concepts for what we perceive. This intuitive thinking is what Steiner calls "pure thinking," which is in essence transcendental. In the second part, in an examination of the motives from which we act, he writes about the reality of freedom. We cannot arrive at a free act when we follow our instincts and desires, or even our moral standards, but only when we act from moral *insight*— i.e., from our personal moral intuitions. We then act from love for the act we are performing, and with understanding of the will of the

The Preparation For Their Missions

other. This, according to Steiner, is the fundamental rule for the action of the free human being.[5] However, because we are not yet completely free human beings, most of our actions are not yet free.

As he wrote in his autobiography, our moral intuition is the force that leads from the morally neutral world of natural scientific ideas to the world of moral impulses. The book opened a path into the spiritual world in which our higher consciousness is rooted. The resonance of this book in the philosophical world was, however, not as great as Steiner had expected. Only 400 copies were sold in fourteen years. In the anthroposophical movement, the book was later read by many thousands. With his radical *ethical individualism*, in which "the individual is the source of all morality and the center of all life," as he wrote in his book, he did not endear himself to others. Bernhard Suphan, the leader of the Goethe publication on which Steiner collaborated, rejected his ideas, and thus his chance for a teaching position in Jena was lost.

Steiner had no connection to the outer Christianity of his time. In his view, there was no room for a God standing outside of visible reality. For him, God was present in the world. Steiner did not accept commandments and moral guidelines imposed by a divine authority or by the external world. A free man is his own lawgiver. For Steiner, the divine was the Idea, which lives in man as spirit. Man's true destiny is that he unites with spirit. "He who lives in spirit is free," Steiner wrote in his manuscript "Credo: The Individual and the All" from 1886/87.[6]

Only around 1900 did Steiner's view of God change, after he gained insight into the incarnation of the divine being Christ in the man Jesus, his death and resurrection (the Mystery of Golgotha), and its fundamental significance for the development of humanity.[7]

---

5. The importance of love towards the deed in our moral choices, rather than considerations of pleasure, utility, or the good feelings that may determine our choices, paves the way for asking a question, which Steiner and Deunov advise asking when we don't know what to do: "What would Christ do now?" We then follow what the Christ-impulse of love tells us.

6. Rudolf Steiner, Credo, in *Truth-Wrought-Words* (CW 40).

7. Wolfgang Gädeke, first chapter of his recent book *Die Gründung der Christengemeinschaft* [The Founding of the Christian Community], Stuttgart 2022.

Rudolf Steiner and Peter Deunov

In the spring of 1894, an unexpected development occurred. The sister of the philosopher Friedrich Nietzsche (1844–1900), who Rudolf Steiner so highly esteemed, visited the archives in Weimar. Her brother had been in a state of insanity since 1890. She came to inquire about the possibilities of publishing his estate. In 1889, at the end of his Viennese time, Steiner had read Nietzsche's 1886 book *Beyond Good and Evil*. In his autobiography, he called Nietzsche "one of the most tragic men of the time." Nietzsche sought access to the spiritual world, but could not free himself from materialistic thinking. Steiner was fascinated by Nietzsche's virtuoso use of language, but criticized the way he presented his ideas. These ideas were not new to him, and they appeared to him distorted and caricatured. To Steiner, Nietzsche was not a philosophical problem—but a *psychological* one.

In May 1894, Steiner and some of his colleagues from the Goethe Archives visited Nietzsche's sister in Naumburg, which was not far from Weimar. Eager to help publish his work, Steiner delved further into it. In doing so, he experienced Nietzsche as a "martyr of knowledge," a free spirit who had left conventional Christianity and traditional morality behind. His thoughts, however, needed further elaboration. That is why Steiner was saddened that Nietzsche would never read his book *The Philosophy of Freedom*. In November 1894, he wrote to Rosa Mayreder that he experienced this as grief. About Nietzsche's 1888 book *Antichrist*, he wrote to Pauline Specht in Vienna on December 23, 1894, that it was one of the most important books written for centuries and that he had recognized his own feelings in every sentence. Steiner had crept completely into Nietzsche's skin and then formed his own image of his philosophy. He was used to fully empathizing with others and then developing their thoughts further.

In May 1895, Steiner's book *Friedrich Nietzsche: Fighter For Freedom* (CW 5) was published. In it he described ideas of Nietzsche that he himself could support, and these he developed further. He was often at the Nietzsche Archives in Naumburg, and in January 1896 compiled a catalogue of the books in Nietzsche's library. He was also allowed to enter the room where Nietzsche was living. In his autobiography, he later wrote that Nietzsche's soul then stood

The Preparation For Their Missions

before his soul, "floating above his head, boundlessly beautiful in its spiritual light, freely surrendered to spiritual worlds—which it had longed for before insanity, but had not found."

In a January 1896 letter to Anna Eunike, Steiner called Nietzsche "the greatest spirit of our time."[8] But he was forced to withdraw in August 1898, due to the intrigues of Nietzsche's sister (who later became infamous for her anti-Semitism), as well as to opposition from the publisher of Nietzsche's collected works. Until early 1899, he shared Nietzsche's radical criticism of Christianity. His assessment of Nietzsche's work now echoed criticism. He realized that there were dangerous aspects to this philosophy (which indeed later found a place in National Socialism). In his later anthroposophical days, he presented a balanced view of Nietzsche and his work.

In his spiritual research, Steiner discovered that in Nietzsche's previous life he had been a Franciscan monk who had subjected himself to ascetic exercises and self-flagellation.[9] He also noted that Nietzsche's last works, such as *Antichrist* and *Ecce Homo*, had not been written by himself, but by the spirit of darkness Ahriman (called Satan in the Old Testament), who in this way for the first time manifested himself as a writer.[10] In 1917, Steiner remarked that the spirit of the German composer Richard Wagner, who had died in 1883 and whom Nietzsche had for a time idolized, caused him to become insane, so that Ahriman could no longer write other books through Nietzsche.[11] Thomas Meyer has pointed out that Steiner helped Nietzsche spiritually. On June 1, 1914, Steiner made known that he had struggled for years with Ahriman to give back to "someone" his intellect, which he was in danger of losing to Ahriman in the spiritual world. Everything speaks for the fact that this "someone" had been Nietzsche.[12]

---

8. Rudolf Steiner, *Letters*, vol. II (1890–1925) (CW 39), 278.

9. Rudolf Steiner, lecture of March 15, 1924, in: *Karmic Relationships*, vol. 1 (CW 235), 162–66.

10. Rudolf Steiner, lecture of July 20, 1924, in *Karmic Relationships*, vol. 6 (CW 240).

11. Rudolf Steiner, lecture of November 11, 1917, in *The Working of Individual Spirits in Human Souls* (CW 178).

12. Meyer, *Milestones in the Life of Rudolf Steiner*, 47.

Rudolf Steiner and Peter Deunov

In 1896 Rudolf Steiner's work in the Goethe and Schiller Archives came to an end. He also brought to a close his work on the Kürschner edition of Goethe's natural science writings and summarized his work as a Goethe specialist in the book *Goethe's World Conception* (CW 6), published in 1897. He had elaborated Goethe's method of research and shown that in his work lay the seeds that should "bring modern natural science to maturity." He had hoped that Goetheanism might be brought into German spiritual life, but this was not the intention of the Goethe Archives. Steiner's hopes had not been fulfilled, nor did he now have any prospects for an academic career. In the spring of 1897, he decided to take over the Berlin literary magazine *Magazin für Literatur* and settle in the metropolis of Berlin as an independent editor. He wanted to highlight spiritual impulses in this magazine. He moved back in with Anna Eunike and married her on October 30, 1899.

A new period in his life commenced. During his Berlin years, Steiner had had to focus on his readers as a magazine editor and on his listeners as a speaker in various circles. Until 1899, in the literary circle of his co-editor Otto Erich Hartleben, he could often be found in cafes until late into the night, in the company of people living on the fringes of society. He published on literature, theater, and dramaturgy, as well as on sociological, psychological, and political issues. Moreover, he wrote about contemporaries and recently deceased people. In addition, he was personally involved in literary activities and theater performances. Because it was difficult to keep the journal afloat financially, he turned it over to others at the end of the summer of 1900. He had not yet abandoned the idea of an academic career, for in September of that year he attempted to secure a lectureship at the Humboldt Academy in Berlin, but his application came too late.

Between 1899 and 1905, Steiner taught at the Socialist Workers' Formation School in Berlin, where he gave lectures on historical subjects based on his own spiritual insights, and presented exercises in elocution. In his autobiography, he wrote, "I had to raise [the conscience of the workers] from materialism to idealism." A popular lecturer, he participated with Anne Eunike in the workers' Sunday outings. He also gave lectures to other groups of workers.

The Preparation For Their Missions

Rudolf Steiner in 1900, 39 years old

Eventually, his activity was prevented by socialist leaders at the school. They rejected his freedom impulse. In 1900 Steiner joined the Giordano Bruno circle, founded by the writer Bruno Wille. Here, lectures on spiritual topics took place and discussions were held. Steiner was active in this circle until 1905.

From his 35th birthday, on February 27, 1896, a profound inner change began to take place in Steiner's soul in Weimar, which continued in Berlin. Now a greater attention to the world of the senses awoke in him. Before that time (as he writes in his autobiography), he had great difficulties in perceiving and remembering details of sensually visible things. He had hitherto lived in the world of ideas, but was now able to make observations in the spiritual world with heightened mental perception. In addition, sensory perception of other people led him to a much more direct revelation of their spirit and soul.

In his autobiography, Steiner emphasized the significance of meditation for gaining insights into the spiritual world. He had lived a meditative life before, but now determined that his soul life needed meditation. In his soul, he experienced that his thinking and willing connected more strongly. His noted that his inner spiritual man also anchored himself more firmly in the spiritual world, and he understood that his encounters with people during these first years in Berlin belonged to his destiny and were meaningful.

Another aspect of the turnaround in his soul concerned the ordering of his life. He used to sometimes put off work; now he kept appointments. He had always drunk a lot of alcohol with his friends. This he already did in Vienna, and it continued in Berlin. By consuming alcohol we weaken the connection with the spiritual world, and Steiner may have needed this to get a sharper perception of the sensory world—and perhaps also to get rid of his innate clairvoyance. But on a certain day in the summer of 1899 his use of alcohol, tobacco, and meat suddenly ceased, as the Eunike family noticed.[13] He now limited himself to drinking coffee.

In his autobiography, Steiner described the first years in Berlin, from 1897 to about 1899, as a time of hard trials, of karmic resistances, that he needed for his spiritual development. During this period, he passed through his second lunar node (May 1898). For him, the objective study of nature (as practiced in natural science) was the basis for spiritual knowledge. He also knew that the spiritual beings he later called *ahrimanic* are led by the fallen angel Ahri-

---

13. Gädeke, "Rudolf Steiners Weg zum Christentum und zur Religion," chap. 1 of his book *Die Gründung der Christengemeinschaft*, referring to a letter of Emil Bock of August 27, 1927, to his wife.

The Preparation For Their Missions

man. They inspire people to conceive of nature materialistically, as a mechanism, thereby bringing hardening tendencies into the soul. Against these demonic beings Steiner had to wage an inner struggle. He writes: "I then had to preserve my spiritual conceptions during inner storms."

On the basis of these views, he took issue in his book *Haeckel and His Opponents* (published in 1900) with the controversial German biologist Ernst Haeckel, who propagated Darwin's theory of evolution. Steiner emphasized the importance of evolutionary thought because he saw in it the basis of a spiritual theory of evolution. He knew Haeckel personally and dedicated to him the book *Welt- und Lebensanschauungen im 19. Jahrhundert*, published in 1901. In 1914, he published an expanded version of this book, *The Riddles of Philosophy* (CW 18), which is a history of philosophy.

Steiner also had to contrast his ethical individualism with the views of German philosopher Max Stirner and his followers, including his friend John Henry Mackay, now in connection with other beings he later called luciferic. Their operation is opposite to that of the ahrimanic beings, in that they bring people into a world of illusions and into a state of pride. Steiner felt himself drawn into "a kind of abyss" here around 1898, and he wrote about this in his 1899 article "Egoism in Philosophy." He was himself concerned with an individualism that is purely human in the inner life and should not be drawn into politics.

We can consider this period of spiritual struggle against ahrimanic and luciferic forces as part of Steiner's path of trials on his yet to be described path to the Holy Grail.[14] These trials he had to overcome in his spiritual development. At the same time, Steiner also felt that the new century would bring to humanity a new spiritual light. This he would later confirm in his vision that in 1899 an age of spiritual darkness, the Kali Yuga, had ended and the Satya Yuga, the age of light, had arrived. Earlier, Blavatsky had described the years 1897/98 as the end of the dark age.

On the occasion of Goethe's 150th birthday, Steiner published the

---

14. Ewald Koepke, *Rudolf Steiner und das Gralsmysterium* [Rudolf Steiner and the Grail Mystery], Stuttgart, 2005, chap. VIII.

article "Goethe's Secret Revelation" in his journal on August 28, 1899, discussing the contents of his *Fairy Tale of the Green Snake and the Beautiful Lily* in an esoteric way.[15] He had been studying it for more than ten years and was now, for the first time, able to "bring out the esoteric that lived in it."

In his interpretation of Goethe's *Fairy Tale*, Steiner showed that by 1899 he had found a new access to the essence of Christianity. Because he had not been raised as a Christian at home, he could explore the essence of Christianity more open-mindedly. As an outsider, he had observed the narrow-mindedness of the Christianity of his time. It had made men unfree and God omnipotent, which is why in 1892 he had written down as a sort of motto "In God's place the free man!!!"

Rudolf Steiner was a freethinker. He found his views on Christianity confirmed in the thoughts of Friedrich Nietzsche. When asked by Rittelmeyer if he thought about Christ during his natural science days, as he did later, Steiner said, "I remember that already about my 25th year in a conversation [with Father Neumann, around 1886] I thought about Christ in that way. After that, it temporarily faded into the background. I had to go through all that. It was a karmic necessity."[16] Steiner first had to make his "journey to hell," his "journey into the underworld," in order to learn about Ahriman's world. He saw no contradiction in his biography in terms of his relationship to Christianity. Compared to the time before 1900, his spiritual powers of perception had grown. He would later remark that his 1893 book *Philosophy of Freedom* was "built on the Christ impulse."

In the early years of his Berlin days, Steiner sought the path from outer Christianity to the living Christ. In his autobiography he wrote that, after his inner struggle in the spiritual world, he had to immerse himself in Christianity. Like a seed, its contents began to unfold in his soul between the summer of 1899 and the summer of 1901 as an inner phenomenon. He writes: "The evolution of my soul

---

15. Johann Wolfgang von Goethe, *Fairy Tale of the Green Snake and the Beautiful Lily*, Stourbridge, 2007.
16. Friedrich Rittelmeyer, *Rudolf Steiner Enters My Life*, Stourbridge, 2013, ch. 6.

The Preparation For Their Missions

rested upon the fact that I stood before the mystery of Golgotha [the death and resurrection of Christ] in most inward celebration of knowledge."[17] This inner transformation must have taken several years.

Rudolf Steiner was very reticent about his spiritual experiences during these years. He went through an initiation such as he described in his book *Knowledge of Higher Worlds* (based on articles from 1904/05). On this path, trials and inner struggles are triggered by an encounter with the lesser guardian of the threshold, who holds up to man a mirror of his positive and negative qualities. Weaknesses must be overcome before entering the spiritual world in full consciousness. Steiner must have faced and overcome his inclination to alcohol and tobacco. As we have seen, he battled with luciferic and ahrimanic beings. In the next stage, man meets the greater guardian of the threshold, who asks him whether he wants to work for others and thereby follow Christ—or, to only seek his own salvation. In this encounter, Steiner must have chosen to go the way of *Imitatio Christi* and work for the spiritual development of mankind.

His encounter with Christ, his having stood before the mystery of Golgotha, possibly had another dimension as well. Heinz Eckhoff noted that, when asked by Ernst Lehrs how a scar had appeared on his left temple, Steiner is said to have replied that it had happened when he received an imprint of the I of Jesus.[18] Shortly before the baptism in the Jordan (we will come back to this), the I of the Solomonic Jesus left the spiritual bodies of the Nathanic Jesus of Nazareth[19]—including his I-organization,[20] with which it was pre-

---

17. Rudolf Steiner, *The Story of My Life*, end of chap. XXVI.
18. Benjamin Schmidt, "Rudolf Steiner und die 'Ich-Abbilder des Jesus Christus'" [Rudolf Steiner and the "I-imprints of Jesus Christ"], in *Der Europäer*, July–August 2009, 45–48. See also T.H. Meyer, *Rudolf Steiner's Core Mission*, Forest Row, 2010.
19. The Solomonic Jesus, whose birth is described in Matthew's gospel, is descended from King Solomon, a son of King David. The Nathanic Jesus in the gospel of Luke is descended from Nathan, another son of King David.
20. The I-organization or I-carrier, formed by the I, is the expression of the immortal I, which through its incarnation intervenes in the body and works on the transformation of its sheaths.

viously deeply connected. After-effects of the connection with the I of the Solomonic Jesus remained in this Nathanic I-organization. More important, however, is that during the next three years this I-organization received the powerful effect of the macrocosmic Christ-I and was thereby transformed, "elevated." After the Mystery of Golgotha, an imprint of this Christ-working, as it were, remained in the I-organization of the Nathanic Jesus of Nazareth. Thus, by virtue of the occult law of multiplication, copies of this I-organization then came into being. The imprint of the I of Jesus of Nazareth, which Steiner may have received, corresponds to such a copy.

After Nietzsche's death on August 25, 1900, Steiner gave three lectures in his memory. When this became known in Countess Brockdorff's Theosophical circle, he was invited to give a similar lecture at the Theosophical Library in Berlin on September 22, 1900. At this time he had given up his editorship of the *Magazin für Litteratur* and applied in vain for a university lectureship. We can speak here of a dramatic turn of destiny, for his Theosophical listeners were so moved by his way of speaking that he was asked to give another lecture. As early as September 29, he spoke on Goethe's *Fairy Tale*, and a week later began a series of more than twenty lectures on German mysticism. These lectures continued into the spring of 1901 and were attended by about twenty people. In the winter season of 1901/02, he held a lecture series on Christianity as mystical fact and the mysteries of antiquity. The contents of both lecture cycles appeared in book form (CW 7 and 8).

On November 17, 1901, one of the listeners, Marie von Sivers (1867–1948), asked him "whether it was not very necessary, after all, to create a spiritual movement in Europe," and whether it might not be possible to bring the Theosophical wisdom in a way that would be more appropriate to European spiritual life and take into account the impulse of Christ. To this, Steiner replied, "It is certainly necessary to create a spiritual-scientific movement; I will only allow myself to be available for such a movement that ties in with Western occultism, and exclusively with it, and develops it further."[21] Later, according to Johanna Mücke, he said, "With that, I had been given the opportu-

---

21. Quoted in Christoph Lindenberg, *Rudolf Steiner*, Stuttgart, 2011, vol. 1, 326.

nity to work in the sense I had in mind. The question had been put to me, and I could, from the point of view of spiritual laws, begin to answer such a question."[22] Countess Brockdorff wanted to engage the 40-year-old Steiner for Theosophical work in Germany; and as early as December 1901, consultations were held on the subject. A new period in his life began in 1902, when he acted as a spiritual teacher within the German branch of the Theosophical Society.

There are indications that this major turning point in Steiner's life was the result of a spiritual intervention, and that he was guided to his new mission by a spiritual master. On September 28, 1911, in Neuchâtel, Switzerland, Steiner spoke of such interventions by Christian Rosenkreutz to bring people out of a karmic crisis that could lead to the end of their lives, and in fact that it was along such lines that he calls his disciples.[23] Steiner told Friedrich Rittelmeyer around 1917 that he was once suddenly saved by a Master when he was about to do something that would have "brought him death."[24] This might have happened in a situation where Steiner was possibly in danger of succumbing to alcohol in 1899, and thus would have lost his spiritual mission.

Behind his decision to become active in the Theosophical Society was probably Christian Rosenkreutz, who had previously sought to reopen access to esoteric Christianity through Blavatsky. Of this, Steiner wrote in a letter to Marie von Sivers dated Jan. 9, 1905:

> I can only tell you that if the Master had not managed to convince me that, in spite of all this, Theosophy is necessary for our time: then, even after 1901, I would have written only philosophical books and spoken literarily and philosophically.

He was then "instructed to take care of the Christian element." The writing of the articles on the path of schooling collected in the book *Knowledge of Higher Worlds* (CW 10) and of his book *Outline of Occult Science* (CW 13) was apparently done under the inspiration of Christian Rosenkreutz.

---

22. Conrad Schachenmann, *Marie Steiner-von Sivers*, Basel, 1984, 64.
23. Rudolf Steiner, lecture of September 28, 1911, in *Esoteric Christianity and the Mission of Christian Rosenkreutz* (CW 130).
24. Rittelmeyer, *Rudolf Steiner Enters My Life*, chap. 8.

Rudolf Steiner and Peter Deunov

Peter Deunov

Rudolf Steiner's adult years until the beginning of his spiritual mission cover a period of about 20 years (1882–1902). In the life of the three years younger Peter Deunov, we now describe such a period of about 15 years (1885–1900). For the 20-year-old Deunov, a decade of training as a Methodist pastor and theologian began in 1885. According to Tsvetan Tsvetanov, one of his classmates in the school of Svishtov, he was a very good and intelligent student and his skills in preaching were second to none. Like the elementary school in Hadurcha and the high school in Varna, the American school in Svishtov also offered an excellent education.

Peter Deunov (back right) in 1886 with fellow students

The Preparation For Their Missions

After completing his education in the school year 1887/88, the 23-year-old Deunov gained practical experience during a year as pastor and teacher in a small Methodist congregation in Hotantsa (near Ruse, on the Danube). The congregation's school had twenty pupils. There he wrote his first song, a hymn of praise to Melchizedek, the priest of the Most High God, who in the Old Testament performed an offering of bread and wine and blessed Abraham.

> To the heavenly King
> Forward! Forward into battle
> For the glory of the heavenly King,
> The King of justice, peace, and love.
> Peace and love, peace and love, love, love!
> Glory, glory is due to You.
> You are King of justice and peace,
> You are King of justice and peace,
> Peace and love, peace and love,
> Peace and love, peace and love, love, love!

In the reminiscences of Angel Zhelyazkov we read:

> The children of Hotantsa who passed through the class of their teacher Peter Deunov have unforgettable memories of the days of their first education. Central to these memories is the image of this dedicated and strange teacher who performs the dual task of an education in the atmosphere of the classroom and beyond its walls. An educator who enlightens the mind and shapes the heart and soul. An educator who simultaneously introduces you to an outer world of objects and to an inner, incomparable world of small and large processes that leave lasting traces. An educator who seeks your well-being and that of your fellow human beings. An educator who is not sparing with his knowledge, but wants you to know what he knows, to act in the Spirit of Truth, which is not a personal possession. An educator who has passed on his love to those who have had the privilege of hearing him in the classroom and outside the walls in life.[25]

Teachers at the Svishtov school made it possible for graduates to continue their education at Methodist Drew Seminary in Madison,

---

25. *Mladiyat Peter Deunov* [The Young Peter Deunov], 34–35.

Rudolf Steiner and Peter Deunov

New Jersey, about 50 miles from New York. On their recommendation, the 24-year-old Deunov made the sea voyage to New York in August 1888, which must have been via Hamburg or Liverpool, and attended a two-year theological course in Madison with eminent professors during the years 1888–1890. He was not a regular student, for he was already a pastor. However, he could not earn an American bachelor's or master's degree because he did not have a Bachelor of Arts. The first year was preparatory. He attended college and read much. In the second year, he practiced preaching. During this time, he obtained a license to practice as a preacher in the United States.

Probably he had originally planned to return to Bulgaria after two years, but he wanted to augment his knowledge and take advantage of the opportunities he had at the seminary in Drew. Starting in 1890, he stayed at the seminary for two more years and did a practicum in congregations in New Jersey. He worked as a Methodist missionary in New York City, in Manhattan's Chinatown. In this city, he was introduced to the musical culture of the time. In addition, he worked to pay for his stay, among other things by playing his violin in the streets and lugging suitcases for travelers.

Peter Deunov in 1891, 27 years old

The Preparation For Their Missions

In October 1892, the 28-year-old Deunov enrolled at Boston Methodist University, where he graduated in theology shortly before his 29th birthday on June 7, 1893. As a non-regular student, he did not obtain a bachelor's degree in theology. During this academic year, he wrote the thesis *The Migration of the Germanic Tribes and Their Christianization.*[26] In it he pointed out the important role of the Visigoth bishop Wulfila, who in the fourth century had translated the Bible into Gothic. This was a language that all Germanic tribes could understand, and in this way Christianity could spread among the Germanic people within the Roman Empire. It was important to Deunov that Wulfila had made this translation in northern Bulgaria, not far from Svishtov, where he himself had been educated. In Boston, he participated in the weekly pastors' conferences of the Protestant churches. He remained in Boston for another year and in the academic year 1893–1894 studied at the medical faculty of Methodist University, where he took a basic course in medicine for missionaries.

About many events of Deunov's time in American we have no information, because in 1944 he burned his diary about this period. In Boston he learned about new spiritual currents. Between 1830 and 1850, transcendentalism had emerged there, made famous by the work of Ralph Emerson, Henry Thoreau, and Walt Whitman. These authors assumed the goodness of man and nature. Deunov visited Concord near Boston, where Thoreau had been born and had lived for two years in a cottage built by himself on Walden Pond. The transcendentalist movement inspired communes in the woods of Massachusetts.

Deunov often made excursions into nature that took him away from the Boston area for several days. Associated with the Bulgarian Freemason Velichko Grablashev (who was interested in the Rosicrucians and had studied theology and law in America in the early 1890s) is a puzzling story of such a trip about which no further information is known. It is not even documented that Grablashev

---

26. Peter Dunoff, *The Migration of the Teutonic Tribes and their Conversion to Christianity*, Sofia, 2007. Transcription by Harrie Salman, https://petardanov.com/DUNOFF-Diplomna.pdf.

studied in Boston during the years 1892–1894. Grablashev himself wrote in 1922 that he had not met Deunov until 1902. Therefore, the story may be about someone else, or it may have been made up.

The story goes that Deunov had taken Grablashev on a train ride to northwestern Massachusetts after a promise of secrecy. After a carriage ride and crossing a lake, they arrived at a house built into a hillside like a temple. There Deunov was received by a group of people who sat at a round table, stood up, and bowed to him. They held conversations with each other about occult and religious issues, which Grablashev did not understand. When he later wanted to return to this place, it proved impossible, for which reason he believed the trip with Deunov had not taken place in the visible world. According to him, they had probably had a spiritual encounter with a circle of Rosicrucians.[27]

Indeed, there were circles inspired by the Rosicrucian tradition in the northeastern United States, such as the Fraternitas Rosae Crucis, founded in 1861, but it is not known whether Deunov was in contact with them. It is possible that his spiritual-scientific studies, both in America and later in Bulgaria, were inspired by these circles or by a spiritual encounter with Christian Rosenkreutz. He must also have heard about the Theosophical Society (which had been founded in New York in 1875), spiritualism, and Mary Baker Eddy's Christian Science movement, which were attracting much attention on the east coast of the United States at the time.

In late 1894 or early 1895, Deunov traveled from the United States by boat to Liverpool. He probably stayed in London for several months before returning to Bulgaria,[28] where he initially lived (again) with his sister Maria in Varna, and from 1898 with his father in Novi Pazar. He found that his seven-year sojourn in the big world had alienated him from the Methodist circles in his country. Several congregations asked if he would become their pastor, but he only wanted to do so without pay and without an official position. He was working for God. His father found him a job in the office of the bishop of the Orthodox Church in Varna, but he turned it down. A

---

27. *Izgrevut na Bialoto Bratstvo* [From the White Brotherhood], 249.
28. *Mladiyat Peter Deunov* [The Young Peter Deunov], 190.

meeting with the leader of the Bulgarian Theosophists led to him being asked to give lectures, but he did not do that either. He maintained contacts with Protestant pastors, Orthodox priests, spiritualists, and Theosophists, but remained independent.

Peter Deunov in 1895, 31 years old

From the summer of 1895 to 1900, Deunov devoted himself in Bulgaria to the preparation of his later spiritual work—of "God's mission," as he called it—and had intensive contact with the invisible world. In 1896, his first book, *Science and Education*, was published.[29] In it he placed education in the context of his views on the origin and development of man, society, and the world. For him, education was a spiritual activity aimed at transforming man's lower nature into his higher, spiritual nature. Here he referred to theological visions as well as to the knowledge produced by science. During

---

29. Peter Deunov, *Science and Education,* Sofia, 2004.

his stay in America, he had had the opportunity to study the science of his time. He believed that religion should take into account insights from science. The truth, which enlightens people, had to be studied. Thus we see Deunov as a reformer of traditional religious thought, inspired by ideas that he expanded upon in his later teachings. His pedagogical ideas about the importance of love, freedom, music, artistic and creative work, and the connection with nature run parallel with what Rudolf Steiner developed in his pedagogy.

At the end of 1896, Deunov was one of the founders of the Varna Reading Room, which he headed for several years as librarian. Such reading rooms, in addition to the Bulgarian Church (which had become independent, and for which his father and grandfather had worked) were centers of the revival of Bulgarian culture after about five centuries of Ottoman-Turkish oppression. In 1897 and 1898, Deunov gave free lectures here on the descent of man, ancient and modern philosophy, science and philosophy, and why and how we live.

In March 1897, the 32-year-old Deunov had a profound spiritual experience. He was with his father at an inn in Tetovo when a bright light appeared around him in which his father perceived Christ and heard within a voice that said, "I make him my solid rock upon which I build my kingdom." Deunov later said, "I was inspired, and this happened on March 7, 1897 [March 19 according to the present calendar]. I received a mission from heaven and I was told that I am a teacher for all mankind. The mission assigned to me is connected with the new path of the Slavic peoples and with the coming of the sixth race [the new cycle of cultures]."[30]

That Deunov was now ordained as a teacher of humanity could mean that he had attained the rank of a bodhisattva.[31] Bodhisattvas are teachers of humanity who, according to Steiner, are animated by an archangel all the way into their physical body, or else only into their etheric body. The human being in whom a bodhisattva incar-

---

30. Peter Deunov, *Harmonizing of the Human Soul*, Sofia, 2013, 386. https://ia80 0703.us.archive.org/3/items/PeterDeunov/HARMONIZING_OF_THE_HUMAN_ SOUL.pdf. Following Theosophical usage, Deunov called the cycles of cultures races.

31. This does not mean that he was the Maitreya Bodhisattva.

The Preparation For Their Missions

nates (between the ages of 30 and 33) will, according to Steiner, experience "a tremendous change" in his life. In the process, his soul will be "exchanged," so that he will become "a very different man than he has been until then." This might have been the case with Deunov, if we look at his activities after 1897, and especially at his deep connection with the archangel of the Bulgarian people, whose task it is to prepare the Slavic culture of the future. As we shall see, in 1898 this archangel spoke through him to give a message to his people.

After this initiation experience, Deunov founded in 1897 the Society for the Elevation of the Religious Spirit of the Bulgarian People, which became the germ of the later School of the White Brotherhood. In 1898 an extensive correspondence began with his first three students, Protestant teacher Penyu Kirov (1868–1918), Catholic physician and spiritualist Georgi Mirkovich (1826–1905), and the Orthodox court secretary Todor Stoimenov (1872–1952). They were, together with Maria Kazakova, Milkom Partomian, and the physician Anastasia Zhelyazkova, among the co-founders of the Society. As editor of three journals on occultism and natural medicine, Mirkovich was a well-known figure in Bulgarian spiritual life.

Georgi Mirkovich

Between 1897 and 1900, Deunov united in his first circle these three people, who represented the main currents of Christianity (Protestantism, Catholicism, and Orthodoxy). During these years he wrote several prophetic texts that arose from his contact with the invisible world.[32] In his letters to them, he wrote about these revela-

---

32. Published together with some shorter texts from 1903 and 1904 in D. Kalev (ed.), Peter Deunov, *Toy ide, Nachalno slovo 1896–1904* [He is Coming, Words for the Beginning 1896–1904], Sofia, 2004.

tions. The first text from 1897 was titled *Hio-eli-meli-mesail, The Voice of God*. In it, Deunov brought the message that the time of the Kingdom of God is approaching, and that this requires a radical

Penyu Kirov (left) and Todor Stoimenov, 1915

preparation in which humanity awakens. God revealed in this text Deunov's election and the divine blessing that was poured out upon him—to accomplish the great work that is coming. On September

The Preparation For Their Missions

20, 1898, he writes the text *The Elect of God and the Leader of Truth*, which confirms his mission. God has sent an angel to him with a command that he must fulfill. In so doing, the Holy Spirit will enlighten and guide him. In letters to his disciples, he wrote that the Spirit of God inspired him and that several of God's emissaries had already come to him to give him commands.[33]

On October 8, 1898, he received a message from the angel Elohil, who has guided the Bulgarian people for about a thousand years as its inspiring national spirit. He is "one of the great princes in heaven," Deunov wrote in a letter to Georgi Mirkovich on November 14, 1898. Possibly he is part of the angelic hierarchy of the Elohim.[34] This message is called *A Call to My People, Bulgarian Sons of the Slavic Family*. In the same month, Deunov read this message at an evening of the charitable association Miloserdi'e (Mercy) in Varna. In 1994, this text was first published in a brochure.[35]

As an emissary of God, the angel Elohil revealed through Deunov that he had allied himself with the Bulgarian nation when, in 865, Tsar Boris I adopted Christianity as the state religion. At that time, the mission of the Bulgarians began. It was guided by Elohil, who led them through their sufferings (caused by their sins as a nation) to purify their souls along a path of patience and humility, toward a "good and holy life." In the second half of the 19th century, he initiated the liberation from Ottoman rule. Now he came to his people again, to confront them with the misuse of the gifts of the new freedom and to remind them of his mission.

According to the angel, the Bulgarians share their mission with other members of the Slavic family, to whom he provides leadership. Elohil revealed that God had chosen the Slavic house as a dwelling place for himself. Just as the Old Testament prophets called the Israelite people the "bride" of Yahweh, so Elohil called the Lord (Christ) the "bridegroom" of the Bulgarian people and, in a broader sense, of the Slavic peoples generally. They are the "chosen children of truth"

---

33. S. Tchorbadzhiyev (ed.), Peter Deunov, *Pisma do purvite uchenitsi* [Letters to the First Pupils], Sofia, 1999.

34. Some editions give "Elohim" instead of "Elohil."

35. Translated and commented by Harrie Salman in: *Peter Deunov: Prophet of the New Age*, Sofia, 2014. The *Call* can be read on https://prizvanie.bg/English/.

and the "seed of the new humanity" of which the Slavic family, as a new Israel, will be the hearth.

The opening of the *Call to My People* reads, "Heaven has granted you a holy ministry in the Kingdom of Peace, which is coming and is approaching in its power." Elohil will lead his nation into the Kingdom of God. Christ will return; the New Age is coming. Heaven has given "a sacred promise of great mercy and love" to the Bulgarians, but they must act in accordance with their calling. The angel describes them as a "tribe of discord" and as a "wayward people," suffering from the "general lack of unity and from the discord" of the Slavic family.

The angel had come to warn them. The Bulgarian people needed to wake up and turn away from the evil path, to repent and develop pure virtues. They needed spiritual guidance and formation from their archangel. When they heeded his call, their redemption and spiritual renewal would begin. By heeding it, according to Elohil, they would avoid the "total destruction" that was even then hanging over their heads. Such words of warning and threat of punishment are reminiscent of the words of the Old Testament prophets. A people who do not heed the divine instructions, as articulated by the prophets, must face the consequences.

Peter Deunov connected himself with the archangel's call and took on the task of working for the mission of the Bulgarian people as part of the preparation for the Slavic culture of the future. He did not receive the messages from the invisible world in the night, as did the Old Testament prophets, but during his meditations and as answers to his prayers to God.[36] We have seen that, in his own words, he had been ordained a world teacher a year earlier. He was God's chosen one and had a mission to fulfill for humanity in preparation for the coming of the Kingdom of God. On February 13, 1899, he received the *Testimonies of the Spirit*, ten questions from the Spirit of God to those willing to dedicate their lives to the service of God and bear witness to it.

---

36. Peter Deunov's prayers to God and the answers of God from the years 1897–1900 were published in *Dnevnik na Uchitelya Beinsa Douno: Peter Deunov* [Diary of the Teacher Beinsa Douno], Sofia, 2001.

The Testimonies

Here is our promise to God, heaven, and you, our brother in Christ the Lord, which we sign in the following ten testimonies, which the Spirit of Truth gives us:

First Testimony: *Do you believe with all your heart and soul in the one eternal, true, and good God of life who spoke?*
I believe with heart and soul in the one eternal, true, and good God of life, who always speaks, and who by speaking His Word created all visible and invisible things!

Second Testimony: *Do you believe in me, your Lord and Savior, who is speaking to you now?*
I believe in the Lord, my Savior, who speaks to me now; and by the power of His Word I have consciously come to the knowledge of the Truth!

Third Testimony: *Do you believe in my eternal and kind Spirit, who brings your salvation?*
I believe in the eternal and good Spirit of God, who is now working on my salvation, constantly sanctifying and enlightening me and leading me on the journey of my life to know Him as He is known.

Fourth Testimony: *Do you believe in your Friend and Savior, the Lord Jesus Christ, and in all your brothers?*
I believe in my Friend, the Lord Jesus Christ, and in all my brothers, the servants of the living God, who walk with me.

Fifth Testimony: *Will you do the will of the only true and just God without hesitation?*
I accept to do the will of the only true and just God without hesitation. His word will be my law!

Sixth Testimony: *Will you renounce yourself and everything of the world for His love?*
I renounce myself and everything of the world for God's love.

Seventh Testimony: *Will you devote your life and health and all precious things to His Glory and to the Glory of His work?*
I will dedicate life and health and all things dear to me to the Glory of God and to the Glory of His Work.

Eighth Testimony: *Will you listen to My voice and to My advice when I speak to you?*

> I will listen, O Lord, to Your voice and to Your counsel when You speak to me.
>
> **Ninth Testimony:** *Will you readily follow my orders without doubt?*
> I am willing, O Lord, to do your commandments without any doubt.
>
> **Tenth Testimony:** *Will you always meet my eyes with all the innocence of your heart and never grieve Me?*
> O Lord, I will endeavor to always walk before You with the integrity of my heart, and I will endeavor to never grieve You.
> Amen.

Peter Deunov was the first to answer these questions and to endorse his testimony with his signature. Until 1922, all new disciples did the same. On February 24, 1899, he received a *Promise from God*, which he also sent to his disciples. It contained the following:

> From now on, I Myself will lead you, I Myself will work and arrange everything for you. I will teach you everything you need to do. You will lie down and rise under My wings. I will be a watchman over you, and My eye will watch over the fate of your heart. You will call to Me early, and I will answer you at dawn. Before you call I will answer you, and before you desire something I will give you My divine gifts. I will attend to all your needs. See that you do not profane My name. Know that I abhor evil, that I abhor iniquity, that cruelty grieves Me.
>
> Finally, always be ready to carry out every commandment I will give you. The rule of your life will be to do everything, to give thanks for everything. When you lie down, when you rise, when you eat, when you drink, when you do all things, you will give thanks in your heart for all things.
>
> I AM, I, the One God, will confirm you in all things, and your peace will rise like the morning sun of life.

On March 31, 1899, Peter Deunov wrote in his diary:

> And the Lord speaks to me and gives me His Word and says, I have made you the solid rock on which I build My Kingdom. I am with you to deliver you from all your enemies. I will deliver you from the hand of Evil and set you free from the hand of the oppressors. I will make you a light of the nations: you will go before me and

The Preparation For Their Missions

you will gird the earth with the scepter of your hand. My Word is already working for your spirit and will reign in the hearts of those I have chosen to serve me.[37]

Early in the summer of 1900, Deunov had *Seven Conversations with the Spirit of God*, in which he received advice and instructions for his upcoming mission. The angel Alphael was their conveyer. These conversations made clear to him what he had not yet understood. He had yet to pass a test in which he had to overcome his last doubts. Then he would experience the inner change that all those born of God undergo. With that, his heart would come under the direct guidance of God. In the final message, the angel spoke these words, which give a picture of Deunov's activity:

> A certain power will pass through this land [Bulgaria]. A man will come forth from God and proclaim the Truth. In his words will be power and strength. He will be a man whose countenance will shine like that of an angel, and in his eyes will be a hidden divine fire.[38]

From July 19 to 23, 1900, the 36-year-old Deunov and his disciples Penyu Kirov, Georgi Mirkovich, and Todor Stoymenov gathered for the first summer meeting of the Society for the Elevation of the Religious Spirit of the Bulgarian People. An earlier attempt to meet at Easter of that year had failed because the 74-year-old Mirkovich was still reluctant. The three disciples were surprised that they were the only ones present, but that, as Deunov told them, the chairs were occupied by invisible beings, and thousands would join the Society in the future. The text of the *Seven Conversations with the Spirit* was read and discussed. They understood the importance of this first meeting. Deunov's mission had begun. On November 5, 1900, he wrote in his diary:

> The Lord has done good to my soul. He has blessed me with the abundance of His grace. He has sanctified my innermost being and applied the seal [stamp or imprint] of His Spirit. The Lord has

---

37. Ibid., 18–19.
38. *Sedemte razgovora na Alfael* [The Seven Conversations with Alphael], Sofia, 1998, 46.

not deemed it beneath His dignity to dwell in my heart, to make my soul a dwelling, and my mind a school for my thoughts, that I might learn of his Holy Spirit. Trust in me and you will see what I will do for you, says the Lord.... This is the day that God has overshadowed me with His Holy Spirit. This is the day that the Lord has forgiven my sins and visited me with His presence. The Lord will go with me.[39]

Peter Deunov around 1900, about 36 years old

This concluded the process of Deunov's initiation as a world teacher, which had begun on March 19, 1897. He had overcome his last doubts and was now born of God, as the angel Alphael had told

39. *Dnevnik na Uchitelya Beinsa Douno: Peter Deunov*, 164–65.

him in the summer of 1900. His heart was now under the direct guidance of God. We can assume that he had received an imprint of the I of Jesus Christ (the "seal" of the Spirit of God).

On November 27, 1900, he sent to his disciple Penyu Kirov a prayer dictated to him by the Holy Spirit in 1899. This is the *Good Prayer*, which he said was a prayer not only for humanity, but for the entire universe and all the angels.

The Good Prayer

Lord our God, our merciful heavenly Father, who has bestowed upon us life and health, that we may rejoice in You, we pray to You to send us Your Spirit to guard and deliver us from any cunning and evil thought.

Teach us to do Your will, to sanctify Your name, and to glorify You always.

Enlighten our spirit and guide our hearts and minds so that we may keep Your commandments and precepts.

With Your presence, inspire Your pure thoughts within us so that they may lead us in serving You with joy.

Bless our life, which we dedicate to You, for the good of our brothers and neighbors, Lord.

Help and support us so that we may grow in all knowledge and Wisdom, to learn from Your Word and abide in Your Truth.

Lead us in everything we think and do in your Name so that your Kingdom on earth is glorified.

Nourish our souls with Your Heavenly Bread and strengthen us with Your power so that we may succeed in our life.

As You bestow upon us all Your blessings, so give us Your Love and make it our eternal law.

For Yours is the kingdom, power, and glory for ever and ever. Amen.

Retrospective

In the life of the adult Rudolf Steiner, we can distinguish three phases of six to eight years, marked by his moves from Vienna to Weimar to Berlin. He occupied himself from 1882 to 1890 in *Vienna*, describing the scientific method of Goetheanism—which was to become the basis of anthroposophical research. This period began when Steiner was 21 years old and ended at the age of 29.

Between 1890 and 1897, he lived in *Weimar*. His work in the Goethe and Schiller Archives was not his main occupation. It was, rather, the elaboration of his philosophy of freedom. He was concerned with the free man, which he perceived in certain respects in the philosopher Nietzsche, despite the latter's entanglement in the thought world of materialism. According to Steiner, the free man can, through intuitive thinking, take a conscious path to the spiritual world. When he was 29 years old, he came to Weimar, which he then left at the age of 36. Already a year before his departure, a turning point in his consciousness had begun in him that led him to a more conscious perception of the sensory world.

In *Berlin*, in 1897, the natural scientist and philosopher Steiner had to stand on his own two feet and find an audience willing to read his work and hear his lectures. At the time of his second moon node (May 1898), he faced the question of what his life's mission was to be. In the process, he went through an inner experience that confronted him with himself. In the background, Christian Rosenkreutz was his spiritual master and savior. Steiner was going through an inner struggle that paved a path to the living Christ. This process was concluded in 1903. In 1901, his mission in the Theosophical Society began, at which time he was 40 years old.

Peter Deunov had fallen behind in his schooling. In 1887, when he was 23 years old, he began his first task as a preacher and school teacher. From 1888 to 1893, he continued his theology studies in the United States. He was 29 when he began an additional study of medicine in 1893. It was at this same age that Steiner left for Weimar.

By early 1895, 30-year-old theologian and educator Deunov was back in Bulgaria. There he wrote his first book, *Science and Education*, in which he developed a vision that he later elaborated as his country's spiritual teacher. This book was published in 1896, when he was 32 years old. Three years earlier, also 32 years old, Steiner had published his book, *The Philosophy of Freedom*.

Between 1897 and 1900, Peter Deunov went through an intensive spiritual development in which he communicated with God and his

The Preparation For Their Missions

angels. In 1897 he was initiated as a world teacher; and in the three years that followed, he prepared himself step by step for this task. His disciples he sought out himself. He was 36 years old when his mission began in 1900. We may assume that, in November of that year, he received an imprint of the I of Jesus Christ (the seal of God's Spirit).

In the same years, Steiner (who was three years older than Deunov) was also preparing for his task in Berlin. He set out on the path of his Christ initiation, and on this path found access to the living Christ, in whose *imitatio* he entered. Probably around 1900, standing before the mystery of Golgotha, he also received an imprint of the I of Jesus Christ.

3

The Creation of Their Spiritual Circles

From the beginning of the 20th century, Rudolf Steiner and Peter Deunov gathered their disciples. Steiner did this as general secretary of the German Section of the Theosophical Society. Three phases of seven years can be distinguished in his work, each with its own character. As for Deunov, he had his own society since 1897, soon called the Veriga (Chain). He first traveled around in Bulgaria before settling in Sofia, the country's capital. In the early 1920s, their circles took on a new form. Deunov founded the School of the White Brotherhood in 1922, which emerged from the Chain of Divine Love. And at the 1923 Christmas Conference, Steiner reorganized his Anthroposophical Society, which had emerged from the German Theosophical Society in 1912/13.

Steiner did not make it easy for himself in his attempt to make room within the Theosophical Society for a European-Christian spiritual path. In 1900, his opinion of Theosophy was negative, and he had not yet read the books of Helena Blavatsky (1831–1891) and Annie Besant (1847–1933). In Germany at that time, about a hundred people were members of the Theosophical Society. Many of them were devoted to the Hindu-Buddhist vision of life propagated by Theosophy. Steiner wanted to join an existing spiritual movement and could build on the support of the leadership of the Berlin lodge and of Marie von Sivers. Without her 1901 request for a Christian Theosophy and her active cooperation, he would not have done it. His motivation was to address people who had an honest desire for insights from the spiritual world.

In his 1907 notes to the French writer Edouard Schuré and in his

The Creation of Their Spiritual Circles

lectures of October 10 and 11, 1915, Steiner looked back at the history of the Theosophical Society.[1] In the mid-19th century, when materialistic thinking had reached a certain peak, a small group of initiates wanted to counterbalance it by making some of their spiritual knowledge public. Others were opposed to this. And so, in 1845, the compromise was made to demonstrate the existence of the spiritual world through spiritistic séances. In 1864, the initiates concluded that this effort had failed, because the mediums' messages did not come from the spiritual world, but were mostly from deceased people still haunting earthly realms.

In 1874 it was decided to spread spiritual truths with the help of the extremely gifted medium Helena Blavatsky. For this purpose, the Theosophical Society was founded in New York in 1875 by Helena Petrovna Blavatsky, Henry Steel Olcott, and William Quan Judge. Blavatsky now became a pawn in the conflict between initiates who served general human interests and others who served certain political interests. Initially, she received inspirations from Christian Rosenkreutz, the teacher of Christian esotericism, which, however, she presented in a confused way. She had acquired much knowledge she wanted to bring out into the open, but this was not to the liking of American lodges. They placed her in an "occult prison." She was freed from that by Indian occultists, who in turn

Helena Blavatsky in 1887

---

1. Notes made by Rudolf Steiner, written for Edouard Schuré, September 1907, in Rudolf Steiner and Marie Steiner-von Sivers, *Letters and Documents 1901–1925* (CW 262). Lectures of October 10 and 11, 1915, in *Occult Movements in the Nineteenth Century* (CW 254).

had their own intentions with her, namely to spread old Asian occultism in the world. From what Steiner said about Blavatsky, it can be inferred that after her death he freed her from this second "occult imprisonment," and that she then became his disciple.

Steiner entered into this minefield when he responded to Countess Brockdorff's request that he take on the leadership of the Berlin lodge. The intention was also to establish a German section of the Theosophical Society. Steiner became a member of this society on January 17, 1902. With Annie Besant's approval, the German section was then formed in October 1902, headed by Steiner and numbering about 130 members. Besant had accepted that Steiner would teach in his own way, oriented toward esoteric Christianity, and on the basis of his spiritual experiences.

His goal was to guide spiritual disciples on their inner path. Until the end of his active life (Sept. 1924), he counseled his students. For him, individual development also included dealing with one's karma. At the founding of the German Section in 1902, he wanted to talk about practical karma exercises, but its members demurred: such an approach was too concrete for them. He had to hold this intention back and was unable to address this topic until 1923. He noted in 1924 that Theosophy thus entered a theoretical arena.

Anna Eunike

Marie von Sivers

The Creation of Their Spiritual Circles

He now began to build up the German section with all his strength, in cooperation with Marie von Sivers. This led to problems with his wife Anna Eunike, who found no access to Theosophy. These problems intensified when Marie von Sivers, who was fourteen years younger than Anna Eunike, had also rented an apartment in the same house for practical reasons in the beginning of 1903. A year later, Anna Eunike left her husband. She died in 1911. She and Rudolf Steiner were not legally separated.

In the first phase of the development of his Theosophical work (1902–1909), Steiner held lectures in Berlin and other German cities. As a result, membership grew to about 2,000 by 1910. In June 1903, the first issue of the new Theosophical journal *Luzifer* (meaning light bearer and symbolizing the search for higher knowledge) was published. In 1904, his first main work, *Theosophy* (CW 9), was published, providing an introduction to supersensory knowledge of the world and man's destiny. In 1904 and 1905, articles appeared in the magazine *Luzifer* that were later compiled in the book *How to Know Higher Worlds* (CW 10). Between 1904 and 1908, articles appeared that were subsequently published in the books *Cosmic Memory* (CW 11) and *The Stages of Higher Knowledge* (CW 12). After Steiner had elaborated on the two faces of evil (Lucifer pulling us away from the earthly world and Ahriman wanting to chain us to it) in 1907/08, another book followed, *Outline of Occult Science* (CW 13), which among other things describes the evolution of the earth and man. This book appeared in 1910.

During this period, Steiner was invited twice, in 1906 and 1908, to Russia by Russian Theosophists. The Holy Synod of the Orthodox Church turned against his coming in 1906, so he was denied a visa, and in 1908 he himself declined a trip to Russia.

Starting in 1906, lecture cycles were published for members. At first, Steiner was not in favor of his lectures being stenographed and printed in books. They were intended for a particular audience that was expected to work with these contents. Moreover, Steiner had no time to correct them. But the pressure on him to publish them anyway became too great.

In 1904, he received permission from Besant to create an esoteric school within the Theosophical school founded by Blavatsky and

Rudolf Steiner and Peter Deunov

Rudolf Steiner around 1905, about 44 years old

headed by Besant. He built up the German branch of this esoteric school with its own contents. To its members he gave instructions for meditation and personal advice. In a letter dated January 2, 1905 to Anna Wagner, he wrote that the school was founded and directed by the masters themselves, by which he meant the two masters of the West, Christian Rosenkreutz and Master Jesus. In his book *How to Know Higher Worlds,* Steiner elaborated the path of initiation, which he called the modern Rosicrucian path. On June 26, 1906, he said that Master Jesus represents "the intimate in man." This master

The Creation of Their Spiritual Circles

was associated with the Christian path of initiation that was undertaken in seclusion by hermits and in monasteries in the Middle Ages.[2] At its center were meditations on the Passion of Christ. Steiner did not discuss this path in detail, and Deunov did not mention it. In the School of the White Brotherhood, the mystical tradition of Christianity took a modern form for working on ourselves.

In 1906 Steiner acquired the right to establish within the Memphis-Misraim order of Freemasonry a chapter with its own rituals called Mystica Eterna.[3] He did this at the request of members of his theosophical esoteric school. It was an attempt to renew Freemasonry, which, in his opinion, no longer had any real content. Therefore, he explained the *meaning* of all the rituals. During the meetings, there were times when spiritual masters of humanity spoke through him, such as Master Morya and Master Kuthumi. Furthermore, after having received personal permission from Besant in 1907 to separate his German esoteric school from her general Theosophical school, he incorporated the rituals into the upper classes of his own esoteric school. (During World War I, which broke out in 1914, esotericism could not be practiced. Only in 1924 was esoteric work resumed.)

The conversation with Besant about founding an independent German esoteric school took place after the Theosophical Congress organized by the German Section in Munich in May 1907. Here Steiner made it clear that his work stood in the tradition of the Rosicrucians. Unlike what the Theosophists were accustomed to, the design was artistic. This was due in part to Marie von Sivers, who had trained in dramatic art and recitation. The Congress took place in a room decorated like a Rosicrucian temple. Seven occult seals were hanging in the hall and there were seven columns, all designed by Steiner. Here was performed *The Sacred Drama of Eleusis* by Edouard Schuré, whom Steiner and von Sivers had met personally

---

2. Gerhard von Beckerath, *Rudolf Steiners Leidensweg* [Rudolf Steiner's Path of Suffering], Dornach, 2011, 54–55.

3. See Rudolf Steiner, *Freemasonry and Ritual Work: The Misraim Service* (CW 265).

in Paris in 1906. The text had been translated by Marie von Sivers and adapted by Rudolf Steiner.

At the Congress, Steiner delivered the lecture "The Initiation of the Rosicrucian," followed by a series of fourteen lectures on "The Theosophy of the Rosicrucian." After the congress, he made extensive trips to Italy, Prague, Austria, the Netherlands, Denmark, Sweden, Norway, and Hungary. In addition to introductory courses in Theosophy, he began to give more specialized lectures, such as on the gospels, mythology, cosmology, and the folk souls.

After this first period, in which Steiner wrote his main works and laid a foundation for the spread of Theosophy with his lectures, a second phase (1909–1916) followed in which artistic life flourished and Steiner brought new insights into the life and work of Christ. In

Rudolf Steiner and Annie Besant in 1907

The Creation of Their Spiritual Circles

the middle of this period fell the founding of the Anthroposophical Society. As a follow-up to Schuré's performance of *The Sacred Drama of Eleusis*, his drama *The Children of Lucifer* was staged in Munich in 1909. In the subsequent lecture series "The East in the Light of the West—The Children of Lucifer and the Brothers of Christ," Steiner made it clear that the ancient Eastern mysteries could be resurrected in Rosicrucian Theosophy by the Christianized wisdom of the West.

In Steiner's 1909 lectures on the principle of the "spiritual economy," he described that after the resurrection of Christ, several people had "incorporated" into their being copies of spiritual bodies of Jesus.[4] In the early Middle Ages this included some Irish monks (Columbanus and Gallus) who received imprints of the etheric body of Jesus, and in the late Middle Ages some saints and mystics who received a copy of the astral body of Jesus. These were imprints of his sentient soul (Francis of Assisi and Elisabeth of Thuringia), his intellectual soul (Thomas Aquinas), and his consciousness soul (Meister Eckhart and Tauler). These imprints were multiplied in the spiritual world after Christ's resurrection. From the end of the Middle Ages, imprints of the Jesus-I became available, of which Christian Rosenkreutz was the first recipient. In the future, every human being can receive such a copy. These copies, according to Steiner, are kept in the spiritual world by the Brotherhood of the Holy Grail.[5]

Steiner called Anthroposophy the "Science of the Grail" in his book *Outline of Occult Science*. Therefore, the initiates of modern times are initiates of the Grail. From the knowledge of the Grail comes the highest ideal of human development. And from this ideal, according to Steiner, we can work on our spiritualization, which leads to our connection with Christ. In the aforementioned lectures on "spiritual economy," he explained that we then become, like Parzival, Grail seekers: "Christians of the future." We set out for a Grail initiation, which may only lead to our spiritual rebirth in the next life. As Parzival had to learn, it is an active path of searching,

---

4. Rudolf Steiner, lectures from 1909 in *Principles of Spiritual Economy* (CW 109).

5. Ibid., lecture of April 11, 1909.

and then awakening to ask decisive questions. This path suits the development of the modern consciousness soul.[6]

Between 1908 and 1910, Steiner gave lectures on the four gospels and the Book of Revelation. In them he revealed that the two lineages of Jesus, which appear in the gospels of Matthew and Luke, refer to children born into two different families. This disclosure[7] came as a shock to many. Added to this was the fact that, according to Steiner's research, these two families united, and the I of the Matthew child passed on to the Luke child when he was 12 years old.

Rudolf Steiner's Research on the Two Jesus Children[7]

Gospel of Matthew	Gospel of Luke
Family tree: Abraham to Joseph *via* King David and his son Solomon.	Family tree: Adam to carpenter Joseph *via* King David and his son Nathan.
Joseph from Bethlehem (early deceased), married to Mary from Jerusalem	Joseph from Nazareth, married to Mary (died early), remarried Mary from Jerusalem.
The Solomon Jesus Child	**The Nathan Jesus Child**
Visited by the wise men from the East, fled to Egypt, then to Nazareth.	Visited by the shepherds, returned from Bethlehem to Nazareth.
Incarnation of the sage Zarathustra, one of humanity's oldest souls	Incarnation of the pure etheric aspect of the cosmic Adam from Paradise.
Dies after his I passes on to the other child.	Receives the I of the other child at age 12.
This I leaves this child before baptism in the Jordan.	Receives the Christ-I at the baptism in the Jordan.
This I further incarnates as Master Jesus.	Thereby, this Jesus becomes the New Adam.

Every human being can transform into a "new man" by the reception of copies of the spiritual bodies of Jesus, which are available to all people after His resurrection.

In 1909, Steiner made another discovery: that the return of Christ was imminent. On January 12, 1910, he spoke about this for the first

---

6. The consciousness soul is an aspect of the soul that has developed since the end of the Middle Ages. It enables self-awareness and an objective attitude toward the world outside us.

7. Bernard Nesfield-Cookson, *The Mystery of the Two Jesus Children*, Forest Row, 2005.

The Creation of Their Spiritual Circles

time during a lecture in Stockholm. He said that starting from the year 1933, with their developing natural clairvoyance, people would be able to perceive the etheric figure of Christ—at first a few, and later more and more. In 1910, Steiner toured Europe from north to south with this message as a prophet of Christ. In the course of 2,500 years, he said, the etheric Christ would be perceived by all mankind.

Moreover, in October 1913 in Oslo and in December 1913 in Cologne, Steiner gave a total of seven lectures on the Fifth Gospel, revealing unknown aspects of the life of Jesus. In two lectures, he described how the deceased Mary of the Luke gospel connected spiritually with the still-living Mary of the Matthew gospel during Jesus's conversation with her shortly before his baptism in the Jordan.[8] The deceased Mary carried within her the soul aspect of the cosmic man from paradise, which had not joined in the Fall. This aspect is associated with Sophia, the divine wisdom. Leading up to Pentecost (in AD 33), the living Mary, called the "mother of Jesus" in the John gospel, was thus able to develop into Mary-Sophia.[9]

In 1910, Rudolf Steiner decided to write mystery dramas himself in order to make visible and experienceable the karma of an interconnected group of people in the succession of dramatic entanglements from different incarnations. They show the paths people can take when seeking access to the spiritual world. Steiner said of these dramas that they contain the whole of Anthroposophy. If people absorbed the content deeply, lectures would no longer be necessary. In 1910, the first drama, *The Portal of Initiation*, was performed; in 1911, *The Soul's Probation*; in 1912, *The Guardian of the Threshold*; and in 1913, *The Soul's Awakening*. Owing to the outbreak of war, this series of dramas was not continued. These mystery dramas were in fact a metamorphosis of Goethe's *Fairy Tale*. Its characters were replaced or supplemented by people Steiner had come to know, such as the herbalist Felix Koguzki (cast as Felix Balde).

The artistic impulse that came to life in the dramas brought with it a whole stream of new impulses. A new mystery art developed, a

---

8. Rudolf Steiner, lectures of October 6 and December 17, 1913, in *The Fifth Gospel: From the Akashic Record* (CW 148).

9. Michael Debus, *Mary and Sophia*, Edinburgh, 2013, 191.

new style of speech, a new art of movement (eurythmy), a new plastic art and painting. A new organic architecture appeared in the building project of the Goetheanum. Through this blossoming of spiritual artistic expressions, a large number of artists connected themselves with Anthroposophy. One such was the Russian writer Andrei Belyi, who attended Steiner's lectures between 1912 and 1916 and wrote a book that portrays Steiner in a very warm way.[10]

The production of the Mystery Dramas in Munich raised the question of a suitable building in which they could be staged (as well as where the Theosophical work could take place). This initiative did not come from Steiner himself. In 1911, a design was made for a "Johannes Building," but the authorities in Munich worked against it, so Steiner was forced to find another location. Its name was connected exoterically with Johannes Thomasius, the principal figure in the Mystery Dramas, and esoterically with John the Evangelist (Christian Rosenkreutz), who years earlier, on July 18, 1904, Steiner had declared to be the same individual called Lazarus in the gospel. He even spoke in this lecture of a Johannes Society that "will bring a true understanding of Christianity."[11]

On September 20, 1913, the first foundation stone for the Johannes building was laid in the Swiss town of Dornach, near Basel. This building project gave birth to an anthroposophical colony there. From 1918 on, the building was called the Goetheanum. This change of name from the figure of John to Goethe as representative of German culture had not come from Steiner himself. It was symbolic of the change from deep Christian esotericism to exotericism, the world of the mundane, which had been prepared for some time due to the lack of interest of members in the Christian mysteries (the four gospels, the Fifth Gospel, the Grail). This is why, according to Gerhard von Beckerath,[12] Steiner was silent on these mysteries even before 1914. But even so, the theme of the Grail did not disappear entirely. Anthroposophy as a "science of the Grail" increasingly narrowed down to a path of insight: as Ehrenfried Pfeiffer wrote in 1959

---

10. Andrei Belyi and others, *Reminiscences of Rudolf Steiner*, Ghent, 1987.
11. Von Beckerath, *Rudolf Steiners Leidensweg*, 60.
12. Ibid., 49–77.

The Creation of Their Spiritual Circles

in a retrospective,[13] the esotericism of the "mystery Christianity" of John was lost in the Society.

Steiner expected war and wanted the construction to be completed by August 1, 1914. This did not succeed, however, and the outbreak of war meant that the building could not be opened until 1920. It was constructed of wood with two unequal domes. Volunteers from seventeen countries participated in its construction. They provided the artistic work. The spectator area was surrounded by two rows of seven planetary columns that carried the large dome. The domes were painted, and colored glass windows were inserted in the side walls. The small dome was supported by twelve columns.

The audience hall with the large dome represented the outer world, the world of the mundane, lower self (the ego); while the stage with the small dome represented the spiritual world, the world

The First Goetheanum

of the higher Self. At the back of the stage, an eight-foot-tall wooden sculpture was to have been placed. Created by Steiner with the English sculptor Edith Maryon (1872–1924), it was called the Representative of Man. It represents Christ balancing the opposing forces Lucifer and Ahriman, thus creating the space for man to evolve. Entering this temple of humanity, which Steiner called the

---

13. Thomas Meyer (ed.), *Ehrenfried Pfeiffer: A Modern Quest for the Spirit*, Spring Valley, NY, 2010.

House of the Word, and walking from west to east—past the pillars with their seals, under the painted domes, to the great statue—evoked an experience of inner awakening in many who entered the First Goetheanum.

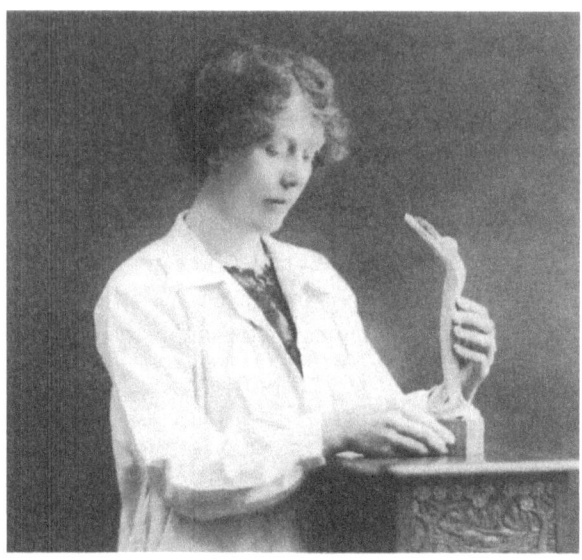

Edith Maryon

Starting in 1909, the idea was spread within the Theosophical Society by C.W. Leadbeater and Annie Besant that Christ would reappear on earth in the person of the young Hindu Jiddu Krishnamurti (1895–1986). He was also said to be the Maitreya Bodhisattva, the future Buddha. In 1911, the Order of the Star of the East was established to prepare for his mission. This prompted Steiner to take a stand against this idea with all his might. This conflict led from December 1912 to the founding of the Anthroposophical Society, which was celebrated in Berlin on February 4, 1913. Most of the approximately 2,500 Theosophists joined it, as well as Theosophists from other countries. The board was formed by Marie von Sivers, Michael Bauer, and Carl Unger. Steiner had used the word "anthroposophy" as early as 1902 in lectures outside the Theosophical circle in Berlin. By this he meant "the wisdom of our humanity."

Krishnamurti later saw through the game that was being played with him, and on August 3, 1929 in Ommen, Netherlands, dissolved

The Creation of Their Spiritual Circles

the order that had been built up around him. As will be described later, Peter Deunov may have had an important part in this.

The outbreak of World War I (1914–1918) was a catastrophe for the deeply shocked Steiner. He believed it was the result of the karma of materialism. According to Marie von Sivers, the day the German army was mobilized (on August 1, 1914) was the hardest day in his life. Steiner's work for a spiritual culture was in danger of being destroyed. He realized that the founding of the German Empire in 1871 was not linked to a *spiritual* mission, but to an impulse to rule; whereas for Steiner, Central Europe had instead a *cultural* mission of eminent importance for the future of humanity. In his lectures during the first war years, therefore, he often spoke of the "German mission." Anthroposophy is "an answer to the call that the German spirit let ring out in the voices of the best representatives of its spiritual life. The heart of Europe cherishes a deep yearning for spirituality," he said on September 30, 1914.[14] In his view, Central Europe was a culture of the I, in which people strive to develop their individuality. In a public lecture in Berlin on January 14, 1915, Steiner reminded Germans that they had a mission—to be fulfilled by the German spirit as it stands under the direction of the German folk-spirit to which they must remain faithful:

> The German spirit has not finished
> What it should create in the making of the world.
> It lives, full of hope, in its concerns for the future;
> It hopes, full of life, for future deeds.
> In the depths of its being, it deeply feels
> Something hidden, that even while yet maturing must do its work:
> How, in the power of the enemy who lacks understanding,
> May the desire for its end be brought alive,
> As long as a life reveals itself to him
> That keeps him creative in the roots of his being.[15]

Shortly before, on December 24, 1914, Rudolf Steiner and Marie von Sivers had married. Until 1923 they lived alternately in Berlin and in Dornach.

---

14. Rudolf Steiner, lecture of September 30, 1914, in *Karma of Untruthfulness*, vol. 2 (CW 174b).

15. Rudolf Steiner, lecture of January 14, 1915, in *Aus schicksalstragender Zeit*

Rudolf Steiner and Peter Deunov

The third period in the development of Anthroposophy began in 1916 and ran until the end of 1923. This phase was marked by a turn toward practical life. Steiner was committed to a renewal of social life and wanted to contribute from Anthroposophy to the spiritual renewal of culture. At the end of this period, he was forced to reorganize the dysfunctional Anthroposophical Society.

In 1917, WWI took a dramatic turn with the entry of the United States into the war and the outbreak of the Russian Revolution. President Woodrow Wilson had drawn up a peace program based on the self-determination of nations. Steiner saw great danger in this because it would draw borders in Central Europe in an area where people of different nations had lived together for centuries. He developed his own ideas about the functioning of a society that was based on his 30-year study of the functioning of the human organism. In this, he had discovered a threefolding of three organ systems (the nervous-sensory system, the rhythmic system of blood circulation and respiration, and the digestive-limb system). He had also elaborated this threefold division in the form of thinking, feeling, and willing at the level of the soul in his book *The Riddles of the Soul* (CW 21), published in 1917. He had come to the conclusion that, in a healthy society, the elements of culture, politics, and economics must work together in a similar threefolding.

At the request of Count Otto Lerchenfeld, an anthroposophist with political connections, he took action. He wrote two memoranda in July 1917 addressed to leading politicians in Germany and Austria, calling on them to proclaim his proposed social threefolding as a Central European peace program.[16] He elaborated his vision in many lectures. For culture, freedom should be the guiding principle; for politics, the equality of all citizens; and for economics, fra-

---

[From Our Destiny-Laden Times] (CW 64). The German text is: "Der deutsche Geist hat nicht vollendet, was er im Weltenwerden schaffen soll. Er lebt in Zukunfts-sorgen hoffnungsvoll, er hofft auf Zukunftstaten lebensvoll. In seines Wesens Tiefen fühlt er mächtig Verborgnes, das noch reifend wirken muss. Wie darf in Feindes Macht verständnislos der Wunsch nach seinem Ende sich beleben, so lang das Leben sich ihm offenbart, das ihn in Wesenswurzeln schaffend hält!"

16. Rudolf Steiner, "Memoranda," in Stephen Usher (ed.), *Social Threefolding: Rebalancing Culture, Politics and Economics*, Forest Row, 2018.

The Creation of Their Spiritual Circles

ternity (solidarity). Steiner emphasized in his memoranda that, with the program of social threefolding, Central Europe could be prevented from being absorbed into Anglo-American world domination. However, the responsible political leaders did nothing with this proposal. Instead, they accepted Wilson's program and the Treaty of Versailles (1919), which placed the blame for the war solely on Germany. Steiner had already foreseen this and even wanted to establish a press office for objective reporting in Switzerland in 1916.

After the failure of the action for the transformation of the centralist-ruled unitary state, he concentrated instead on freeing cultural life from the grip of the state and on establishing "works councils" in enterprises. He held lectures in factories in the Stuttgart region, where he was thwarted by the entrepreneurs, socialist parties, and trade unions. In anthroposophical circles he found little support. In 1919 he wrote his book *The Threefold Social Order* (CW 23), which was read by many outside Anthroposophy, including in England and the United States.

After the end of the war, he saw the need to make contributions from Anthroposophy for the reconstruction of culture. This had been his commitment from the beginning of his Theosophical days, but this form of practical spirituality was too concrete for the Theosophists. He had to work with the impulses of the new generation, those born after 1899. Meanwhile, the geopolitical situation had changed. On December 14, 1918, Steiner argued that, by eliminating Germany, the Anglo-Saxon peoples were destined for world domination, which would be a domination by *materialism*. This would lead to the downfall of spiritual life. The German people no longer bore responsibility for the future of the world, but only as individual persons. They would have to nurture the new seeds of spirit.[17] Steiner saw this as the task of anthroposophists who should go out into the world to plant these seeds.

Between the fall of 1921 and May 1922, Steiner undertook major lecture tours of Germany, reaching thousands of people. At the end of these, an attack on him in Munich on May 15, 1922 by German

---

17. Rudolf Steiner, lecture of December 14, 1919, in *Michael's Mission: Revealing the Essential Secrets of Human Nature* (CW 194).

nationalists was foiled. A large East-West congress was still held in Vienna in June 1922, but from the end of 1922 Steiner held no more lectures in Germany or Austria. His intentions were no longer actively taken up there. He came to Germany only for anthroposophical initiatives and still gave lectures in Great Britain and the Netherlands. He even traveled to Great Britain three times in 1922 and once each in 1923 and 1924. In August 1922, he was the principal speaker at the conference "Spiritual Values in Education and Social Life," held in Oxford. During his two-week stay in this town, he visited an industrial company. According to Paul Emberson, he later said he had a physical encounter there with Christian Rosenkreutz.[18]

In England, Steiner struck up a friendship with the Scottish anthroposophist Daniel Dunlop (1868–1935), who held a leading position in the energy industry. He called Dunlop his brother. Steiner understood English, and with the help of his secretary, Günther Wachsmuth, he improved his speaking skills. It has been reported that he wanted to make a trip to the United States. About this he may have already spoken with Dunlop, who had worked in the electricity industry in America. Not the Germans, but the Anglo-Saxons, it was said, should make Anthroposophy a world movement.[19]

In the last years of his life (1918–1925), Steiner sowed seeds of the spirit. He was in a hurry and put his hopes in young people. Besides Marie von Sivers, the Dutch physician Ita Wegman (1876–1943) now appeared as the mainstay in the development of the "new mysteries" —in which people will cooperate with spiritual beings in a conscious way. She had known Steiner since 1902, but it was only in working intensively with him 21 years later that it became clear to her that they had been connected for many lifetimes. This cooperation began in August 1923 when, in Wales, she asked Steiner whether the medicine that used to exist in the mystery temples could be

---

18. Paul Emberson, *From Gondishapur to Silicon Valley*, vol. 3, Tobermory, 2020, 1576.

19. According to Paul Emberson, Steiner's work in Central Europe had failed and Steiner still saw a future for Anthroposophy in Britain, the Netherlands, and Scandinavia, and perhaps Switzerland. See his book cited in note 17.

The Creation of Their Spiritual Circles

revived. This collaboration led to a book they wrote together, *Fundamentals of Therapy* (CW 27), which was published in 1925.

In 1919, the first Waldorf School was founded in Stuttgart. Steiner directed it. Starting in 1920, the first anthroposophical enterprises were founded, which demanded much attention. These included Ita Wegman's clinic and the pharmaceutical laboratory, where medicines developed by Steiner were prepared. This was the basis of anthroposophical medicine, which had begun in 1920 with a course for doctors. In 1922, the Christian Community as a movement for religious renewal was founded by a group of theologians and theology students around Friedrich Rittelmeyer and Emil Bock: they had turned to Steiner in 1921 with questions regarding the possibilities of a religious activity in the sense of the anthroposophical movement. In 1922, young people came to him asking how they could work in the service of the spirit of the age of Michael. Steiner held a pedagogical youth course for them in October 1922. Twelve participants asked Steiner for meditative content for their work. From this emerged the Esoteric Youth Circle, which still exists today. In 1924, a course by Steiner led to the beginning of remedial pedagogy, working with people with disabilities. Also in 1924, biodynamic agriculture emerged after a course given by Steiner near Breslau (now in Poland).

Since 1914, Steiner had been attacked from many sides: from scientific and left-intellectual circles, by representatives of the Protestant and Catholic churches (including Max Kully, the priest of Arlesheim and the Jesuit Otto Zimmermann, who applied the July 1919 condemnation of Theosophy by Pope Benedict XV to Steiner's anthroposophical writings), by the bourgeoisie, trade unions, and businessmen who opposed Steiner's vision of social threefolding, by Hitler's nationalist movement, which plotted attacks on him, and by lodges that did not want him to reveal occult secrets and develop new rituals. The Society was no match for these opponents. On December 31, 1922, a fire was set in the wooden Goetheanum. It could not be saved.

For Steiner, whose life forces were connected to this building, this meant a huge drain on his health. Ita Wegman would later write that he had "lived since then only from the strength and power of his higher spiritual being, while his body was actually already a corpse."[20] Moreover, he complained, the fire had become possible because the Anthroposophical Society had become hollow inside. The daughter movements had forgotten the mother: the Anthroposophical Society.

On the night of the fire, 23-year-old Ehrenfried Pfeiffer, who was a close student of Steiner despite his age, sought out his teacher and found him all alone. Steiner told him "he could not go on any longer." Pfeiffer summoned all his courage and replied "that he had to go on and that he, Pfeiffer, would do everything in his power to ensure that there would be no interruption in the course of things."[21] The next day Steiner resumed all his duties.

In the spring of 1923, Günther Wachsmuth came to Steiner asking how members could protect him from attacks. Steiner invited him and others who had the same question to join him on May 27, 1923. That became the first of three times he gave an esoteric lesson as a follow-up to the esoteric school Mystica Eterna, which had been shut down in 1914. This continued on October 23, 1923 and January 3, 1924. From the 24 participants, the new board of the society emerged at the end of 1923. Steiner now demonstrated the cultic words and exercises from ancient mystery schools. For Ita Wegman, who participated in these three esoteric lessons, this led to a further awakening of her memory of initiations in a past life.

The problem of the Society becoming hollow occupied Rudolf Steiner intensely in 1923. He spoke of an "internal opposition" to what he wanted, of a bureaucratic board in Stuttgart that did not function, and of "sleeping" anthroposophists. Within the Society, the old generation with their often sectarian behavior and the impetuous young generation did not get along, so that in 1923, for the young people, he founded the Free Anthroposophical Society.

Willem Zeylmans van Emmichoven has described that, on November 17, 1923, Steiner expressed his doubts in a small circle in The Hague as to whether he could continue with the Society. He complained about the members' lack of understanding for what was spiritually necessary: "The members do not want to… They are

---

20. Rudolf Grosse, *The Christmas Foundation: Beginning of a New Cosmic Age*, Gt Barrington, MA, 1984.
21. Von Beckerath, *Rudolf Steiners Leidensweg*, 138.

The Creation of Their Spiritual Circles

full of good intentions... What should I do?... Should I then found an order?" he said.[22] Steiner was at the precipice. According to Daniel van Bemmelen, also present, Ita Wegman then said to him, "But Herr Doktor, surely you cannot abandon the Society. You told me this summer [in Wales] how you want to build the new Society under your leadership." Steiner then stood up, walked over to her, took her hands and said warmly and intimately, "Ja Frau Doktor [Wegman], if you help me, I will risk it."[23]

Her words helped in his decision to reorganize the Society. This happened during the Christmas Conference of 1923, attended by about 800 members out of a total of about 12,000. Here the foundation stone of the new Society was symbolically laid. Rudolf Steiner became its president, which he had not been in the old Society. With this, he assumed responsibility for everything the members would do as anthroposophists in the world.

Steiner was guided in his work in the Theosophical Society and later in the Anthroposophical Society by the masters of Christian occultism in the Western world: Christian Rosenkreutz and Master Jesus. He said that, at the laying of the foundation stone during the Christmas Conference, Christian Rosenkreutz with his hosts entered the room where the conference was held.[24] Steiner worked closely with him, as is visible in the meditation image he gave to Wegman, in which Christian Rosenkreutz in a blue stole and Steiner in a red stole stand side by side before an altar.[25]

Steiner's problem with the Anthroposophical Society was that he had started in a theosophical circle in which there was little interest in making spirituality fruitful in social life. For this purpose, younger people later wanted to get involved; but they belonged to other karmic groups. The Society suffered from the passivity of its members, the inner opposition to Steiner's intentions, and from the

---

22. Emanuel Zeylmans, *Willem Zeylmans van Emmichoven*, Arlesheim, 1979, 121, 124. (*W. Z. van Emmichoven: An Inspiration for Anthroposophy*, London, 2002.)

23. J.E. Zeylmans van Emmichoven, *Wer war Ita Wegman*, vol. 1, Heidelberg, 1990, 264. (*Who was Ita Wegman: A Documentation*, vol. 1, Spring Valley, 1995.)

24. See Margarethe and Erich Kirchner-Bockholt, *Rudolf Steiner's Mission and Ita Wegman*, Forest Row, 2016.

25. Judith von Halle, *Rudolf Steiner: Meister der Weissen Loge* [Rudolf Steiner: Master of the White Lodge], Dornach, 2011, 86.

conflicts that arose among its members. At the Christmas Conference of 1923, he wanted to create a new framework for spiritual work.

Peter Deunov

After Peter Deunov gathered his first three disciples for the initial meeting of his spiritual circle in July 1900, he confidently continued his work. Until 1942, these conventions took place almost every year in August. Until 1915, he invited the participants personally; after that, anyone who associated with his circle was welcome. From 1926, the annual conventions no longer took place in the east of the country (Varna, Burgas, and Veliko Turnovo), but in the west, in Sofia and in the mountains, near the seven lakes of Rila.

Several phases can be distinguished in the period up to 1922, which are not as clearly marked as in Steiner's work. In September 1901, Deunov passed through his second lunar node. In this year his travels throughout Bulgaria began, which for eleven years brought him into contact with a large number of people in many towns and villages, where he held lectures on popular science subjects. In his lectures he showed that the mysteries of life and of nature are determined by laws. His work was always aimed at elevating the religious spirit of the Bulgarian people. This was a metamorphosis of the work for which he had been prepared as a Methodist pastor and missionary. He prayed for the people who needed help. And at the same time, he brought attention to the principles of spiritual science, such as in the area of curing diseases.

Deunov conducted physiognomic and phrenological research in Bulgaria on the shape of heads and skulls to determine people's abilities and talents. He measured thousands of skulls and studied faces. People came to him of themselves because, he later said, it cost nothing and "the Bulgarians are very curious." He had probably learned about this kind of research, which had become a popular form of science, in America.[26] Through his clairvoyant abilities, Deunov was able to make statements about the development of chil-

---

26. Diagrams of the skull from that time show about 35 areas of different abilities. For example, even today we speak of a "language nodule" or a "math nodule." Phrenology as practiced by Deunov is to be distinguished from the materialistic phrenology discredited by Italian criminologist Cesare Lombroso.

The Creation of Their Spiritual Circles

dren, but through his research he also gained psychological insight into the character and abilities of the Bulgarian people. In 1901 and 1902, he published five articles on "Skulls and Faces." In the famous Rila Monastery, he examined skulls of monks who died long ago.[27]

Along the way, Deunov familiarized people with his mission. Among them were pupils of Tolstoy, Theosophists, pacifists, vegetarians, and advocates of Esperanto. A large number of his first pupils were connected with spiritualism. Deunov told them to examine the "spirits" that appeared at séances and to pay attention to what they produced in one's inner life. When he himself participated in séances, he demonstrated that these "spirits" submitted to him. Gradually his students lost interest in spiritualism.

From 1901, more participants came to the annual summer conventions of Deunov's association, which in 1899 was already informally called the Chain. From 1906, this name appears in the protocols of the conventions. Deunov was addressed as "Mr. Deunov" during the conventions. Only from 1922 did everyone call him the *Uchitel* (Teacher).[28] Sometimes this word is also translated as Master, but this is a term from Theosophy. Many people kissed his hand out of respect, as they were used to doing with older people, priests, and monks. Members of the Chain were expected to contribute the "divine tithe." This is the ten percent of the harvest that was earmarked for God in the Old Testament. Even today, people from the School of the White Brotherhood donate ten percent of their income or time to the school.

In these conventions, which lasted a week, participants rose early to meditate around sunrise and then did gymnastic and breathing exercises, praying and chanting. Deunov held lectures, which the participants then discussed in groups. He prepared a *naryad*, an order of service with chants, prayers, mantras, and texts from the Bible. He also gave exercises for spiritual concentration and health, and instructions to local groups for work in the coming year. Partic-

---

27. Omraam Mikhaël Aïvanhov, *Life with the Master Peter Deunov*, Fréjus, 2014, 250–52.

28. The convention protocols of the August 8, 1915 meeting described Peter Deunov as "the Master" for perhaps the first time.

ipants sang spiritual songs, took walks with each other, and had conversations with Deunov. There was also a ritual meal, the "last supper," for which participants brought bread, wine, fish, vegetables, and fruit. This was not a Eucharist, but a commemoration of the life of Jesus. For the eighth convention in 1907, Deunov had a silver set of ritual objects made (a chalice with 14 cups), for a meal of bread and wine. His disciples could also perform this ritual.

The atmosphere during the meetings was mystical. The participants experienced that they were participating in a sacred ritual and communicating with the Spirit. Just as spiritual beings spoke through Rudolf Steiner during meetings of his esoteric school, the same happened in the meetings of the Chain. Peter Deunov relayed messages from Christ, angels, and those among the deceased who participated in the gathering.[29] Maria Kozakova wrote about the 1905 convention to Georgi Mirkovich:

> There is something supernatural, something divine, regarding Mr. Deunov. He often speaks on behalf of Christ, or as if he is Christ himself. In our sessions, God said about Mr. Deunov, "He is my prophet and your teacher. Listen to him! He is my image, and meek and humble like me. Peter Deunov is a ray of my Spirit. He is permanently in association with me and knows everything, but he is not allowed to reveal it all at once to you. He will do that gradually, according to your spiritual elevation."[30]

During this time, Deunov passed on the word of Jesus Christ in letters and sermons to his disciples.[31] In 1909, he explained that the members of the Chain were in the chain of divine love. In this context, he gave them three commandments: love the Lord your God, love your neighbor as yourself, and be perfect.

When participants expressed their doubts, he said that God had brought them together, had taught them, and had spoken to them.

---

29. For example during the convention of 1906: see Peter Deunov, *Verigata na bozhestvena lyubov* [The Chain of Divine Love], Sofia, 2007, 11–13.

30. Kraleva, *The Master Peter Deunov*, Sofia, 33.

31. See Beinsa Douno, *The Teacher*, vol. 1, "The Dawning Epoch," London, 2016, 1–14.

The Creation of Their Spiritual Circles

Christ, about whom he preached, was in their midst; you can hear his voice, he said, but you cannot see him. "What I say is dictated by the one who sent me. The new religion is the teaching of Christ on the physical plane. It is the religion of pure forms, music, harmony, and poetry."

Peter Deunov in 1907, 40 years old

In 1904, Deunov settled in Sofia, where he lived in a room in the house of a Protestant couple who belonged to the circle of his disciples. There he began lecturing on Sunday mornings at 10 AM to a small circle of friends. Starting in 1910, these were public lectures, which, like almost all of his lectures, began with a quotation from the Bible or a prayer. They were very lively, and included anecdotes, instructive stories from folk tradition and literature, as well as events from the lives of people he had met. His listeners noticed that they received answers to the questions that lived in them, which also happened at Steiner's lectures. When there was not enough room inside at these Sunday lectures, a window was opened and the listeners stood in the garden, even in winter. Peter Deunov then sat in front of the open window. A neighbor at the time was the young socialist Georgi Dimitrov, who was once hidden by Deunov when the police were looking for him. In 1946, Dimitrov became communist head of state and left the White Brotherhood in peace.

Rudolf Steiner and Peter Deunov

Peter Deunov in 1907 (seated right)

Starting in 1910, Deunov spoke at various conventions of the Chain about the symbol of the pentagram, which he had received as an inner revelation in 1898. In 1911 he gave to all participants a black and white image of the pentagram, which was the symbol of their spiritual work, of the development of their souls. This image, with the many symbols on it, was meant to be studied. Inscribed around the pentagram is the phrase "In the fulfillment of the will of God lies the strength of the human soul." The five connecting lines between the corner points of the pentagram are the paths of the five great creative forces: goodness, justice, love, wisdom, and truth. The qualities of these paths, which each had their own color, were to be applied in daily life. In 1922, a colored version of the pentagram was made.

The instructions that the members of the Chain had to carry out included acquiring these five qualities. For example, Deunov gave a method for strengthening Goodness: "This year each of you will plant ten plum seeds, ten apple seeds, ten cherry seeds, and ten pear seeds. Nourish them and take good care of them." A method for strengthening Justice: "During the coming year, you are to water forty fruit trees. As you do so, ball your fists and say 'I want to be righteous!' The meaning of this is: 'As I take care of the trees, so God

The Creation of Their Spiritual Circles

will take care of me.'" And a method for reinforcing the truth: "During the coming year, you will find forty beings trampled and in need in some way. You will comfort them in the name of Truth."

In 1911, Deunov bought a house for the Chain in the village of Arbanasi near Veliko Turnovo. Thereafter, meetings were held here. In June 1912, he retired here for several months to work on his second book, *The Testament of the Colored Rays of Light*.[32] On August 15, 1912, he presented a copy of *The Testament* to each of the 63 participants of the convention of the Chain in Veliko Turnovo. In this book, he had arranged quotations from the Bible into ten groups as manifestations of the Spirit: the Spirit of Love, the Spirit of Life, the Spirit of Holiness, the Spirit of Wisdom, the Spirit of the Soul, the Spirit of Truth, the Spirit of Strength, the Spirit of Grace, the Spirit of Christ, and the Holy Spirit. Each of these manifestations has its own color. By meditating on the texts and enveloping ourselves in a visualization with the corresponding colors, we can develop certain qualities. This book is commonly used in the brotherhood. It appeared in the same year as the book of weekly meditations by Rudolf Steiner (*The Calendar of the Soul*), who also began the development of eurythmy this same year.[33] *The Testament* closed with the "sacred commandment of the master":

> Love the perfect way of Truth and Life. Place Goodness as the foundation of your home, Righteousness as the measure of your life, Love as its adornment, Wisdom as the wall of defense, and Truth as the light of your path. Only then will you come to know me, and I shall reveal myself to you.

In early September 1912, the then 48-year-old Deunov was on a mountain near Arbanasi when the Spirit of Christ appeared to him

---

32. Beinsa Douno (Peter Deunov), *The Testament of the Colored Rays of Light*, Sofia, 1995.

33. Paneurythmy teacher Svetoslav Costoff considers *The Testament* to be the primal form of paneurythmy. It opens with 28 bible quotations, just as the first section of paneurythmy includes 28 exercises. The section "The Father of All Light" anticipates the Sun Rays; and the section "The Fruit of the Spirit," with the five spiritual forces, refers to the Pentagram.

asking, "Peter, will you give your body, your heart, your mind—and will you work for me?" He answered, "I listen, my Lord. Your will be done in heaven as well as on earth." Then the Spirit of Christ entered him.[34]

In 1912, Peter Deunov had reason to act. There was strife among members of the Chain, and gossiping. On September 6, 1912, he warned that this disharmony was being used by the Dark Lodge. Its dark forces were hindering his work, so he required a promise that the members would restore harmony. If they did not, he would leave the Chain within three years. Only in an atmosphere of love and self-sacrifice could Christ work; and, he added, "Christ and I are one."[35]

On October 8, 1912, the First Balkan War broke out. The allies Bulgaria, Serbia, Montenegro, and Greece attacked the Ottoman Empire to expand their territory. In November, Deunov unsuccessfully advised the Bulgarian king to make peace with the Turks and not attack his allies. After the May 1913 peace agreement, Bulgaria was not satisfied with what it had received. It began the Second Balkan War in June 1913 by attacking Serbia and Greece to capture Macedonia, which had been connected with Bulgaria in the Middle Ages and where a language is spoken that is very closely related to Bulgarian. The war lasted several months and ended in complete defeat. Two years later, Bulgaria entered World War I after declaring war on Serbia in October 1915, again hoping to gain Macedonia after a victory by Germany and Austria-Hungary. Deunov had advised the king, who was of German descent, to remain neutral. Like Steiner, he had seen the war coming.

On Sunday, March 22, 1914 (according to the modern calendar), at the beginning of spring, Deunov invited the spiritual circle that had gathered for several years for his lectures to a banquet in Sofia. After reading texts from the last chapter of each of the four gospels, he spoke the following words:

---

34. Krustev (ed.), *Izgrevut na Bialoto Bratstvo*, [From the White Brotherhood], vol. 2, 33. Another source gives the year 1914.

35. Beinsa Douno, *The Teacher*, vol. 1, 59.

The Creation of Their Spiritual Circles

"Not many realize the importance of today's date, but for some it will be a day to remember, because today one epoch has ended and a new one is beginning." In the course of his speech, he said, "This day is a great spiritual day. There is a gathering up above, from where all our friends are sending you their greetings.... Today a new epoch is beginning in the spiritual world." The closing words of his speech were: "Let us uplift ourselves and imagine the divine picture of today's celebration in heaven. The spirits will descend from heaven to make human beings satisfied with what they have, and Christ will come with them. Either they will come with a blessing, a renovation of the contemporary order, or—if it is seen that it cannot be renovated—they will come with a catastrophe that destroys everything from the foundations, after which the building will begin completely anew. We must not be afraid of this possibility. Christ is always above us and among us. Let us leave this meeting with Christ in our souls. Let us open our souls and hearts, so that Christ can enter them and bless us. Amen."[36]

On March 22, 1914, according to Deunov, a new chapter in human history began. It was the realization of the prophetic message of 1898—the beginning of the return of Christ. Since 1914, this day, March 22, has been celebrated in the School of the White Brotherhood as the first day of the spiritual New Year. A week after this meeting, on March 29, 1914, public Sunday readings officially began, which continued through November 28, 1943. They were collected in the volumes of *Sila i Zhivot* (Strength and Life). Informally, these lectures had already begun in 1911. They present the new teaching on the development of consciousness in the age of the returning Christ. From the perspective of the spiritual world, the new age of Aquarius began on March 22, 1914, as Deunov said on that day. This date for the beginning of the new age is not related to the visible constellation of Aquarius (the vernal equinox does not enter the constellation of Aquarius until 2374), but to the beginning of the "end of time" with the return of Christ in the etheric.

In February 1917, Deunov began a series of Thursday lectures for married women, which continued until June 1932. As wives, moth-

36. Ibid., 119–22.

ers, educators, and teachers, they could contribute much to changing society. These 36 lectures were published in 2006 under the title *Velikata Majka* (The Great Mother). According to Deunov, child rearing began during pregnancy. Mothers had to raise their children to be pacifists, for then wars would cease. About the woman's task, he noted:

"She must first elevate herself and then her husband. The good and graceful woman represents the ideal for the man. She instills within him the impulse towards the sublime, forces him to think, and at the same time she brings peace and tranquility to his soul." On October 18, 1932, he pronounced: "The present state of the social order is due in every field to the degradation of women. The salvation of the world lies in the upliftment of the woman."[37]

Peter Deunov in 1914, age 50, on Cherni Vruch

During the wars, Deunov passed messages to widows of fallen officers from their spouses. This is evident from a 1917 report on him by Sofia's beleagured city commander Svinarov.[38] Because his criticism of the Bulgarian government's war policy and his teachings would undermine the morale of soldiers in this time of war, he was interned in a hotel in Varna from August 1917 to June 1918. He corresponded with his disciples and many visited him. In Varna, he could watch the sun rise on the beach. He was also able to visit his old father, who lived as a hermit in the church of the Archangel

---

37. Beinsa Douno (Peter Deunov), *The Woman: Source of Love and Life*, Sofia, 2001, 27–29. https://ia600703.us.archive.org/3/items/PeterDeunov/Woman_source OfLoveAndLife.pdf.

38. Thomas Heinzel, *Weisse Bruderschaft und Delphische Idee* [The White Brotherhood and Delphic Idea], Erfurt, 2013, 115.

The Creation of Their Spiritual Circles

Michael and died in 1918. During this time he met Michael Ivanov (1900–1986), who became an important disciple.

Peter Deunov in 1920, 56 years old

After the war, many students, artists, and intellectuals (including teachers, doctors, and officers) joined his movement. His influence and teachings spread throughout Bulgaria. The country had failed to achieve its war aims and ruined its economy, leading to political and social unrest. There was a need for a new teaching that linked faith and science and that had a moral message—one of practical significance, based on love. The teachings Deunov propagated offered a perspective for the renewal of Bulgarian society and provided a new identity and mission for the Bulgarian people.

At the 1919 summer convention, Deunov recommended that participants call themselves disciples of the White Brotherhood. He explained that this is a spiritual brotherhood that exists not on earth, but in the invisible world. It consists of intelligent beings who have completed their evolution and can manifest themselves to help humanity. They are beings from all the hierarchies of angels, as well as highly evolved human beings who give guidance to humanity. At the head of these is Christ.

The publication of Deunov's lectures began in 1919. Deunov wanted to investigate whether an occult school could be established as early as the following year. To this end, at the beginning of 1920, he held three lectures ("Electricity and Magnetism" for men, "Gentleness and Humility" for women, and "Suffering" for both). He spoke about the requirements of discipleship, and noted: "Do not think it is easy to be a student of an occult school. Its purpose is not to help improve your temporal life, but to consciously do the will of God." His disciples were not ready for that, nor were the five women who formed a circle in the summer of 1920 to study the five qualities of the pentagram. From this emerged a "class of virtues" with ten women. In the difficulties of life, this initiative collapsed in 1926.

At the summer convention in 1920, about 1,200 participants were present. Deunov spoke of a "great occult school," in which the students are given the requirements of absolute purity and self-control. At this meeting, excursions into nature were made for the first time. There were plans to establish communes in which disciples would live together. Deunov advised them at the 1921 convention to begin with a few families. Five circles were then chosen and given practical tasks. Their purpose was to awaken the talents and abilities of the disciples, to develop the common work, to help each other, and to pass on knowledge and experiences to others. For this purpose, groups of five to twenty disciples were formed throughout the country, who now began to address each other as "brother" and "sister." The leaders of these groups could be either men or women.

The Creation of Their Spiritual Circles

The members of these groups were instructed to research themes from natural science, Theosophy, and occultism, and to write essays on them.

The esoteric School of the White Brotherhood was founded in Sofia on February 24, 1922. Deunov also called this school "the school of God" or the "school of Christ, where the powerful forces of the invisible world express themselves, the luminous advanced beings, working for the elevation of all humanity." The school was open to anyone who wanted to become a student of it. Over the course of 22 years, Deunov had brought together a circle of disciples with whom he could work in an occult school like the Teacher. He brought not his own teaching, he kept saying, but the teaching of Christ, who is also the head of the School of the White Brotherhood on earth.

This school had no organizational structure; there was no formal membership. Deunov instructed students to observe the ethics and laws of the White Brotherhood, and to be worthy people. On the value of the school's teachings to society, he said:

> We can show you how to apply the science of life. We will draw knowledge from living nature. However, this should be taken up by many men and women, by many workers. We will experiment and show the world the first model of renewing modern society. We do not demand blind faith and we will not call on you: come with us, be our followers. We want to present a model that anyone can follow and be devoted to the law of love.[39]

Retrospective

Rudolf Steiner began to gather his disciples in the German Theosophical Society, where he found over a hundred people who were open to his Christian-esoteric teachings and path of schooling. A decade later, through his lectures, he had gathered about 2,500 people who had become members of the Anthroposophical Society. Peter Deunov also traveled around giving lectures to find people who were open to the task of elevating the religious spirit of the Bulgarian people. At the annual conventions of the Chain, he him-

---

39. Kraleva, *The Master Peter Deunov*, 41.

self invited the disciples with whom he wanted to work intensively. Here a community of people who did inner work was formed.

The Christ initiates Rudolf Steiner and Peter Deunov became proclaimers of the return of Christ in 1910. The German Theosophical Society in those years was a center of artistic impulses arising from Steiner's work with Goethe's *Fairy Tale* and its metamorphosis into the Mystery Dramas. In Bulgaria, the nuclei of a brotherhood—in which, though Deunov, Christ acted as Teacher—spanned the entire country. In the local groups, people performed the tasks he gave them. They worked on themselves and made studies of nature.

In 1923, the Anthroposophical Society was going through a difficult time. Its enemies had set fire to the living center of the movement, the Goetheanum. The members were not awake, and the board was not functioning properly. Steiner considered continuing with a small group of students, but decided to take charge of the reorganized Society of 12,000 members. In Bulgaria, the government and church kept a close eye on Deunov, but they could not hinder the fruitful development of his work. By the summer of 1920, 1,200 disciples had already gathered. By 1922, this work had progressed to the point where an occult school could be established.

4

The Work in Their Spiritual Schools

Shortly after each other, Peter Deunov and Rudolf Steiner founded their esoteric schools. The 57-year-old Deunov did so in February 1922. He would have another 22 years to build the White Brotherhood school until his death in 1944. At the end of 1923, the 62-year-old Steiner was faced with the choice of leaving the Anthroposophical Society and continuing with a small group of members, or else refounding it on another basis. He chose the latter, and called the members together for a Christmas conference. After nine months, however, illness forced him to cancel his lectures and courses. He died six months later, on March 30, 1925, and so the new spiritual school remained unfinished.

The re-establishment of the Anthroposophical Society took place at a conference held from December 24, 1923 to January 1, 1924. Steiner had developed a threefold structure: a spiritual school (the Free School of Spiritual Science), the Anthroposophical Society with its 12,000 members, and a third part, which included Marie Steiner's publishing house, Ita Wegman's clinic, the Society's membership administration, and the management of assets and property.

Steiner had worked out the statutes of the Anthroposophical Society and proposed a board, in which he would assume the chairman's role. The Swiss poet Albert Steffen became vice president, Günther Wachsmuth became secretary-treasurer; Marie Steiner, Ita Wegman, and Elisabeth Vreede were the other board members. This board was to function as an esoteric board by being connected with the spiritual world, and it would take initiatives. Steiner also expected the members to take initiatives with their will-power and in openness to the questions of our time.

Rudolf Steiner and Peter Deunov

The foundation on which the new Society was to be built consisted of the spiritual foundation stones that the members carried in their hearts. In their work in the world, in their harmonious cooperation, they were to build upon these foundations stones a spiritual Goetheanum. Steiner gave the Foundation Stone Meditation for this purpose. The situation in which the new Society had to be founded in the hearts of the members was dramatic. The wooden "first Goetheanum" (the Johannes Building) had burned down a year before. Steiner had created a model for the second Goetheanum, which was to be built from concrete on the foundations of the first. Its construction began in 1924 and was completed four years later.

Rudolf Steiner in 1924, 63 years old

Steiner also became the leader of the Free School of Spiritual Science, which included sections for the various areas in which practical work was to be done from Anthroposophy. The School was to be created with three classes under his general direction—with a First Class led by Ita Wegman, a Second Class led by Marie Steiner, and a Third Class under his own leadership. On February 15, 1924, Steiner gave the first of a total of nineteen class lessons, which included meditations for entering the spiritual world and communicating with spiritual beings. The last class lesson was given on August 2, 1924. All class lessons were held in Dornach. From April 3 to September 20, 1924, he repeated lessons in Prague, Bern, Breslau, Torquay, London, and Dornach. It is notable that, except for Breslau (where he was present to give an agricultural course), he did not repeat class lessons in Germany. According to Ita Wegman, it was his intention to hold class lessons later in Germany, and other countries as well. These nineteen lessons were part of the content of the First Class.

The Work in Their Spiritual Schools

Further parts, as well as the contents of the two other Classes could no longer be given due to Steiner's illness and his death in 1925.[1]

The Free School of Spiritual Science was a mystery school, the center of what Steiner called the "new mysteries." The temples of the ancient cultures used to have attached to them mystery schools in which priests trained people who were to perform leading tasks in these cultures—for example, as kings, doctors, or master builders. For this purpose, they underwent training in which they developed their inner capacities and were subjected to tests of courage leading, in due course, to an opening of their organs of spiritual perception (chakras). The latter occurred during an initiation that lasted three-and-a-half days, during which they were put into a state of deep sleep. In this *unconscious* state, they made a journey through the spiritual world. By contrast, in the new mysteries, a *conscious* state was to enable communication with the spiritual world.

Steiner did not know whether the spiritual world would accept his leadership of both the Anthroposophical Society and The Free School of Spiritual Science. This was a great sacrifice for him because it meant that he became responsible for everything the members would do as anthroposophists. It was therefore a great relief to him that the spiritual world accepted his decision and made possible an abundant flow of revelations in the field of karma research. However, the success of the new Society depended upon the members coming to an understanding of their own karma and taking up the new impulses. Steiner set the condition that the members harmonize their mutual karma. The members came from different karmic currents and now had to cooperate with each other. In June 1924, Steiner told the priest Rudolf Meyer that the new impulses of the Christmas Conference had not been taken up, but that there was still time—until autumn, until the Feast of Michael (nine months after the Christmas Conference). If that did not happen, the ahrimanic powers would strike.[2]

In the new Society, Steiner needed cooperation with Ita Wegman (1876–1943), just as he had needed cooperation with Marie von

---

1. Steiner had intended three Classes. See pages 103–4 for further notes on this.
2. Von Beckerath, *Rudolf Steiners Leidensweg* [RS's Path of Suffering], 228–29.

Rudolf Steiner and Peter Deunov

Ita Wegman

Sivers from 1901. Through his own spiritual research, Steiner knew that he had been connected to Wegman in five lifetimes. She, however, did not know this. Building a new mystery school thus depended on her inner development. When she was a Theosophist, Wegman had met Steiner in Berlin as early as 1902, and in 1905 was accepted into his esoteric school. In this year, she realized that Steiner had already been her teacher in a past life and would also be her teacher in the future. On the New Year's Eve of 1922/23, when the first Goetheanum burned down, her relationship to Steiner changed. It dawned on her that he was completely alone in his work. She then decided to support him completely. Thus began for her a process of inner awakening.

Ita Wegman later stated that her karmic connections with Steiner were revealed to her a few months after the fire.[3] In August 1923, in Wales, she asked him about a contemporary "mystery medicine" that would be based again on the principle of initiation. As she wrote in 1925,[4] her karma had been fully revealed to her in Wales. Steiner gave her meditation texts to support her awakening.[5] Among them was a text, probably from October 1923, in which he listed the places where they had worked together: on the Tigris (in Sumeria), in Ephesus, with the Kabirs (on the island of Samothrace), on Odilienberg (in Alsace), in a monastic cell and on the hill of Dornach.[6] In November 1923, she asked Steiner not to abandon the Society.

---

3. J. E. Zeylmans van Emmichoven, *Die Erkraftung des Herzens* [The Power of the Heart], Arlesheim, 2009, 99.
4. J. E. Zeylmans van Emmichoven, *Wer war Ita Wegman?*, vol. 1, 319.
5. This process is described in *Die Erkraftung des Herzens*.
6. Ibid., 148.

The Work in Their Spiritual Schools

Prior to the 1923 Christmas conference, Steiner spoke about the initiation methods of the ancient mysteries; and during the conference, he spoke about some of his past lives and his previous cooperation with Wegman's individuality. Few attendees will have understood this. He spoke of Enkidu and Gilgamesh in Mesopotamia, of the temple of Ephesus, and of Aristotle and Alexander the Great.[7] From January 4, 1924, he called Wegman "Mysa" in his letters to her (invoking her previous life as temple priestess at the temple of Artemis in Ephesus, where he had been the priest Cratylus). In a later incarnation, he was the Greek philosopher Aristotle, and she Alexander the Great. The letters Steiner wrote to her are deeply moving and show how important this renewed collaboration was for him. They are letters of a purely spiritual love.

In a letter to Albert Steffen dated August 21, 1925, Wegman wrote:

> Before his illness, the Doctor [Steiner] gave me a small cross with small rubies set in roses, which he used to wear on a red ribbon around his neck. He put it on me with his own hands after we had performed a ritual act.

The other members of the Society's board knew nothing about this. They, along with leaders of the national societies, did not hear about it until April 25, 1930, when Wegman spoke about it and echoed Steiner's words, "From this moment we will be there together for the Michael School."[8]

This transfer of the rose cross may have taken place in August 1924 in Torquay (on England's south coast), after Steiner and his associates had made an exhausting car trip to Tintagel on August 17, 1924. He described that a knight met them inside the grounds of King Arthur's former initiation site. According to Paul Emberson, this was a knight of the Round Table, who had come for a meeting with Steiner. In the process, a connection would have been established between Steiner's *new* esoteric Michael school and King Arthur's *old* Michael school. Steiner may have given the rose cross

---

7. Rudolf Steiner, in *Mystery Knowledge and Mystery Centres* (CW 232) and *World History and the Mysteries in the Light of Anthroposophy* (CW 233).

8. For this and the preceding quotation, see Peter Selg, *Rudolf Steiner and Christian Rosenkreutz*, Gt. Barrington, MA, 2012, 97.

to Wegman immediately afterwards, so that the Michael school which they now led together was linked as well to the spiritual stream of Christian Rosenkreutz.[9]

Emberson points out that during the class lessons of August 19 in Torquay and August 27, 1924 in London, Steiner introduced a new cultic element for the protection of the class: the occult sign of Michael. Moreover, Wegman received the great Rosicrucian meditation from Steiner at some point.[10] This may have occurred at the time of her ordination as co-leader of the First Class. After practicing this meditation in her imagination, she had to take from her heart each evening the spiritual rose cross she had previously placed in her heart and with it ascend a mountain, where she gave this cross to a "brother of the rose-colored and golden cross." The next morning she had to ascend this mountain again and receive the cross again from the brother. This spiritual cross can be considered an inner image of the golden cross that Steiner had given to Wegman. Emberson saw in this brother an Arthurian knight from Tintagel, who, like a knight of the Rose Cross, watched over the esoteric Michael School at night when Wegman slept.

After the Christmas conference, from January to August 1924, Steiner wrote a weekly piece to members for the Society's weekly newsletter *Das Goetheanum*, in which he presented his views on questions of principle and the objective of the new Society.[11] In addition, starting in February 1924, members received the *Anthroposophical Leading Thoughts*, in which Steiner wrote texts in very concentrated form with which members could deepen their anthroposophical work (CW 26).

He had hoped that the conference participants would understand the meaning of the evening lectures on the ancient mysteries and begin to understand their teacher's karma. After the members of the German Theosophical Society in 1902 had prevented his intention to concretely explore issues of karma and reincarnation, now, 21 years later, he was finally able to realize this intention. On February

---

9. Emberson, *From Gondishapur to Silicon Valley*, vol. 3, 1605, 1616–626.
10. Emmichoven, *Die Erkraftung des Herzens*, 167–77.
11. Rudolf Steiner, *The Michael Mystery: Letters to Members* (CW 26).

The Work in Their Spiritual Schools

16, 1924, he commenced a series of revelations of karma that continued until August 27, 1924, amounting in the end to 81 lectures.[12] On May 4 and 9, 1924, he described the well-known karma exercise that spans three nights and four days.[13]

In Arnhem, on July 20, 1924, he spoke for the first time about the Michael School in the spiritual world, in which Michael acted as teacher to a large group of human individualities, angels, and nature beings from the 15th century to the beginning of the 19th century.[14] Here the future anthroposophists were prepared for the work that was to begin from the end of the Kali Yuga in 1899. In this work, individualities from the currents of Plato and Aristotle would join together to reconnect human intelligence with the spiritual world. From this was to emerge the new spiritual sciences, based on the principle of initiation.

Steiner gave an unimaginably large number of lectures in the half year between March and September 1924, sometimes as many as four, or even five, a day. Although at the outset of each lecture he gave an impression of exhaustion, as he entered into each lecture he was revived by an influx of forces from the spiritual world. In June of that year, he was in what is now Poland for the first course on biodynamic agriculture; his teaching on remedial pedagogy began at the end of June with a course in Dornach; and in August, he was in England with a course on the consciousness of the initiate.

That he was ill was apparent to all. As in the year 1923, when his life forces were exhausted by the fire at the Goetheanum, he had to drag himself to the speakers' podium; but as soon as he began to speak, he was filled with an unprecedented flow of power. On September 28, 1924, he delivered a lecture on John the Baptist and Lazarus-John. He felt inner resistance from the circle of listeners when he spoke about the entanglement of the karmic lines of these two

---

12. Rudolf Steiner, *Karmic Relationships*, six volumes (CW 235–240). In his lectures, Peter Deunov did not speak about concrete cases of reincarnation. Sometimes, however, he did this in conversations.

13. Rudolf Steiner, lectures of May 4 and 9, 1924, in *Karmic Relationships*, vol. 2 (CW 236).

14. Rudolf Steiner, lecture of July 20, 1924, in *Karmic Relationships*, vol. 6 (CW 240).

individualities. He was unable to finish this lecture and had to cancel those already scheduled.

Thus began Steiner's final illness, which would last six months. During this time he was cared for by the physician Wegman. He cherished hope in November 1924 that he would recover and be able to continue his work. In February 1925, he even ordered a wheelchair. In the early morning hours he was able to write. To the last, he continued work on the medical manual he wrote with Wegman, and on his autobiography. He read widely and maintained communication with members through letters and through the *Anthroposophical Leading Thoughts*. He could receive only a limited number of people. During his illness he was attacked by demons that had their origin in jealousy and other negative feelings toward Wegman from those close to him.[15]

On March 30, 1925, after a sudden deterioration in his condition, Steiner's life came to an end. He died on that day by 10 AM, at the age of 64. Earlier in his life, he himself had expected to live to over 80 years of age, which age had been common among his ancestors. In that case, he would have lived until the early 1940s and would have had time to develop Anthroposophy further. But the task he had set himself was too great, and the resistance from inside and outside the Society was immense.

Steiner's illness had its causes on several levels. On the physical level he suffered greatly from hemorrhoids, digestive problems, and a severe prostate enlargement. On the etheric level, he was exhausted by the many conversations about people's personal problems. His etheric body had already been greatly weakened by the conflagration of the first Goetheanum. This building was a living organism connected to his own life forces. One consequence of this was that his etheric body was no longer well-connected to his digestive organs.

On another level, his health had been undermined by his failure to bring to realization the new impulses with which he had intended to inaugurate an initiation culture at the Christmas Conference. He had actually come to understand this by the end of the conference,

---

15. Emmichoven, *Die Erkraftung des Herzens*, 379.

The Work in Their Spiritual Schools

because the resistance to the new impulse was strong. The members should have developed karmic consciousness and harmonized their mutual karma. By the end of September, the nine months in which these impulses should have begun to live among the members had run their course. Steiner expressed openly that the Christmas Conference had failed. He said so in September 1924 to the lawyer Bruno Krüger ("This impulse has been crushed") and to the eurythmist Ina Schuurman ("The Christmas Conference has failed"). In September 1924, he told Austrian anthroposophist Ludwig Polzer-Hoditz that the attempt of a Free School of Spiritual Science had also failed.[16]

Nevertheless, in a subsequent conversation with Polzer-Hoditz on November 11, 1924, he spoke of the further establishment of the school, with Ita Wegman leading the First Class, Marie Steiner leading the Second Class with 36 members, and he himself leading the Third Class with 12 members, who together would form the esoteric board.[17]

For many anthroposophists, everything had remained the same, and tensions within the Society were not lifted. The earlier opposition among members to karma revelations had led to the formation of anti-Michael demons who attacked Steiner himself, but could be neutralized at the Christmas conference. The German anthroposophist Gerhard von Beckerath speaks of Steiner's way of the cross in this regard, which left deep marks through his life with the Theosophists and anthroposophists—who did not understand, and even ignored, his intentions.

In addition, he was attacked from the outside world. Church circles, materialistic scientists, German nationalists, and occult groups targeted him. He was not adequately protected by the members. Circles around Hitler wanted to physically eliminate him. He would have been on their death list. Guardians of cultic traditions, possibly from the Freemasonic lodges and the Catholic Church, resented him for receiving a new cult for the Christian Community from the spiritual world.[18] Indeed, the fire that destroyed the first

---

16. Von Beckerath, *Rudolf Steiners Leidensweg*, 229.
17. Meyer, *Ludwig Polzer-Hoditz*, Basel, 1994, 665 ff.
18. Meyer, *Milestones*, ch. 18, "A Light in the Darkness of German Nationalism."

Rudolf Steiner and Peter Deunov

Goetheanum began behind a wall in the White Hall, where in September 1922, the Christian Community had been founded. And there were other groups that opposed Steiner's revelation of occult secrets they wanted to keep hidden.

According to some eyewitnesses, on January 1, 1924, immediately after the conclusion of the Christmas Conference, an attempt was made to poison Steiner. He was handed something during a gathering with many participants and immediately noticed that he was being poisoned. After collapsing, he drank a quantity of milk to neutralize the poison. Only a few knew about this, and Steiner did not want it to become known among the members.[19] That same evening, he gave another lecture.

While traveling, Ehrenfried Pfeiffer had met the person who ordered the poisoning. In a lecture he gave at the Goetheanum in the late 1950s, Pfeiffer said that this person had told him: "This poisoning should not have had a fatal consequence, but should have put Rudolf Steiner into a state in which he could no longer use his great occult faculties sovereignly and which would have had the practical effect of extinguishing them." In this way, a circle of occultists had wanted to discredit Steiner's path of schooling.[20]

As early as December 17, 1950, during a lecture in Spring Valley, USA, Pfeiffer had highlighted Steiner's illness and death from yet another perspective. During a train trip in 1934, presumably in the United States, he met a doctor and occultist who told him that Steiner's illness had been caused by occultists who wanted to prevent Steiner from telling more about the spiritual function of the heart. Therefore, they directed forces at him against which he could not defend himself.[21]

For Steiner himself, these outside forces were not the main cause of his passing (if we take as authentic the communications Countess

---

19. See the reports of eyewitnesses in: Wilfried Hammacher, *Marie Steiner*, Stuttgart, 1998, 263–65; and Meyer, *Milestones*, 148–49.

20. Meyer (ed.), *Ein Leben für den Geist: Ehrenfried Pfeiffer*, 233–34.

21. This would involve changes in the heart which, according to Pfeiffer, would gradually form a fifth heart chamber. Rudolf Steiner does not mention a fifth ventricle in his lectures. Possibly he discussed this with Pfeiffer, or this is an interpretation

The Work in Their Spiritual Schools

Johanna Keyserlingk received from the deceased Steiner on the morning of his cremation). The actual cause was that the "culture of the heart" was prevented. According to Steiner, Countess Keyserlingk had the clairvoyant abilities of a future culture. She recognized in Steiner's message the way he always spoke:

My mission has ended.
What I could give to the maturity of human beings, I have given to them.
I leave, because I did not find ears that could perceive the Word of the Spirit behind the word.
I leave, because I did not find eyes that could see images of the Spirit behind the earthly images.
I leave because I did not find people who could realize my will.
The mysteries will remain veiled until I come again.
I will come again, and will unveil the mysteries when I can establish in spiritual worlds an altar, a temple for human souls. Then I will come again. Then I will continue to unveil the mysteries.
Those who have prevented the culture of the heart are guilty of my death.
If the people had reached into the depths of their hearts, they would have found the strength to meet the requirements of the current tasks.[22]

Rudolf Steiner was cremated, but he himself had not wanted that. He had told Ludwig Polzer-Hoditz that he wanted to be buried on the grounds of the Goetheanum; but when Polzer arrived in Dornach, the cremation had already been arranged and the board did not want to change that.[23] On the way back from the cremation, a heated argument broke out between Marie Steiner (who, as a widow, wanted to take the urn home) and Ita Wegman (who felt that Steiner's ashes belonged to the Society). These two women did not like each other. Marie Steiner saw Wegman as a rival, with

---

of Pfeiffer or of the unknown occultists. After Steiner's death, however, these occultists would have noted that this new knowledge about the heart was necessary for the salvation of mankind. See Ehrenfried Pfeiffer, *Heart Lectures*, Spring Valley, 1982, 1–12. See also Meyer (ed.), *Ein Leben für den Geist: Ehrenfried Pfeiffer*, 135–47.

23. Meyer, *Ludwig Polzer-Hoditz*, 253.

whom Steiner had taken a new direction. Marie Steiner represented the Theosophical beginnings of Steiner's work and Ita Wegman the continuation of his work in the new mysteries.

Here is not the place to pass judgment on the controversies between these two women that devastated the Society after Rudolf Steiner's death. Two months after his passing, in a May 1925 board meeting, Marie Steiner asked Wegman if Rudolf Steiner had told her that she had been Alexander the Great in a previous life. When Wegman confirmed this, Marie Steiner was puzzled and uncertain, and according to Elisabeth Vreede, at the end of the session—half in jest, half shyly—she made the unfortunate comment that it probably did not bode well for the board that Alexander was also ingloriously known in history.[24] She could not distinguish between Wegman in her present incarnation and the person she had been in one of her previous lives.

After Rudolf Steiner's death, Marie Steiner saw it as her task to *preserve* his work; Ita Wegman, however, wanted to *continue* it. She had been appointed by Steiner to lead the First Class (which Marie Steiner did not know), and so she continued the lessons further. This gave Marie Steiner the impression that Wegman wanted to take over the leadership of the Society. Wegman represented the young generation of anthroposophists who wanted to *apply* Anthroposophy. This rising generation could be found in Germany, but was especially active in the Netherlands and England.

Peter Deunov

Peter Deunov expected that it would take 20 years for the School of the White Brotherhood to function properly. With this prospect, on February 24, 1922, he began another great stage of 22 years until his death in 1944. At that time he pronounced:

> In this school you will be become acquainted with the methods and laws with which the White Brothers rule over Nature. You will get an idea of the greatness of Nature that surrounds us. We are now founding this mystical occult school. However, the danger is

---

24. Meyer, *Rudolf Steiner's Core Mission*.

The Work in Their Spiritual Schools

that occult knowledge may be used for the achievement of personal ends. This is why you need to cultivate the upright and steadfast morality of love, wisdom, and truth. In this great school of Christ, you will find the true methods of the new life your souls are seeking.[25]

In the school, anyone who wanted to could join the General Occult Class. Until the end of his life, Deunov lectured in this class every Wednesday at 5 AM, in fall and winter. These lectures were occult because they contained knowledge beyond the understanding by the human mind. In the meetings of this class, Deunov gave scientific explanations of spiritual phenomena and described the laws governing the human soul. His students had to study and work on themselves in order to participate in the new culture. He gave assignments to write articles, perform tasks, and do exercises. Each lecture was actually a mini-workshop. Everyone studied at their own level, gaining experience and receiving attention from Deunov. The disciples' lives became a series of lessons in which the laws of nature were learned. They were not to expect their situation to improve. It would first deteriorate before there would be improvement. This was their learning process, Deunov said. In October 1922, this class had 52 members.

Also on Feb. 24, 1922, the Special Youth Class began, to which Deunov invited young men and women, mostly students, who were not yet married. (After their marriage, they generally left this class.) New members could be recommended by older members and join after Deunov's approval. He called this the "Class of Purity" and gave lectures to them on natural science, astrology, occult sciences, poetry, music, the science of life, nature, and God. All these included for him the science of man's spiritual flourishing. These lectures, which included assignments, also continued until the end of his life. They were given on Friday mornings at 5 AM, also only in autumn and winter. In October 1922, 45 young people participated in them.

There was another inner circle in the school besides these two classes, called the "Internal Chain" or the "Internal School." It was

---

25. Kraleva, *The Master Peter Deunov*, 50.

Rudolf Steiner and Peter Deunov

not known who belonged to this "third" class. These were the most advanced disciples, who on a their inner path received the "call" of Peter Deunov and were guided by him in a spiritual way. In White Brotherhood school circles, it is believed that this internal school still exists and is directed by Deunov from the invisible world.[26]

Among the people who gathered around Deunov in the School of the White Brotherhood, we can distinguish three groups. In the first place, the disciples, who applied the rules in their lives. In the second place, the followers, who accepted the teachings but did not follow all its rules. And in the third place, interested people, who attended the public lectures.

Deunov employed a wide range of methods, of which the spoken word was the most powerful. A song was sung at the beginning and end of each lecture. Under the influence of music, the human mind opened to the content of his words. Music transforms the mind and heart; according to Deunov, it connects the physical and spiritual worlds. Beginning in 1922, he ultimately composed more than 170 pieces of music, which he was able to play on his violin with virtuosity. Among them were many songs with lyrics written by him, as well as musical exercises that he used in the two classes and that, because of their purity of tone, activated certain brain centers. Sometimes in his songs he used words from a language he called "Vatan," which he said was an ancient sacred language, as in the 1922 song "Fir-fyur-fen, tao bi aumen." The first three words, according to Deunov, mean "without fear, without darkness." In a paneurythmy song, "zoon mezun, zoon mezum (2x), binom tometo" is sung, confirming that our aspiration will be fulfilled.

Other methods he employed, besides the spoken word and music, were physical exercises, performing tasks during the meetings, working out themes after the lectures, conversations with him, excursions into nature to get in touch with the intelligent beings in nature, the communal life during the conventions and in the summer camps, and correspondence with his disciples. Deunov was reserved with his disciples so that they felt free in his presence. For

---

26. Kovacheva, *Die Weisse Bruderschaft* [The White Brotherhood], 83.

The Work in Their Spiritual Schools

him, prayer was the breathing of the soul and the most powerful method of achieving something and of growing inwardly.

The Bulgarian Orthodox Church was alarmed by the development of a spiritual school that could reach the entire population. As the son of a priest, Deunov had good personal connections with priests. Conventions included prayers for the priests, for the Bulgarian people, for the government, and for the peasants. Until 1914, Deunov asked his students to attend church and love the priests, but to live with Christ. He himself did not go to church, saying, "With our lives we show the priests how one should live, and we tell them how the teachings of Christ can be applied in all its parts."[27]

After earlier attacks from the Orthodox Church, a council of bishops declared on July 7, 1922 that Deunov had excommunicated himself and that his teachings were "heretical and dangerous to domestic peace and morality in society." The Church soon began to exclude his disciples. He was attacked in church publications, but the government left him alone. Protestant pastors, who often attended his lectures, took issue with his free interpretations of Holy Scripture. He maintained to them: "Mankind has outgrown many modern religions, for they are incompatible with the development of the human soul and do not meet the present needs of the heart and mind of man."[28] The main goal of life, according to Deunov, is not man's *salvation* (the central Protestant theme), but his *self-perfection* (the Orthodox theme of *theosis*, man's becoming divine).

Alexander Stamboliski, the prime minister of Bulgaria and leader of the Agrarian Party, invited Deunov to a conversation on July 26, 1922. He asked him questions about the nature and purpose of his teachings and gave him permission to hold conventions. They appeared to share the same opinion about the Orthodox Church. When asked about his teachings and his relationship to the Church, Deunov replied:

> "We follow the teaching of Love, the teaching of Christ, which is Love, Wisdom, and Truth. We seek the truth of soul, light of mind, and purity of heart. We try not only to believe in these principles,

---

27. Quoted in Kovacheva, ibid., 27.
28. Kraleva, *The Master Peter Deunov*, 56

but also to live them and manifest them in society, preparing thus to be of help to all humanity. We are not opposed to the Orthodox Church; but its ministers have strayed from the path of their calling and serve the dark lodge of their leaders, deceiving the entire Bulgarian people and turning service into a trade."

Stamboliski replied: "This is true. No priest is there because this is his calling; it is just a career, a way to gain a position. Now they want to divert you and us from the Church. But I know this: when there are too many sinners in a country, they lay their sins at the door of the pure."

Deunov: "Inside the Orthodox Church there is much darkness and discord; what it has adopted and applies from Christianity is obsolete. Young people are not satisfied with old traditions; they want something modern, capable of giving them light and scope for thinking."

Stamboliski: "You are right. Young people cannot be satisfied with what the priests have to offer them, and their wicked deeds discourage the young from going to church."

Deunov: "The church is in need of a reform, and the reform would consist in changing the ministers. They should serve with purity and sinlessness, in the name of the Spirit and Truth. The young generation should be given the food its development demands."[29]

On August 19, 1922, the feast day of the White Brotherhood, Deunov held the morning lecture "The New Life" in Veliko Turnovo. In attendance were more than a thousand of his disciples, citizens of this city, and a large number of representatives of the Orthodox clergy from all over the country. A disputation had been announced for the afternoon. Deunov predicted that, due to heavy weather, which indeed broke loose, this disputation would not take place; and he challenged his opponents to hold it on the top of the highest mountain in the country, Musala (2925 meters). This calls to mind the confrontation on Mount Carmel between the prophet Elijah and the 450 Old Testament priests of Baal, whose sacrifice was not accepted and who were subsequently killed. The Bulgarian

---

29. Ibid., 54.

The Work in Their Spiritual Schools

clergy did not want it to come down to a judgment of God, and so did not accept the proposal.

Later in 1922, Deunov, who was accustomed to going into the mountains, organized the El-Shadday camp in the Vitosha Mountains, immediately south of Sofia. On Thursdays, he and his disciples went to Vitosha to meditate at sunrise. Sometimes they left at 2 AM. for this purpose. A new activity was the youth camps, which took place annually, from the beginning of July 1923 until 1930. In late August 1923, Deunov and his disciples climbed Mount Cherni Vruch in the Vitosha Mountains. During the second youth camp in 1924, Mount Musala was climbed, which since then has been done every year. In the mountains, as well as in other situations, anyone could sit down with Deunov and ask him questions. Boyan Boev[30] recorded many of these conversations.

Peter Deunov conversation with his students, Boyan taking notes

In February 1925, Deunov had a chance meeting with King Boris III at his residence in Chamkoria (now Borovets). What they discussed is not known. The king was interested in printed texts by Deunov, which he received from his adviser Lyubomir Lulchev, a disciple of Deunov. Through Lulchev, the king sought Deunov's advice on government matters. These included questions about Hit-

---

30. To be pronounced in two syllables: Bo'ev.

ler and other foreign politicians.[31] In 1923, Prime Minister Stamboliski had been assassinated in a right-wing coup. On April 16, 1925, in the ongoing political chaos, Communists attacked the Holy Nedelya Church in Sofia. In this situation, Deunov was questioned and released by the police on July 21, 1925, after giving the statement below.[32]

> ### Protocol of an Interrogation, July 21, 1925
>
> I declare that my teaching is based on three main principles: Divine Love, Divine Wisdom, and Divine Truth.
>
> From these three principles it follows that we need absolute peace, mutual understanding between people, and mutual help for universal benefit.
>
> My teaching excludes any violence and demands absolute purity of thought, feeling, and action. One of the most important requirements for all followers is flawless morality.
>
> In order to be able to adopt and apply all truths of Christ's teaching, a disciple of the divine school must be pure in a physical, moral, and spiritual sense. Any violation of this requirement is an important obstacle to his development. A student must be flawless in every respect, both to himself and to others, to society, and to the state. I recommend the observance of established laws and regulations. Every imperfection and flaw in the social and state order can be corrected by means of self-perfection, for it has been said, "Be ye therefore perfect, even as your Father in heaven is perfect."
>
> The Church must always be in full accord with Divine Love, Wisdom, and Truth.
>
> I am not involved in politics, because that is not among our objectives. Only people who have yet to study life go into politics. I only preach about what is good and wise.
>
> Knowledge of life is required to grasp Divine Wisdom and to understand Divine Truths. This knowledge is taught to those who study and grow by their own will. If they are mentally and morally sound, they can easily learn the lessons; if they are not, they can give up this task, which is beyond their powers.

---

31. Heinzel, *Weisse Bruderschaft und Delphische Idee*, 102.
32. Kraleva, *The Master Peter Deunov*, 55.

The Work in Their Spiritual Schools

> I neither call nor force nor detain anyone against his will. My teaching applies the law of reasonable freedom.
>
> Whoever comes will not be rejected; whoever wants to go will not be stopped. No one is coerced; I help them all as they desire, with advice, instructions, and rational means, following the laws of Living Intelligent Nature. All this I do without self-interest. The Lord whom I serve provides for my subsistence.
>
> In view of the above, I declare that any complaints, testimonies, and criticism against me, no matter where they come from, are absolutely groundless. My teaching, elaborated in more than six volumes, and my life, are open to all, and this statement can be verified any time; therefore, no defense is required.
>
> This teaching assures the physical health, moral purity, and spiritual growth of all its followers, and my life is admittedly exemplary. The minor exceptions and delays in development are evidently due to atavistic reasons. That is to say, if among my many listeners there are one or two cases of spiritual hesitation or taint, this is due to themselves or to their parents. Their lives, both previously and presently, demonstrate that clearly. But they are not my disciples, although they may have come to me.
>
> This is all I have to say.

On August 29, 1925, Deunov was arrested during the convention in Veliko Turnovo for not having permission for the meeting. He was released again and decided to relocate his activity to Sofia after the city council held a citizens' signature campaign to ban the conventions thenceforward. Earlier, rioters dressed in black, incited by the Church and occultists, had tried to disrupt a public lecture in Veliko Turnovo.[33]

In the spring of 1926, in a clearing in the forest southeast of Sofia that had been purchased in 1921, a cottage was built for Deunov, where he could live and receive people. Here, from 1924, the community of Izgrev (Sunrise) emerged, where many young people built simple wooden houses until World War II. In 1926, the annual summer meeting, with 1460 participants, was held on this property.

---

33. Aïvanhov, *Life with the Master Peter Deunov*, 242–44.

Rudolf Steiner and Peter Deunov

Among the visitors was the journalist Stoyan Vatralski, who wrote a very positive report and noted that the School of the White Brotherhood would make Bulgaria known all over the world. In July 1927, a wooden hall for lectures was built, in which Deunov took a room. This hall became the center of the school. This is considered the foundation of Izgrev. One night, during the same year, an arson attempt was made by right-wing activists, which Deunov prevented. He turned on all the lights when the arsonists entered the Izgrev premises.

The center of the Brotherhood in Izgrev

In 1929, Deunov sent his disciple Magdalena Popova to Holland with a letter for Krishnamurti. A summer congress of the Order of the Star of the East was being held there in Ommen. This order had been set up by the leaders of the Theosophical Society to launch Krishnamurti as the world teacher, who was said to be the reincarnation of Christ, and the Maitreya Bodhisattva. On August 3, 1929, Krishnamurti renounced this claim and dissolved the order. He said that this was the conclusion of two years of deliberation. Possibly, Deunov's letter was decisive in this regard. Bulgarian Theosophist Atanas Dimitrov, who was also associated with the brotherhood,

The Work in Their Spiritual Schools

went to Ommen on foot. There, on his morning walks, he spoke with Krishnamurti several times and told him about Peter Deunov. According to these two Bulgarians, Krishnamurti is said to have declared in Ommen, "The World Teacher is in Bulgaria. It is Peter Deunov."[34] However, the text of the speech he then delivered, on August 3, 1929, lacks any reference to Deunov.[35]

In this same year, 1929, Deunov went with a group of disciples for the first time to the Rila Mountains, south of Sofia, where, according to him, there is the oldest esoteric school on earth. During the summer, the first Rila summer camp was held in the area of the Seven Lakes, at an altitude of more than 2,000 meters. A year later, on September 21, 1930, a new series of lectures began, held every Sunday morning at 5 AM in Izgrev, and open to all. The lectures dealt with the problems of life from scientific and pedagogical points of view, and continued until September 24, 1944.

Around 1930, Deunov's work received international acclaim. Articles about him appeared in Japan, Czechoslovakia, Italy, France, Switzerland, Germany, the Netherlands, England, Hungary, Brazil, Serbia, and Poland. Groups studying his teachings arose in a number of countries. Some years later, several of his lectures were translated into other languages, including Esp-eranto. People came from many countries to speak with him. After Deunov asked Michael Ivanov (1900–1986), who had been his student for 20 years, "if he would be

Michael Ivanov in 1937

---

34. Kovacheva, *Die Weisse Bruderschaft*, 198–99. Krustev (ed.), *Izgrevut na Bialoto Bratstvo* [From the White Brotherhood], vol. 1, "Reminiscences of Maria Todorova," 277–78.

35. https://jkrishnamurti.org/about-dissolution-speech.

Rudolf Steiner and Peter Deunov

willing [to go to France]," the latter settled in France in 1937.[36] From there, he spread the teachings of the White Brotherhood throughout the French-speaking world and far beyond.

In 1932, Deunov presented to his disciples a small booklet, *The World of Great Souls*. It contained eight chapters of eternal truths and was intended for daily contemplation. His disciples could reflect on these truths and discover how they manifest in the physical, spiritual, and divine worlds. According to Deunov, this method of reading would lead to increasing concentration and intuition and developing virtues. He gave the example of reflecting on the phrase "Do not wash yourself in a river that does not come from a spring." In the physical world, this is a river of muddy water. In the spiritual world, this phrase means living from thoughts, feelings, and desires that are not of divine origin. We then psychically wash ourselves in muddy water and become dirty in our souls. In the divine world, this is like having a transient life purpose. If, however, our life purpose is to serve God and Love, however, our life is like a river from a pure spring.[37]

Deunov had developed some rhythmic exercises to music as early as 1922. From 1932, new exercises were added to these, which developed as a sacred dance with 28 exercises. This was the beginning of paneurythmy (literally: the universal, good rhythm), a combination of harmonic movement, music, songs, and ideas. In 1942, paneurythmy included the first part with 28 exercises, the Sunrays as the second part, and the Pentagram as the third part. This dance is performed early in the morning in spring and summer. Paneurythmy harmonizes, regulates, and transforms the life-energies of the human body. This involves working with the forces of the earth and the sun, which meet in the human being.[38]

---

36. Aïvanhov, *Life with the Master Peter Deunov*, 420. It is well known in the Bulgarian Brotherhood that Peter Deunov sometimes criticized his disciple Ivanov. That Deunov asked him if he was willing to spread the teachings of the White Brotherhood in France, and that they corresponded with each other until the outbreak of war, are facts which are far less known

37. The Master Beinsa Duno, *The World of Great Souls*, Sofia, 2016.

38. https://ia800703.us.archive.org/3/items/PeterDeunov/Paneurhythmy_2004_english.pdf.

The Work in Their Spiritual Schools

Peter Deunov in the circle of paneurythmy in the Rila Mountains

Paneurythmy, according to Deunov, contains the essence of his teachings. In the first part, the forces of the mind, heart, and will are harmonized. In the Sunrays, man is born as an individual. In the Pentagram, he develops the five spiritual forces he needs in his life: goodness, justice, love, wisdom, and truth. People who dance paneurythmy become part of a greater whole—thereby participating in the life of intelligent nature.

On May 4, 1936, Deunov was physically attacked. A member of a political party penetrated the hall in Izgrev and struck him forcefully on the head with his fists. As a result, he suffered a brain hemorrhage, which a month later led to paralysis on his right side and an impairment of his speech. Nevertheless, in July of that year he went to the Rila Mountains and dragged himself up to the camp. By mid-August, his bodily functions had recovered. He later said of this that he had prevented an attack that would have blown up the lecture hall and led to the deaths of a large number of disciples. In a prayer, he had asked God to protect them while he, himself, suffered vicariously.[39]

---

39. Pashov on https://ia800703.us.archive.org/3/items/PeterDeunov/The_Extraordinary_Life_of_the_Master_Beinsa_Douno_Pashov_Vlad.pdf.

Rudolf Steiner and Peter Deunov

This was not the only attempt on his life. According to his student Michael Ivanov, a group of conspirators in Sofia sent a member of their group to Izgrev to kill Deunov with a knife. Deunov knew that danger was imminent, because he could clairvoyantly perceive the people coming toward him, as well as their intentions. When this person stood before him, he said, "I know what you are coming for, try it! But what will you do if your hand remains immobile in the air?" The man was shocked, fell to his knees, and asked for forgiveness.[40]

In June 1939, Ita Wegman made a trip through Bulgaria. She was familiar with Rudolf Steiner's statement that Bulgaria had its own spiritual teacher.[41] It is not known what she heard about Deunov or whether she met him. In the summer of 1939, shortly before the start of World War II, the last major Rila summer camp was held. It included followers from France, Finland, Estonia, and Latvia. Within Bulgaria, Deunov had several tens of thousands of followers.[42] The exact number cannot be determined because there was no membership in the School of the White Brotherhood. There still isn't. Membership was solely a matter of inner connection.

In late 1940, Bulgaria joined Germany and Italy when German troops were about to invade the country. German soldiers could now operate from Bulgaria; but in 1941, Bulgarian King Boris III refused to provide troops for the German attack on the Soviet Union. On December 13, 1941, Bulgaria declared war on Britain and the United States, resulting in Sofia and other cities being bombed several times by the Allies. The Bulgarian government planned to send the country's Jewish residents to concentration camps in the spring of 1943, but this was prevented by the king. That August, shortly after a visit to Hitler, who had not gotten his way on the issues of Bulgarian participation in the war in Russia and the deportation of Jews, the king died mysteriously.

---

40. Aïvanhov, *Life with the Master Peter Deunov*, 422–23.

41. J.E. Zeylmans van Emmichoven, *Wer war Ita Wegman?* [Who Was Ita Wegman?], vol. 2, Heidelberg, 1990, 222.

42. Kovacheva, *Die Weisse Bruderschaft*, 184.

The Work in Their Spiritual Schools

Peter Deunov played an important role in saving the Bulgarian Jews. In the early 1930s, the spiritual leader of Bulgarian Jews, Daniel Zion (1883–1979), who had a deep interest in other religions and philosophy, was invited to meet with Deunov. According to his student Boris Nikolov, Rabbi Zion often came to the Brotherhood community in Izgrev to talk with Deunov and read his printed lectures. He also came to the summer camp in Rila, where he stayed for some time and participated in the Brotherhood's communal life. He received Christianity, Nikolov said, "in spirit and truth" from the teacher Peter Deunov.

The messianic Rabbi Joseph Shulam, born in Bulgaria, and founder of the Netivyah congregation in Jerusalem, wrote about this in 2008:

> Rabbi Daniel was impressed with the lifestyle of this Deunov, and started to implement some of the teachings of this mystic. There were three things that Rabbi Daniel Zion appropriated from Deunov: vegetarianism, getting up early in the morning and starting the day with prayer looking at the sunrise, and daily physical exercise. Deunov did speak of Jesus as the Messiah and Savior. He also spoke of the simple lifestyle of the early disciples of Jesus. These subjects were eye-openers for Rabbi Daniel. He started to think about things that could be called, from an Orthodox Jewish viewpoint, unorthodox—or at least, unusual subjects for a Rabbi to think about. But according to Rabbi Daniel Zion, the major change came into his life when, as he was praying looking at the sunrise, a vision of Yeshua [Jesus] appeared to him. He did not know what this vision meant, so he asked some of the other Rabbis what he should do about it. After the third time the same vision appeared, Rabbi Daniel turned toward the figure and spoke to him. The figure was scintillating right out from the sun, and the impression Rabbi Daniel received from this figure was that it responded to him, identifying himself as Yeshua. It is no small thing for a Rabbi to receive a vision of Yeshua the Messiah. Yet Rabbi Daniel Zion was well versed with the teaching, "Receive the truth by whomever it might come."[43]

---

43. Joseph Shulam, "Remembering Rabbi Daniel Zion," https://ffoz.org/discover/yahrzeit/yahrzeit-of-rabbi-daniel-zion.html.

Rudolf Steiner and Peter Deunov

Daniel Zion (second from right) in 1940

On the advice of Metropolitan Stefan of Sofia, Daniel Zion, who recognized Jesus as the Messiah, remained a rabbi and immersed himself in the gospels, studying them with members of the Jewish congregation. In early 1942, he visited Deunov to discuss the dangerous situation of the Jews in a conversation that lasted for six hours. This relationship of trust between the two men led to a special request. Three representatives of Sofia's Jewish community came to Deunov asking him to take custody of a number of diamonds. They were ritual objects related to the Law of Moses. After the war, they were returned to the Jewish community.[44] That Deunov accepted them can be interpreted as his willingness to take Bulgarian Jews under his protection.

When the government's plans to deport the Bulgarian Jews were

---

44. Boris Nikolov, "Diamantite na evre'ite i skiniata na Moyseia" [The Diamonds of the Hebrews and the Tabernacles of Moses], in Krustev (ed.), *Izgrevut na Bialoto Bratstvo*, vol. 1, Sofia, 1993, 485–86.

The Work in Their Spiritual Schools

in danger of being implemented in early March 1943, Metodi Konstantinov, a disciple of Deunov who worked in a ministry and had been assigned to supervise the transport of the Bulgarian Jews to Poland, reported to him that the king had signed the deportation decree. Deunov ordered his disciple Lyubomir Lulchev, who was the king's adviser, to deliver a message to the king. This message stated that if only one Jew was sent to Poland, nothing would remain of him and his dynasty.[45] The king was untraceable, but Deunov discovered by spiritual means where he was. Thus warned, the king immediately went with Lulchev to the ministry and tore up the decree. This took place on March 9, 1943. Thanks to the efforts of Rabbi Zion, the metropolitan, and others, the Jews were taken to a labor camp in Bulgaria, where they survived the war.[46] Most of them later emigrated to Israel, including Daniel Zion and his circle of "messianic" Jews (Jews who accept Jesus as the expected Messiah).

After a heavy bomb attack on Sofia on the night of January 10, 1944, which caused fire throughout the city, Deunov decided to leave the area. He lived then in the house of Boris Nikolov at the foot of the Vitosha Mountains. With a small group of disciples from Izgrev, he was given shelter in the house of Temelko Temelkov in the village of Murchaevo, located 24 km southwest of Sofia. Here they stayed until October 19, 1944. During this time, excursions into the mountains were made, and visitors came from all over the country. At some point Temelko lost contact with one of his sons, who had gone into the mountains as a guerrilla fighter. He had gone missing. Deunov declared that he had perished and indicated where his body could be found. He also predicted that this young man would be born again into the family of a brother of his.[47]

Every day, Deunov gave lectures in Murchaevo; these were later published in the three volumes of the *Testament of Love*. For Deunov,

---

45. Metodi Konstantinov, "Spasyavaneto na evre'ite" [The Salvation of the Hebrews], in Krustev (ed.), *Izgrevut na Bialoto Bratstvo*, vol. 4, Sofia, 1995, 534.

46. Harrie Salman, "Daniel Tsion (1883–1979): Rabbi and Follower of Yeshua the Messiah," in *Starlight*, 2014/2. https://sophiafoundation.org/wp-content/uploads/2017/04/Starlight_2014_Advent_Sm.pdf.

47. During a visit to this house in 2012, the author met this reborn guerilla fighter.

love has the last word: all difficulties can be resolved by the law of Love. Love overcomes all contradictions and is the only force that can connect people. All relevant statements Deunov made during these nine months were recorded by Boyan Boev and published in 1992 under the title *The Wellspring of Good* (referring to the spring near the house in Murchaevo that had been discovered and dug open by Deunov). It brings together statements on dozens of subjects.[48]

The last photograph of Peter Deunov, in Martschevo, August 1944

48. Boyan Boev and Boris Nikolov (ed.), Peter Deunov, *The Wellspring of Good*, Sofia 2013. https://ia600703.us.archive.org/3/items/PeterDeunov/Wellspring_of_Good.pdf.

The Work in Their Spiritual Schools

In September 1944, the Soviet army invaded Bulgaria. On September 9, a leftist coup took place, abolishing the monarchy. Only in 1946 did Bulgaria, after a referendum, become a communist state led by Georgi Dimitrov. Deunov did not live to see this. After returning to Sofia in October 1944, his health deteriorated. On December 20, he held his last lecture in the General Occult Class. He had heart trouble and then developed pneumonia. After saying his last words ("A small task is accomplished for God") on December 25, he died on December 27, 1944, shortly after 5 AM, at the age of 80. He was buried in Izgrev. A small park was established around his grave.[49]

Retrospective

Rudolf Steiner was given only nine months to build his spiritual school, and another six months to lead it from his sickbed. He knew that it would be difficult to bring a new esoteric impulse into the declining Anthroposophical Society. This impulse had to be carried out into the world by the members. For this purpose, they had to lay, and care for, a foundation stone of love in their hearts. Building on their interconnected foundation stones, they then had to create places where they could work on a new spiritual culture in cooperation with spiritual beings. These are the mystery places of the future. This required that they come to an understanding of their individual karma—and then harmonize their mutual karma. Since this did not happen in the space of the nine months after the Christmas Conference of 1923, it became impossible for Steiner to continue working with the Anthroposophical Society. He had connected the Society with the Michael movement in the spiritual world, but at his death this connection broke down. Both the new Society and the Free School of Spiritual Science were then unable to properly fulfill their task.

---

49. A so-called Testament of Peter Deunov, which he allegedly uttered shortly before his death, is circulating on the internet. No such will exists. The text referred to contains statements Deunov made in the last years of his life, as well as others he *never* made.

Rudolf Steiner and Peter Deunov

Peter Deunov's work was blessed by the invisible world. He was able to work for 22 years from 1922 on, building his school. Like Steiner, Deunov was attacked by enemies of modern Christian spirituality—by the traditional Church and political movements, and perhaps also by some Freemasonic lodges. The occult knowledge he imparted to his disciples, however, may not have been a direct threat to the dark spiritual elites of the Western world. Nor did his work suffer from conflicts among his followers or from bureaucratic structures in the Brotherhood. Nor was there a legacy from a Theosophical period such as was represented in Steiner's environment by sometimes unworldly people from the upper echelons of society. Deunov's followers formed a brotherhood and sisterhood from all walks of life in Bulgaria, the germ of a new Christian community.

5

Who Are Rudolf Steiner and Peter Deunov?

After describing in this chapter the biographies of *Doktor* Rudolf Steiner, the spiritual teacher and universal scholar from Austria, and *Uchitel* (Teacher) Peter Deunov, the spiritual teacher from Bulgaria, we can go deeper into their humanity, their mutual relationship, their missions, their connection to the spiritual masters of humanity, and their previous incarnations.

Many of Steiner's disciples have recorded their memories of him. The book *Reminiscences of Rudolf Steiner* by Andrej Belyi and others has already been mentioned. The book *Wir erlebten Rudolf Steiner* [We Experienced Rudolf Steiner] gives an impressive picture of how he lived on in the memories of his disciples.[1] In Bulgaria, Vergili Krustev has collected texts written by disciples and contemporaries of Peter Deunov, published in a series of 35 thick volumes.[2]

We get to know Steiner in the memories of his disciples as a person who was always ready to help others on their path of inner development, who was grateful for their questions, and who had a deep insight into their life-situations. He left them completely free, even when the stakes were high. He possessed a superior spiritual intelligence that enabled him to connect regular knowledge and spiritual insights. Steiner's working power was unparalleled. In the last years of his life, he usually slept only one hour a night.[3]

 1. Maria J. Krück von Poturzyn (ed.), *Wir erlebten Rudolf Steiner*, Stuttgart, 1988.
 2. Krustev (ed.), *Izgrevut na Bialoto Bratstvo*, 35 volumes, Sofia, 1993–2020.
 3. It is known that Steiner used a method to bring about total relaxation and regeneration of his life forces in short periods during the day. In doing so, however, he noted that normal sleep is needed at least once a week.

Rudolf Steiner and Peter Deunov

He diagnosed diseases and recommended medicines that doctor Ita Wegman had made. Thus, the first anthroposophical medicines arose out of concern for the sick person, whose illness was always understood in a holistic context. He saw in children what they needed for their development and how parents and teachers could stimulate them. This is how anthroposophical education came into being. He was concerned about the quality of our food and gave directives for its improvement in biodynamic agriculture, and expected new food crops to be developed.[4] Moreover, he saw the needs of our time and devoted himself tirelessly to the realization of spiritual impulses for a new culture.

When we imagine Peter Deunov, we see him with disciples walking in the mountains, conversing on a mountainside, meditating with them at sunrise on a mountaintop. We hear him playing the violin in a mesmerizing way as his disciples sing his songs. He gave advice to anyone who asked; he knew their destiny, and with his knowledge of traditional and spiritual healing methods he healed dozens of people.[5] In doing so, he worked with the four elements (earth, water, light, and fire) and knew the healing effects of sunlight. Olga Slavcheva recounted that, in 1918, she had the Spanish flu and was dying. She then had a letter written to Deunov. A day later, recovery set in and a letter came from Deunov, who wrote: "I know you are already healthy again. Drink warm cow's milk and eat potatoes." His successful recipe against the flu was to drink hot water and eat only some boiled potatoes daily.

It is said that he could become physically visible somewhere, bring a message, and then disappear again just as suddenly. He knew

---

4. Ehrenfried Pfeiffer once asked Steiner why the path of schooling is so ineffective, to which he received the following answer: "That is a nutrition problem. The way nutrition comes about today no longer gives people the power to manifest the spiritual in the physical. The bridge from thinking to willing and acting can no longer be built. Food plants no longer contain the powers they should give to human beings." Meyer (ed.), *Ein Leben für den Geist: Ehrenfried Pfeiffer* [Ehrenfried Pfeiffer: A Modern Quest for the Spirit], 149.

5. Stories can be found in Vlad Pashov on https://ia800703.us.archive.org/3/items/PeterDeunov/The_Extraordinary_Life_of_the_Master_Beinsa_Douno_Pashov_Vlad.pdf, and Peter Deunov, *Harmonizing of the Human Soul*, 367–83.

Who Are Rudolf Steiner and Peter Deunov?

of events happening elsewhere at the time (such as the assassination of Prime Minister Stamboliski in 1923) and of future events. He also knew when it would rain. He spoke of how he could influence the weather, such as making it rain or stop raining temporarily.[6] Traveling through an area of Turkish-speaking villages where it had not rained for several years, Deunov was asked if he could provide rain. Their religious leaders had prayed for it in vain. Deunov pledged his help, and a few hours later came a large downpour, falling only on the Turkish villages and not on the Bulgarian villages in the region. When the inhabitants of the Bulgarian villages asked him why it had not rained on them, he replied that they had not asked him for anything.

In the practice of his life, Deunov was the herald of a new culture. About greeting others, he said: a true greeting will be that, when we meet someone, we send light from the depths of our soul to place the other in this light. We can then see the beauty of their soul, because the human soul is beautiful. Then we will love the other person and send them a blessing spiritually. Only then can we greet the other person externally.[7]

With his background as the son of a priest, and as a former Methodist pastor, it was natural that Deunov's talks often took on the character of a sermon. In many cases, they began with a quotation from the bible, which was then explained and related to daily life. They were edifying and educational lectures, in which knowledge about nature and insights from his spiritual research were also imparted. He spoke about the science of love.

Peter Deunov and Rudolf Steiner were gifted speakers, each giving thousands of lectures. However, they had an entirely different character. Deunov's lectures were food for the soul; they served to "elevate the religious spirit of the Bulgarian people." According to Deunov, the Bulgarians had a spiritual nature that they had inherited from the older people, the Thracians, who had lived there two thousand years earlier; but they had no faith. While Deunov came to nurture this faith to prepare them for their mission, Steiner's lec-

6. Peter Deunov, *Harmonizing of the Human Soul*, 364.
7. Ibid., 379.

tures offered thoughts to ponder upon, to elaborate, and to apply in new spiritual sciences and activities.

Anthroposophy speaks of the "shepherds" and the "kings," who come to the Jesus children in Luke's gospel and Matthew's gospel, respectively. Deunov spoke the language of the shepherds, Steiner that of the kings. Deunov said: "I give you love; as for knowledge, you must seek elsewhere." To those of his disciples who wanted to know more about what he was communicating, it has been said that he recommended they should study Steiner's work.

In Deunov and his disciples we see the type of a new religious man who is no longer tied to a church, and who applies the teachings of love in everyday life. As Deunov explained the laws of spiritual life and of nature, there is no longer a separation between faith and knowledge. For him, faith had to be based on insight and knowledge. For his part, Steiner represents the type of a new spiritual scientist, one who brings fresh impulses into culture in cooperation with spiritual beings. By pointing out a path of inner development, he wanted to reconnect modern people with the spiritual world.

In singing together and performing other communal activities, such as took place in Deunov's school, we find the example of John Wesley (1703–1791), the founder of Methodism. The sacred dance of paneurythmy stands in the tradition of folk dances, which originally had a cultic and religious character. In addition, Deunov used a considerable number of other methods to stimulate the development of his disciples, such as meditating at dawn, physical exercises (and other methods of improving health and supporting the processes of rejuvenation), methods of developing qualities and faculties of the soul, such as meditations and prayers, methods of developing virtues, methods of ennobling character, and methods of developing occult abilities, such as intuition and clairvoyance.

As to the acquisition of such occult abilities, Deunov was very reluctant to speak. To the young Michael Ivanov, who wanted to learn the methods for this from him, he said, "It is through love that we become clairvoyant."[8] According to Deunov, a spiritual teacher is needed who helps the student overcome the fears he will pass

---

8. Aïvanhov, *Life with the Master Peter Deunov*, 17.

Who Are Rudolf Steiner and Peter Deunov?

through in the course of his clairvoyant experiences.[9] At another time, he added, "A school dealing with the topic of clairvoyance is needed. However, this would not be for everyone." And, "before anyone is ready to develop clairvoyance, they must have developed the twelve basic virtues."[10] Deunov rarely spoke of the chakras, the organs of spiritual perception. Steiner also dealt with these topics cautiously. With his book *How to Know Higher Worlds*, he gave an impetus to the development of higher spiritual faculties (imaginative, inspirative, and intuitive faculties). To further help his disciples, he gave them personal meditations and advice.

Bulgarian Boyan Boev (1883–1963) was a student of both Rudolf Steiner and Peter Deunov. In 1908, when Sofia University was temporarily closed, Boev studied natural sciences at the University of Munich in Germany. There he attended lectures by Steiner and became a member of the Theosophical Society. On December 20, 1909, Boev, who had been imprisoned in Bulgaria for conscientious objection, asked Steiner in a letter if he could become a student of his esoteric school. In 1910 he had a conversation with Steiner, who pointed out to him that he would find his spiritual teacher in Bulgaria. This indeed happened, and in 1912 Boev was at the summer convention of the Chain on behalf of Deunov's group of disciples in Panagyurishte, where he was a high school teacher. In 1917, he was still a member of the Anthroposophical Society, as evidenced by a letter to Steiner dated March 18, 1917, informing him that Steiner's book *How to Know Higher Worlds* had been published in Bulgarian in 1916.

There are no notes from Boev on the content of his 1910 conversation with Steiner. According to Maria Todorova, Steiner said to him, "You do not have to become my student, because the great teacher is in Bulgaria. Therefore, go back and become his student."[11] Vlad Pashov gave a more extensive version of what Steiner said:

---

9. Regarding clairvoyance and conscious out-of-body experiences, see Peter Deunov, *Harmonizing of the Human Soul*, 263–72.

10. Boev and Nikolov (ed.), *The Wellspring of Good*, 198–203.

11. Krustev (ed.), *Izgrevut na Bialoto Bratstvo* [From the White Brotherhood], vol. 1, 246. On page 247, Todorova describes that around 1930 Peter Deunov gave the fifth apocalyptic seal from Steiner's lectures on the Apocalypse of St. John to Vlad Pashov, to be printed in the journal *Zhitno Zurno* [Grain of Wheat].

Rudolf Steiner and Peter Deunov

A powerful spiritual current will develop in Bulgaria, led by a great initiate. He will not work in Bulgaria as I work here, but in another way. I am working here in a scientific and materialistic environment to enlighten contemporary scientific thinking from a spiritual point of view, and to give a spiritual impetus to the descending Western European civilization so that it can be reborn and make the transition to the sixth race [the sixth cycle of cultures]. But there in Bulgaria you will need to lay the foundation of a new culture, the sixth sub-race [the coming sixth cultural period of the present fifth cycle of cultures], from which the sixth race [the sixth cycle] will be born. Since the sixth race [the sixth cycle of cultures] will have to work on the development of the human heart, you too will work there on the development of the heart, with the gospel in your hand.[12]

Boyan Boev and Peter Deunov

So, Steiner worked for the next cycle of cultures, while Deunov worked for the coming Slavic cultural period (from which the next cycle of cultures will emerge). Another of Deunov's disciples, Georgi Sabev, added that, according to Steiner, the Bulgarian initiate would work with love, in the area of the human heart; and that he, Steiner, worked in the area of the brain.

12. The quotation from Pashov can be found in Emily Michael, *Sealed by the Sun*, Varna, 2014, 343–44, 349.

Who Are Rudolf Steiner and Peter Deunov?

The Christ initiates Rudolf Steiner and Peter Deunov never met on earth, but spiritually they maintained a connection with each other. According to Pashov, Deunov told Boev, who asked if he knew Steiner, that they knew each other from the spiritual world:

> Steiner is a good worker in God's fields: he is very active and dynamic. The White Brotherhood assigned him the task to give a spiritual impulse to Western European culture, to save it from a final collapse, in order for it to be reborn and enter into the new culture.[13]

In Dornach in the 1980s, Steiner was said to have spoken several times about Peter Deunov. Jörgen Smit, board member of the Society, confirmed to Klaus J. Bracker in 1989 that he had already heard this in the late 1930s. It went like this:

> Some Bulgarians came to Rudolf Steiner and asked him to hold lectures in their country and possibly to establish a members' group in the capital Sofia. But he refused, with the explanation: No, you have Beinsa Duno [Peter Deunov]. Later, Bulgarians approached Marie Steiner von Sivers with the request to come to Bulgaria for eurythmy performances and to give eurythmy courses there. After she put the question to Rudolf Steiner, he is said to have replied in the same way: No, they have Beinsa Duno and paneurythmy![14]

Possibly as early as 1908, Boev wrote about Steiner's teachings and translated his texts into Bulgarian. After World War I, other Bulgarians studying in Germany learned about Steiner's work and made translations, which however were often of poor quality and incomprehensible to most Bulgarians. This was also due to Steiner's complicated German way of speaking. Deunov's words were understandable to every Bulgarian. Some got the idea that Deunov took his thoughts from Steiner, and that he simplified them.

---

13. The words of Sabev and the quotation from Pashov in Emily Michael, ibid.

14. Klaus J. Bracker, "Von den Früchten des Lebensbaums" [From the Fruits of the Tree of Life], review of the book of the same name by Omraam Mikhael Aïvanhov, in *Novalis*, February, 2001. Since paneurythmy was not developed until after Steiner's death, the second answer can only be attributed to Marie Steiner, unless Steiner knew with foresight before 1925 that Deunov would develop paneurythmy in 1934.

Rudolf Steiner and Peter Deunov

In 1924, Boev settled in Sofia and, as a stenographer, noted down statements made by Deunov. He became Deunov's secretary. After Steiner's death in 1925, Boev asked Deunov whether great esotericists who had already died ever came to his lectures. The latter replied that only Rudolf Steiner and Paul Sédir (a French mystic who lived from 1871 to 1926) regularly attended them. Deunov had conversations in spirit with Steiner, who is said to have told him, "I am amazed at how you can express such great ideas and truths in so few and such simple words." To this, Deunov is said to have replied: "This language [Bulgarian] is not an ordinary language. It is the most exact language on earth, and is the only one that can convey occult truths."[15] Deunov spoke in a different way than Steiner did, and highlighted other aspects of spiritual science. Each teacher had his own mission, which we can now describe a little more exactly.

In the aforementioned conversation with Walter Johannes Stein in 1920, Rudolf Steiner pointed out that his actual mission was "reincarnation and karma, as well as the social task."[16] Steiner did not, however, get around to developing a new doctrine of karma and reincarnation until 1924. Connected with solving the social question was his commitment to social threefolding (1917–1922). Since Professor Schröer had not worked out Goethe's scientific method, Steiner took over this task from him. Through Schröer, Anthroposophy could already have entered the world that way. As Dutch anthroposophist Hans Peter van Manen points out, Schröer—the reincarnation of the philosopher Plato (according to Steiner)—could also have provided "a Christian metamorphosis of Plato's philosophy on the level of the consciousness soul: a metamorphosis not only in philosophical form, but one further developed in several fields of science and art."[17]

This task of developing a Christian Platonism, a Christian Theosophy, was undertaken by Steiner during the period from 1902 to

---

15. Krustev (ed.), *Izgrevut na Bialoto Bratstvo*, vol. 1, "Reminiscences of Maria Todorova," 247–48.
16. Poeppig, *Rudolf Steiner*, 264–65.
17. Hans Peter van Manen, *Twin Roads to the New Millennium*, 1988, Forest Row, chap. 14.

Who Are Rudolf Steiner and Peter Deunov?

1914. The Mystery Dramas were Steiner's own contribution to this, inspired by Christian Rosenkreutz. They are part of his impulse to reconnect science, art, and religion, as they were in ancient cultures.

A special mission of Steiner was to announce the return of Christ, which he said would take place from the 1930s onward. But actually, this is the task of the Maitreya Bodhisattva—who, as Gautama Buddha's successor, will ascend to the Buddha-dignity in the future. We can imagine that, from 1910, the Maitreya Bodhisattva worked *through* Steiner (and also Deunov) as he spread the message of the return of Christ. In 1908, Steiner declared:

> The movement for spiritual science now has the task of preparing the part of humanity for the return of the Christ that is ready for it.[18]

Moreover, as Steiner said on several occasions, the movement for spiritual science (i.e., the anthroposophical movement) has the task of bringing a "true understanding of Christianity." In 1909, he said, "To incorporate Anthroposophy means to transform the soul in such a way that it can come to the understanding of Christ."[19]

Against the resistance of older occult groups, Steiner was determined to open the previously secret mystery schools and make the path of schooling of the Rosicrucians accessible to all in a new form: as the anthroposophical path of schooling. From the Christmas Conference of 1923, it was his intention to make the principle of initiation active again as the basis for civilization. This intention became more concrete when, in 1924, he began to speak about the Michael School in the spiritual world. There, between the 15th and 19th centuries, the cooperation between the "Aristotelians" and the "Platonists" was prepared—and was to be realized in the course of the 20th century.

Deunov's mission lay in another area. The Bulgarian theologian Eva Kovacheva has summarized this mission.[20] Deunov's primary concern was to apply the teachings of Christ, who is the head of the

---

18. Rudolf Steiner, lecture of May 31, 1908, in *The Gospel of St. John* (CW 103).
19. Rudolf Steiner, lecture of May 16, 1909, in *Principles of Spiritual Economy* (CW 109).
20. Kovacheva, *Die Weisse Bruderschaft* [The White Brotherhood], 221–27.

Rudolf Steiner and Peter Deunov

White Brotherhood in the spiritual world. Deunov saw himself as a messenger of this teaching. He spoke especially about love as a divine principle, and brought insight into the coming of a new culture on earth, the sixth culture (the Slavic culture) of the current cycle of cultures. To spread this insight, he did not found a church or a new religion, but a spiritual school in which he held lectures to prepare people for the new culture.

The work done by Steiner and Deunov was connected with the plans of the spiritual leadership of humanity. As leader of the White Brotherhood, Christ heads the angelic hierarchies and the human individualities who are spiritual leaders of humanity. Theosophy speaks of a circle of twelve Bodhisattvas. Christ, according to Steiner, forms the center of this circle. In addition, he also spoke of twelve masters, who are not identical with the Bodhisattvas. Only in 1911 did he make the distinction that a Bodhisattva who attains Buddha-dignity can henceforth be called a Master.[21]

Of these twelve interacting Masters, according to Steiner, seven are always on earth for long periods of time, including two Masters of the West (Master Jesus and Christian Rosenkreutz), two Masters of the East (Master Morya and Master Kuthumi), and two Masters of the South (Master Hilarion and the Venetian Master). The seventh Master moves among them. They may incarnate as human beings, or work through spiritual teachers in esoteric schools.

It is recorded in a private note by Edith Maryon that Steiner had indicated to her that it was intended that, from the beginning of the Age of Michael (1879), the Masters of the West and East would work side by side: the Masters of the West, giving impulses for the present culture and preparing the next, would work through Steiner; the Masters of the East, giving impulses for the next culture, would work through Annie Besant. According to Rudolf Steiner, the goals of the Masters of the East had, however, been betrayed through Leadbeater and Besant. As a result, these Masters no longer incorporated into Besant's lodge, and now the teaching of the will that emanated from Master Morya was to be taken over by Christian

---

21. Rudolf Steiner, lecture of September 17, 1911, in *Esoteric Christianity and the Mission of Christian Rosenkreutz* (CW 130).

Who Are Rudolf Steiner and Peter Deunov?

Rosenkreutz, and the teaching of truth that should have been brought by Master Kuthumi was to be given by Master Jesus.[22]

Steiner was in communication with Christian Rosenkreutz and Master Jesus. In a conversation with Friedrich Rittelmeyer, Steiner explicitly called them his initiators. Christian Rosenkreutz directed him to the transformation of materialism and the problem of dealing with public opinion. We may further assume that, at some point, he saved Steiner's life. Moreover, we may assume that, after his earlier attempt to work through Blavatsky had failed, Christian Rosenkreutz asked him to become active in the Theosophical Society. He also inspired Steiner to formulate the anthroposophical path of schooling, the Mystery Dramas, and the new impulses of the Christmas Conference of 1923.

Around 1880, Master Jesus pointed out to Steiner the special importance of the study of the philosopher Fichte. From 1897, he may have guided Steiner toward his encounter with Christ and his reception of a copy of the I of the Nathanic Jesus. Christian Theosophy, which Steiner developed until 1914, seems to have been directly inspired by Master Jesus. This Christian-Theosophical stream in early Anthroposophy provides an esoteric framework for the anthroposophical path of schooling. And as the German anthroposophist Klaus J. Bracker has described in detail, this stream leads to a Grail initiation: it is a path to the Grail.[23]

We can now list some of the steps of Rudolf Steiner's initiation:

1880/81 (age 19): teaching of his two initiators, the experience of his eternal I.

1893 (age 32): spiritualization of his thinking in the description of knowledge and moral intuitions in *Philosophy of Freedom*.

c. 1900 (c. 39 years): Christ initiation in standing [i.e., in vision] before the Mystery of Golgotha.

The anthroposophists Judith von Halle and Sergei O. Prokofieff have raised the question of whether Steiner himself was not one of

---

22. Edith Maryon, notes of Steiner's esoteric lessons in von Halle, *Rudolf Steiner: Meister der Weissen Loge* [Rudolf Steiner: Master of the White Lodge], 158–62.

23. Klaus J. Bracker, *Grals-Initiation* [Grail Initiation], Stuttgart, 2009.

Rudolf Steiner and Peter Deunov

the twelve masters. According to von Halle, since 1899, "*in* the personality of Dr. Rudolf Steiner, and *as* his personality, worked Master Serapis—the seventh master, who "passes among the six others" and is their servant.[24] According to her, Master Serapis is the one who represents the perfection of the Self. She also believes that Steiner was already the bearer of a copy of the I of Jesus from birth, but that it had yet to be awakened.[25] For Prokofieff, Steiner was "a human Bodhisattva, standing on the level of a master and possessing certain qualities already belonging to the level of Buddha-dignity."[26] According to him, there incarnated in Steiner a new, "thirteenth" Bodhisattva, formed between 1879 and 1900, in which the time-spirit Michael, the archangel Vidar, and the Nathanic soul worked together.[27] These are two different views of who Rudolf Steiner was.

Deunov used his spiritual name Beinsa Duno once in a letter in 1914. What this name means is not known.[28] It was not until the 1930s that it was used as that of the author in conjunction with some collections of his lectures. In the School of the White Brotherhood, he is referred to as Master Beinsa Douno. He may have received this name at the second step of his initiation. These steps are:

1884 (age 19): Deunov was enlightened by the Holy Spirit.

1897 (age 32): He became a teacher of humanity.

1912 (age 48): The Spirit of Christ entered him

In a lecture on March 22, 1940, Deunov said:.

> Who I am, you will never experience. I am a Son of God, who fulfills the will of God. . . . I am a Son of God, who wants to sanctify His name and introduce Love in its full beauty.[29]

---

24. *Rudolf Steiner: Meister der Weissen Loge*, 154.

25. Ibid., 151.

26. Sergej O. Prokofieff, *Rudolf Steiner and the Masters of Esoteric Christianity*, Stourbridge, 2019.

27. Who these two beings are will be described later.

28. Duno (pronounced as "Doonó") is probably comes from the family name. This was derived from the Bulgarian *duno* (pronounced as "dúno"), which means "bottom" (to stand upon). Later on, his spiritual name was written as Douno.

29. Peter Deunov, "Zhilishte shte napravim" [We Shall Build a Dwelling], in *Putjat kum shasti'eto* [The Path to Joy/Bliss/Happiness], Sofia, 1998, 36.

Who Are Rudolf Steiner and Peter Deunov?

Earlier statements of his are: "I and Christ are one" and "Christ is not I, but Christ lives in me."[30]

In Deunov's school, inner work prevailed, but the study of intelligent nature was also part of the excursions and the summer camps in the mountains. More than in Steiner's work, which is directed primarily to the spiritual development of the consciousness-soul of our present cultural age, the focus in Deunov's work is on the preparation of the new culture. This is in accordance with the inspirations of Master Jesus, who, as Steiner pointed out in 1906, leads humanity from the present culture to the next: "Through the principle of brotherly love, which has its representative in Master Jesus, the union of humanity comes about in the sixth sub-race [cultural period]."[31]

In her book on Anthroposophy, the White Brotherhood, and a Russian-Bulgarian school, Bulgarian anthropologist Svetoslava Toncheva distinguishes between the secular and the mystical biographies of the founders of these movements. For her, Steiner is the scientist-mystic who sought to establish a connection between religion and science. Deunov is the national mystic who worked primarily as an educator of his people.[32] She points to the myths surrounding his life: the prediction of his birth, his extraordinary abilities, his conversations with spiritual beings, his divine mission, the healings he performed, and his appearance as a charismatic prophet with his long white hair and beard.

About his past lives, Deunov spoke once. According to the recollections of his student Maria Todorova, he said the following:

> All of you who are now in the brotherhood in Bulgaria were students in an occult school in Egypt many thousands of years ago, and I was your teacher there. Before that, you were in an occult school in India—of Rama—and I was your teacher. Before that,

---

30. Kovacheva, *Die Weisse Bruderschaft*, 216.

31. Rudolf Steiner, esoteric lesson of February 12, 1906, in *From the History and Contents of the First Section of the Esoteric School: Letters, Documents, and Lectures: 1904–1914* (CW 264).

32. Svetoslava Toncheva, *Out of the New Spirituality of the 20th Century*, Berlin, 2015, 241.

Rudolf Steiner and Peter Deunov

you were students in an occult school of Zoroaster [Zarathustra] in Persia, and I was your teacher. You were as Bogomils [in the tenth century, the precursors of the Southern French Cathars] in Bulgaria, and I was your teacher.[33]

According to these recollections, the individuality manifested in Peter Deunov has been a teacher of the White Brotherhood in four previous cultural periods. His remarkable path of initiation and his extraordinary closeness to Christ lead to the question of whether Master Jesus, in whom the individuality of Zarathustra was incarnated, and who worked in a particular incarnation every century, was also incarnated in Deunov. To this points Deunov's reference to the School of Zarathustra, where, in his own words, he was the teacher. This teacher was Zarathustra.[34]

When Friedrich Rittelmeyer asked Rudolf Steiner around 1920 whether Master Jesus had incarnated at that time, Steiner reportedly replied that he was in the Carpathians, indicating that he (Steiner) was in a purely spiritual connection with him.[35] The Carpathians stretch from Slovakia into Romania. Through a spur, this mountain range continues into the Balkan Mountains in Bulgaria. If Steiner had meant Deunov, this was a somewhat strange way of indicating the country where he worked, but this cannot be entirely ruled out. Perhaps Steiner mentioned another mountain range that Rittelmeyer mistook for the Carpathians. But it could also be that Steiner wanted to protect his colleague Deunov. Beinsa Duno would then be the new name of Master Jesus.

---

33. Krustev (ed.), *Izgrevut na Bialoto Bratstvo*, vol. 1, 263.

34. See also Robert Powell and Harrie Salman, *The Prophecy of Peter Deunov*, on https://sophiafoundation.org/wp-content/uploads/2020/06/Prophecy-of-Peter-Deunov-Beinsa-Douno.pdf; and Robert Powell, "Rama and Krishna Avatars: Karma Research and Star Wisdom," in *As Above So Below: Star Wisdom*, vol. 3, ed. Joel M. Park, Gt Barrington, MA, 2020. At www.sophiaschoolofmovement.org (esp. podcast 81), Powell details the mission of Master Jesus in his incarnation as Peter Deunov. As Deunov clearly stated, this mission was to prepare the Slavic people for the sixth cultural epoch, precisely as spoken of by Rudolf Steiner, who described the bearer of this mission as acting "now" (lecture of Feb. 12, 1906, CW 264, 204).

35. Rudolf Steiner, *From the History and Contents of the First Section of the Esoteric School, etc.* (CW 264), 225. No source is given for this answer, so this account could be wrong.

Who Are Rudolf Steiner and Peter Deunov?

Starting in 2000, some Bulgarians who know the teachings of the White Brotherhood, as well as those of Anthroposophy, put forward the thesis that in Peter Deunov the Maitreya Bodhisattva was embodied.[36] This thesis, which deserves serious consideration, has not been received positively either in the anthroposophical movement or in the School of the White Brotherhood. The arguments adduced are not sufficient to prove this identification of Deunov with the new Bodhisattva.

As mentioned before, in 1888, in response to a comment by the Cistercian Father Wilhelm Neumann, Steiner began to realize that in a previous life he had been the medieval philosopher and theologian Thomas Aquinas. This became an inner experience for him, extending to other past lives as well. By 1906 at the latest, Marie von Sivers had also come to this insight. Later, Ita Wegman came to a karmic insight regarding her lives with Steiner. The previous lives of Steiner and Wegman were at first not openly discussed in the anthroposophical movement. They *were* known, however, in the circles of physicians around Wegman. Only in 1976 were they revealed to members of the Society; this was accomplished in a book that was written by Margarethe and Erich Kirchner-Bockholt.[37] In 2009, Emanuel Zeylmans van Emmichoven published Steiner's letters to Ita Wegman.[38] Steffen Hartmann then elaborated further on the karmic friendship between Steiner and Wegman in 2021.[39]

This friendship between the young soul Enkidu (whose individuality later incarnated in Rudolf Steiner) and the old soul Gilgamesh (Ita Wegman), king of the Sumerian city-state of Uruk in the period

---

36. "Dimiter Mangurov, Beinsa Douno, und Rudolf Steiner als Teil des Christus-Impulses" [The Relation of Dimiter Mangurov, Beinsa Douno, and Rudolf Steiner to the Christ Impulse], lecture given on October 21, 2001, in Varna. See https://erzengelmichaelblog.wordpress.com/2016/10/07/1023/. Filip Filipov, Preslav Pavlov and Dimiter Kalev, *The Bodhisattva in the 20th Century*, Sofia, 2007.

37. Kirchner-Bockholt, *Rudolf Steiner's Mission and Ita Wegman*.

38. Zeylmans, *Die Erkraftung des Herzens* [The Power of the Heart].

39. Steffen Hartmann, *Gilgamesch und Enkidu: Eine weltgeschichtliche Freundschaft* [Gilgamesh and Enkidu: A World-Historic Friendship], Stuttgart, 2021.

between 2800 and 2500 BC began 5000 years ago.⁴⁰ This was followed by a period of about 2000 years, during which these friends were presumably not incarnated. The next incarnation that Steiner revealed to Ita Wegman was in Ephesus, in western present-day Turkey, where they were associated with the temple of Artemis in the fifth century BC: Enkidu (Steiner) as the priest Cratylus, and Gilgamesh (Wegman) as the priestess Mysa. In their next life, Enkidu was born as the Greek philosopher Aristotle (384–322 BC) and Gilgamesh as Alexander the Great (356–323 BC).

In their next incarnation, they were connected with the Grail family of Anfortas. Enkidu became Schionatulander of the Grail, the young knight of the ninth century story of Parzival who was asked by his beloved Sigune (Gilgamesh) to retrieve a dog, but was subsequently killed at Arlesheim by a knight who mistook him for Parzival. In a subsequent life, the reborn Schionatulander, as the Dominican monk Thomas Aquinas (1225–1274), took on the task of connecting Aristotle's philosophy with Christianity. From 1265, the theologian and monk Reginald of Piperno (c. 1230–c. 1290), the reborn Sigune, was his secretary.

In the School of the White Brotherhood, it has been handed down by Maria Todorova that, according to Deunov, Steiner is said to have been the Greek philosopher Pythagoras (c. 570–ca. 495 BC), who had a spiritual school in southern Italy and was associated with the Orphic Mysteries. This tradition raises serious questions.⁴¹

As for the karmic connection between Rudolf Steiner and Marie Steiner, the relationship between Thomas Aquinas and the Dominican monk Albertus Magnus (c. 1200–1280) can be mentioned. Albertus was Thomas Aquinas' teacher in Cologne and, according to

---

40. According to Profokieff, Enkidu was very closely connected with the Nathan Jesus. See Sergej O. Prokofieff, *Rudolf Steiner: Fragment of a Spiritual Biography*, Forest Row, 2021, chap. 3.

41. Krustev, *Izgevut na Bialoto Bratstvo*, vol. 1, 246–47. Peter Deunov is said to have mentioned this before 1922, and after the fire of the First Goetheanum it came up again. According to Deunov, the woman who had admitted Pythagoras to his school was the same woman who also sided with Steiner. This tradition is problematic because there is a very short time between the lives of Pythagoras and Cratylus, of whom we do not know exactly when he lived.

Who Are Rudolf Steiner and Peter Deunov?

some in anthroposophical circles, a previous incarnation of Marie von Sivers—although there are other well-considered views on this.

In 1991, Dutch anthroposophist Hans Peter van Manen addressed Marie Steiner's place in world karma in a lecture. He referred to a 1924 statement by Steiner that she was a "cosmic being," and as well to the words from a letter from Steiner to her: "You are for me the priestess, just as you appeared to me when you looked at me, and I recognized your individuality." Van Manen was thinking here of her connection with the mysteries of Eleusis, located near Athens.[42]

With this we have come to the end of these biographical studies of Rudolf Steiner and Peter Deunov. We will move on to a comparison of their spiritual teachings.

---

42. Hans Peter van Manen, *Marie Steiner*, Dornach 1994.

PART II

Two Spiritual Schools

Anthroposophy is a path of insight that seeks to lead the spiritual in the human being to the spiritual in the universe.[1]

— Rudolf Steiner, February 17, 1924

The purpose of every occult science, which belongs to the great science of life, is to enlighten the human mind and ennoble the human heart. It aims to bring light to the mind and warmth to the heart as necessary conditions for the proper development of people. From this point of view, the mind and the heart must come to help people toward the rectification of their lives.[2]

—Peter Deunov, from a lecture of August 24, 1927

---

1. Rudolf Steiner, first Leading Thought, in *Anthroposophical Leading Thoughts* (CW 26).

2. Beinsa Douno, "The Holy Fire," lecture of August 24, 1927, in *The Way of the Disciple*, Sofia, 1996, 324.

Introduction

The spiritual schools of Rudolf Steiner and Peter Deunov stem from the inspirations of the two masters of esoteric Christianity: Christian Rosenkreutz and Master Jesus. This is the common foundation on which they developed inspirations from the great school of Christ in the spiritual world. This school is under Christ's guidance and includes the spiritual beings associated with him as well as the advanced leaders of humanity. Steiner usually called this school the White Lodge, sometimes also the White Brotherhood. These two terms are already found in Blavatsky's work. Deunov spoke of the Great Universal White Brotherhood, which sends its inspirations from the sun to the earthly School of the White Brotherhood.[1] Steiner saw his esoteric school as a school of the archangel Michael, which received inspirations from the White Lodge. This school is also connected to the sun. In this section, we are going to compare the effect of these inspirations. We will do this on the basis of some central themes from their teachings.

In 1879, according to both spiritual teachers, the age of the archangel Michael had begun. It will last for 354 years. As a *zeitgeist* or time-spirit, this archangel gives inspirations for the battle against evil and for its transformation. His spiritual impulses have a cosmopolitan aspect. Moreover, he protects those who fight in his name for a spiritual culture. In 1907, Steiner gave Ita Wegman the "Michael gesture" (a movement with the right arm made during First Class lessons); and from the end of August 1924, he used this gesture to protect the content of the Lessons from abuse. In Thomas Meyer's interpretation, this sign draws a line from the heights of the spiritual world to the depths of the physical world, then creates an inner space for the soul, and finally points to the needed action.[2]

According to Deunov, the White Brotherhood in the invisible

---

1. Boev and Nikolov (ed.), *The Wellspring of Good*, 262.

Rudolf Steiner and Peter Deunov

world has manifested itself in three earthly branches of the Brotherhood. The first branch, the Egyptian, created the conditions for the coming of Christianity. The second branch, the Palestinian, brought Christianity into the world and spread it. The third branch, that of the Bogomils (known in France as the Cathars), aimed to realize the teachings of Christianity. In this connection, Deunov also mentioned the Orphic Mysteries in Greece, the Essenes in Palestine, and the Hermetic philosophers in Egypt as precursors of this third branch.[3] He pointed out that the schools of Orpheus, the Bogomils, and of the White Brotherhood developed in the territory of present-day Bulgaria. All three drew from the same source in the invisible world. According to Deunov, the Rosicrucians were also an offshoot of this third branch. And we can add Anthroposophy to this.

The schools of Anthroposophy and the White Brotherhood take advantage of the opportunities offered by the transition to the Age of Light. Steiner determined the end of the Age of Darkness to be the year 1899. For Deunov, too, this era had ended.

We can first note that at that time Steiner spoke of the "spiritual" world, and Deunov of the "invisible" world. In Anthroposophy, importance is attached to exact quotation, with the date included; but in the texts of the School of the White Brotherhood, quotations from different lectures are often compiled without mentioning the source and the date. Translations of these texts do not always translate directly from Bulgarian, but use already translated texts in other languages. In the process, the nuances of the original Bulgarian words may sometimes be lost.

In Anthroposophy, Steiner's thoughts on dozens of subjects have been systematically elaborated in books authored by his disciples. This is not the case to anything like this extent in the School of the White Brotherhood. Boyan Boev elaborated Deunov's thoughts on education in a book, but gives no references to lectures. In 1942, he did the same with the subject of conscious breathing. Furthermore, he took stenographic notes of Deunov's conversations with his stu-

---

2. Rudolf Steiner, *The First Class Lessons and Mantras: The Michael School Meditative Path in Nineteen Steps*, ed. T.H. Meyer, Hudson, NY, 2017, 395–400.
3. Kovacheva, *Die Weisse Bruderschaft* [The White Brotherhood], 234–35.

Introduction

dents and arranged them by topic. These notes have been published, and also translated into English.[4] Methodi Konstantinov, Boris Nikolov, Georgi Radev, Vlad Pashov, and Maria Todorova also collected texts on various topics.[5] Vassil Velev and Svetla Baltova have done so for medically relevant thoughts.[6] Baltova also selected texts on certain topics in seven booklets. In this way, statements from Deunov's more than 4,000 lectures can be studied in context.

In the next part we turn to an elaboration of seven key themes from the two spiritual schools: the development of the cosmos, involution and evolution, the return of Christ, the development of consciousness, the new culture of community, the connection of head and heart, and the paths of schooling.

---

4. Boyan Boev, *Der Meister über die Bildung und die Erziehung* [The Master on Education and Upbringing]. Boyan Boev, *Breathing*. Boev and Nikolov (ed.), *The Wellspring of Good*, Sofia 2013. Peter Deunov, *Harmonizing of the Human Soul*, Sofia, 2013.

5. Methodi Konstantinov and others, *Uchitelya* [The Teacher], Sofia, 2005; Georgi Radev (ed.), *The Master Speaks*, Sofia, 1997; Vlad Pashov, *Life after the Death of the Physical Body*, Sofia, 2009 (https://ia800703.us.archive.org/3/items/PeterDeunov/LIFE_AFTER_T HE_DEATH.pdf).

6. Vassil Velev (ed.), *The Master Beinsa Douno, Health and Sickness*, Sofia 2002. Svetla Baltova (ed.), *The Master Peter Deunov: Child of the Universe*, Sofia 2013.

1

The Evolution of the World

In his 1910 book *Outline of Occult Science*, Rudolf Steiner described the origin of the earth within our planetary system. This is a simplification of the system of Theosophy. Steiner dealt with three former phases of development of the earth, which he called Old Saturn, Old Sun, and Old Moon. As he describes it, the earth is now in its fourth phase, during which it has (thus far) passed through a Polar, a Hyperborean, a Lemurian, and an Atlantean epoch. We are now living in the post-Atlantean epoch. According to Steiner, two more such epochs will follow.

In our present epoch (the post-Atlantean), seven culture periods of 2160 years may be distinguished, in which separate cultures develop: the first four (the Old Indian, the Old Persian, the Chaldean-Egyptian, the Greco-Roman) bring us to the present so-called "Germano-Anglo-Saxon" culture. Following upon this latter, according to Steiner, will be a Slavic culture period and an American culture period. The earth itself will in due course also go through three more major metamorphoses, which he called the Jupiter, Venus, and Vulcan phases of earth development. According to Steiner, the Jupiter phase corresponds to the biblical image of the New Jerusalem. Man's consciously performed moral deeds create the substance needed for this new phase. Because technology will radically alter the development of the earth and of man, the importance of a moral and etheric technology is seen in the anthroposophical movement.[1]

All developmental processes are guided by nine hierarchies of

---

1. This is the background of the work of Paul Emberson and his research group and of the American *Mystical Technology* (MysTech) group.

The Evolution of the World

angels, which in the Christian tradition have the names Seraphim, Cherubim, Thrones, Dominions, Virtues, Powers, Principalities, Archangels, and Angels. In other traditions they have other names. In Anthroposophy they are also described by their qualities, e.g., the Spirits of Universal Love (Seraphim). Above them is the Trinity of God the Father, the Son, and the Holy Spirit. Steiner and Deunov used similar descriptions of the qualities of the hierarchies of angels. According to them, humanity will develop into a tenth hierarchy. The spiritual world also includes the nature spirits, which were known in all ancient cultures and described in detail by Steiner. The nature spirits have been under the guidance of the angels, but the time has come, according to him, for human beings to take over this task.

The angels live in the spiritual world, which has its own structure. Its lowest part Steiner called the etheric world. Above the etheric world lies the astral world. And above the astral world comes the spiritual world proper, for which he employed the Theosophical term *devachan*. He described these worlds and the role of angels in the creation of the earth extensively in his books and lectures.

Deunov did not give series of lectures on particular topics. In individual lectures, or in answers to questions, he dealt with many aspects of the invisible world, including the role of angels and the intelligence of nature. He knew the previous stages of earth development and noted in one talk that humanity had lived on the sun and the moon before coming to earth. He spoke of the epoch of Lemuria and Atlantis, as well as the post-Atlantean cultural periods. Following Blavatsky, he called these great eras "races" and the culture periods "sub-races." Steiner changed the old-fashioned Theosophical terms to "epochs" and "culture periods."

Deunov called the third culture period the Middle Egyptian and Assyrian-Babylonian, the fourth the Hebrew and Greco-Roman, and the present the Western European. According to Blavatsky, the sixth culture period would be the Australian-American, but Deunov contradicted her—and already in 1898, before Steiner had done so, he spoke of the coming Slavic culture period, which will be a culture of the heart, a culture of love. Steiner said of this in 1905:

> From the seeds dormant in Eastern Europe, something new must emerge, a fusion with all that has been worked out here. The

proper [future] culture lies in the germinating ethnic elements of Eastern Europe. We ourselves in Central Europe are the precursors.[2]

Insofar as the angels are connected to Christ, they are part of the Great White Brotherhood of Divine Love, Divine Wisdom, and Divine Truth, as Deunov called it. They form a hierarchy of intelligent beings,

> who have completed their evolution millions and billions of years ago and who now direct the entire cosmos. They direct it because they themselves have participated in its creation under the guidance of the Divine Spirit.[3]

From their hearts flow love, joy, and life. They send their light to the whole world and move faster than light. These "great brothers of humanity" care about the spiritual upliftment of man and constantly send their emissaries to earth. These are the spiritual teachers of mankind of whom Deunov and Steiner spoke. According to Deunov, all great men, saints, adepts, scientists, writers, and politicians who support the spiritual advancement of humanity are servants of the Great White Brotherhood.

While Steiner distinguished between the physical world, the etheric world, the astral world, and the world of *devachan*, Deunov spoke of three worlds: the human (physical) world, the spiritual world, and the divine world. According to his teaching, there are three solar systems: the first is the physical world, which is made up of dense matter; the second, which is part of the world of the angelic hierarchies, is made up of the finer matter of the spiritual world; and the third, in its totality, constitutes the divine world, which is formed from the finest matter.[4] These three worlds are also found in man. His body belongs to the physical world, his soul to the spiritual world, and his spirit to the divine world. For physical life, man

---

2. Rudolf Steiner, lecture of November 5, 1905, in *Foundations of Esotericism* (CW 93a).
3. Beinsa Douno, *The Master Speaks,* chapter on "The Great Universal Brotherhood," Sofia, 1997. On angels, see Boev and Nikolov (ed.), *The Wellspring of Good*, 308–19.
4. Ibid., chapter on "The Great Universal Brotherhood."

The Evolution of the World

needs food in which the energy of light is stored; music leads him into the spiritual life; and prayer is the entrance to the divine life.[5]

Deunov spoke of "the living and intelligent nature" because intelligent beings operate in it at all levels. Their wisdom can be observed everywhere in nature. For the wise, Deunov said,

> living nature is a beautifully organized world—a world of harmony, music, and beauty. And one day, when humanity's ears are opened, people all over the world will hear the sublime music of nature.

For Deunov, nature is the feminine face of God. She is the Great Mother. When we respect her, she will reveal her secrets, and we can then work with the forces of nature.

Deunov examined the laws of nature. When people go against them, the result is suffering and disease as well as earthquakes, storms, floods, and famine. Our thoughts, feelings, and lifestyles are the cause of this. He described the electrical and magnetic forces in nature and how they work in the human body. His understanding of the laws of nature becomes apparent in the extensive advice he offered in his lectures on the healing forces present in nature. The White Brotherhood's school uses the healing powers of the four elements of nature (earth, water, air, and fire), electricity and magnetism, sunlight, food, and herbs. In the school, hot water is drunk after waking (to activate the body's cells); breathing exercises and movements are performed, as in the sacred dance of paneurythmy; and a wheat-based diet is followed for ten days in the spring. Singing and music-making have a healing and rejuvenating effect, as do meditating before sunrise and at dawn, and taking excursions into the mountains.[6]

Rudolf Steiner, in collaboration with the Dutch physician Ita Wegman, laid the foundations of anthroposophical medicine, which was intended as a holistic extension of existing medicine. It makes possible diagnoses on the basis of a threefold view of man

---

5. Ibid., chapter on "Life."
6. Velev (ed.), *The Master Beinsa Douno, Health and Sickness*, Sofia, 2002. Baltova (ed.), *The Master Peter Deunov: Child of the Universe*.

Rudolf Steiner and Peter Deunov

(the three organ systems) and a fourfold image of man (physical body, etheric body, astral body, and I). Inspired by spiritual beings, Steiner also developed complex medicines for certain diseases.

In contrast, Deunov's wise insights into the laws of nature and how they work in the human body are spread throughout his work. He has pointed out that the spiritual schools of antiquity developed in the mountains. According to him, the oldest esoteric school of humanity is located in the Bulgarian Rila Mountains. The significance of its sacred centers is that they work for the new culture. The luminous beings who reside there do not appear to people except when they harbor love for them.[7] According to Deunov, the cultures of Egypt and India had their origins in the Rila Mountains, and the initiates from the Himalayas come to study in the "libraries" of Rila. The summer camps in the mountains of Rila were for Deunov's disciples a "school of the mountains," in which, under his guidance, they investigated intelligent nature and became acquainted with the beings who intelligently direct the processes of nature.

---

7. Boev and Nikolov (ed.), *The Wellspring of Good*, 231–35.

2

Involution and Evolution

The biblical story of the Fall is a myth symbolizing that original humanity lost its natural connection to its divine origin. Rudolf Steiner has given greater context to the bible story than traditional theology does. The temptation of Eve by the serpent, behind whom the fallen angel Lucifer hides, is the God-permitted beginning of a great process of development in which man can develop into a free being with a mind of his own. Under the influence of Lucifer and his luciferic angels, forces began to work that detach man from the earth, make him haughty, and lead him into a realm of illusions.

Against this, Steiner contrasted the influence of Satan (Ahriman), known from the biblical book of Job, who chains humans to the earth, exposes them to fear, makes them violent, and traps them in a realm of lies and materialistic thoughts. Later, Steiner would further elaborate his view of the powers of evil in conjunction with his interpretation of the Book of Revelation, which describes how the Apocalypse unfolds. This will be discussed in the next chapter.

According to Steiner, we owe to Lucifer the ancient wisdom that works in the spiritual currents from Asia, trapping people in the past so that they cannot find the way to Christ. Ahriman works from North America, especially in the world of technology. He prevents man's spiritual development.

Between these two evil powers stands Christ, who, according to Rudolf Steiner, has restored man's connection to his divine origin by enabling him to connect his lower self (the ego, which he owes to Lucifer) with his higher Self. This is the birth of the New Man, made possible by the death and resurrection of Christ—the New Adam, as described by the apostle Paul. In Steiner's vision, the old man lives from the powers of the world of God the Father—powers that are withdrawing in our time. But thanks to the sacrifice of Christ, the way has been cleared for the new man, who lives from the resurrection power of Christ. This is the beginning of the new creation.

In the School of the White Brotherhood, Peter Deunov spoke in this connection about the processes of involution (the way of the old man) and of evolution (the way of the new man). During the last year of his life, he said the following about this in several talks:

> Involution is turning away from God, and evolution is returning to God. Involution is leaving home and going to work. Evolution is returning home from work with the experience that we have acquired. Moving down means moving into darkness; climbing up is rising toward the light.
>
> The story of the fall of man into error is one of the great mysteries of life. This story has a symbolic bearing upon the issue of involution. It concerns the time when man was with God and dwelled among the angels. The human being, alone, wanted to come down to earth in order to learn.
>
> People descended to earth to study, and when they had come to its unfavorable constraining conditions, they began to think about their Father, about God. God understands human nature, and for this reason He did not give humans immortality—allowing all who do not fulfill His Will to age. When He sent man to earth, God began to take away from him what he possessed. This is a consequence of the involutionary process.
>
> As long as we were outside the material world, we were idealists: we strove toward God and desired to sacrifice, to share everything. Nevertheless, when we descended into the material world, we forgot everything. In the process of descending, we lost something. We need to return to that state in which we were at the beginning.
>
> Since ancient times, many beings have lost their primordial, sublime life. The infinite love of God strives to permeate them so that He may restore the life and light they have lost. Love wants to awaken all those who have fallen asleep, bringing back to life all of the "dead." History keeps silent regarding the cause of these beings having lost their sublime life. They have experienced a great catastrophe. Their life is a great tragedy. Many legends exist regarding the reasons for this tragedy—through which the whole of humankind has lived.

Involution and Evolution

A new epoch is now coming for humankind in which the Intelligent World will show people the way they can return to their primordial life and come to stand on good, solid ground. At present, most people live amid life's illusions.

During the involutionary process—that is, during the process of descending into the material world—materialized souls descended through great resistance into the densest matter of the earth. In the process of descending, considerable energy is generated. This is the most difficult path, the path of wisdom. Although the teaching of love—that is to say, the path of ascent or evolution—has been taught to people, they still walk on the most difficult path.

The devas, the angels, move along the easiest path: the path of the least resistance. That is to say, the angels move along the path of love, and people along the path of wisdom. Until recently, humankind was descending. As human beings begin to ascend, they will meet the angels and will come to know them.

At present, we are in the transient time between involution and evolution. Because descent is followed by ascent, at the border between the two epochs—that is, in the transient period—the greatest resistance, the greatest suffering, exists. This is why there are so many delays and obstacles at present. Nevertheless, once the evolutionary process begins, the forces will be directed upward. Then there will be no obstacles.

The methods for development of the Eastern nations were good at one time, but now they cannot be applied as they were in the past. This is because we are at the beginning of the evolutionary process, and no longer in that of the involutionary process, when these methods were given. The methods that Hindu philosophy has used before are involutionary. Now, new evolutionary methods need to be given to the Western nations.

At the boundary between the involutionary and evolutionary epochs is *Christ*. His appearance heralds the beginning of the evolutionary epoch. However, the majority of people today continue to descend; that is, they are still on the involutionary path. They will not solve their problems in this way. In such a case, another impulse upward toward the sun needs to come.[1]

---

1. Boev and Nikolov (ed.), *The Wellspring of Good*, 38–41.

Rudolf Steiner and Peter Deunov

The new stage of development, Deunov said, "is the stage of love, the stage of evolution, in which love works as a principle. In the process of involution, wisdom was the main principle of work, and love was a tool." In a similar way, Steiner spoke of the transition from the cosmos of Wisdom to the cosmos of love. Man must help make this transition possible:

> From the earth stage of development, the wisdom of the outer world becomes the inner wisdom of man. Internalized in this way, it becomes the seed of love. Wisdom is the condition for love; love is the result of wisdom reborn in the I.[2]

Deunov has called humanity a "battlefield" on which two forces battle each other. The forces of light and of darkness wage a battle for every human soul. The angels of light (angels connected with Christ) want to bring human beings onto the path of evolution, but the angels of darkness (luciferic and ahrimanic angels, according to Steiner) want to prevent this and subjugate us. These angels of darkness together form the world of *fallen* angels. We must pass through the world of darkness, and that of light, to the divine world.[3]

These fallen angels face the angels of the White Brotherhood. Of this, Deunov said:

> But if men do not follow the right path today, the reason is that, counterbalancing the Great White Brotherhood, another lodge of intelligent beings works—beings who do not understand the deep meaning of life and have a diametrically opposite comprehension of it. They constitute the so-called Black Brotherhood.
>
> Therefore, the White Brotherhood is connected with the positive forces, with the good; and the Black Brotherhood is connected with the negative forces, with evil in the broadest sense of the word. But at present, both forces are necessary for the manifestation of life. Their services are strictly defined.
>
> Besides these two schools, there is a third one—the school of the Great Masters, who are from a higher hierarchy and direct the

---

2. Rudolf Steiner, *Outline of Occult Science,* quotation from the final part of the chapter "Present and Future of the World and Man."
3. Svetla Baltova (ed.), *Peter Deunov za nevidimite svetove* [Peter Deunov on the Invisible Worlds], Plovdiv, 2012, 102–4.

Involution and Evolution

activities of the first two. They make use of the methods of both schools for their great aims, but belong neither to the one nor to the other. They are those Great Masters of the Universal Brotherhood who guide the entire cosmos and who, after the completion of each evolution, create new waves of evolution according to another plan and another rhythm. Under the guidance of their mighty spirit, those advanced spirits who created the solar systems, including our own, at one time descended from the highest peaks of creation. They also created and organized the primal "cosmic" earth—what was once "paradise." On that "cosmic earth" still live those perfected forefathers of men who completed their evolution.[4]

Peter Deunov also said,

> The Black Lodge has deluded the people, and they work only for themselves, settling their own matters; thus, humanity has come into collision with the Divine in itself.[5]

The master of the Black Brotherhood does not know the truth, and pays much attention to his outward appearance. To the hearts of his disciples he brings bondage to the soul, darkness to the mind, and corruption. In contrast, the master of the White Brotherhood brings freedom to the soul, light to the mind, and purity to the heart.

---

4. Beinsa Douno, *The Master Speaks,* chapter on "The Great Universal Brotherhood."

5. Peter Deunov, *Harmonizing of the Human Soul,* 94.

3
The Second Coming of Christ

For Rudolf Steiner and Peter Deunov, Christ's death and resurrection are the turning point in human history. The connection with the higher Self was restored through Christ, so that human beings could once again unite with their origin as the "image and likeness of God." The path of involution, to matter, could now turn to the path of evolution, to a return to the spiritual. However, the Mystery of Golgotha, as Steiner called it, opened this new path for only a small part of humanity.

Christ himself said, "I will be with you always until the end of time" (Matthew 28:20), and he also envisioned his return, but not in a physical body. This latter is what was propagated in the Theosophical Society by Besant and Leadbeater around the person of Krishnamurti. Just as Christ disappeared into the clouds (the etheric world, the world of life-forces) at His Ascension, just so would He also return. This was the teaching of both Steiner and Deunov.

On January 12, 1910, during a member's lecture in Stockholm, Steiner announced the imminent return of Christ to the etheric world. He would appear in an etheric form in 1933 to people who would by then have developed natural clairvoyance, as well as to people with clairvoyance trained from Anthroposophy. Steiner worked tirelessly to make this message known, for such visions of Christ (which would occur not only in 1933, but also between 1930 and 1945 and beyond), had to be recognized. Otherwise, he said, an infinite psychic confusion would be caused. For, around 1933, black-magic circles would wrongly proclaim a physical Christ—or, as we can now say in retrospect, put forward another "savior," like Hitler.[1]

---

1. Notes of Marie Steiner in Harald Giersch (ed.), *Rudolf Steiner über die Wiederkunft Christi* [Rudolf Steiner on the Return of Christ], Dornach, 1991, 107–8.

The Second Coming of Christ

After his announcement in Stockholm, Steiner spoke often to *members* of the Anthroposophical Society about the Second Coming of Christ. This he did in order to prepare them for it. Only once, on June 13, 1910, did he refer to it in a *public* lecture (in Oslo). According to Steiner, the Second Coming of Christ would take place over the next 2,500 years through the emergence of new, natural clairvoyant faculties of the soul, effectuated by the Christ impulse itself and based on the gradual separation of the etheric body from the physical body. These faculties would enable human beings to perceive Christ spiritually and to understand him more and more. This would happen first in few people; but in the course of time Christ would reveal Himself to all people who would take the necessary inner path.[2] This is the path of the conscious development of the new clairvoyance, opened by Steiner in Anthroposophy.

In the fall of 1911, Steiner predicted that Christ would appear to people as a comforter, counselor, and helper in difficult situations of their lives. This has since been confirmed in many ways.[3] During this time, he also spoke of a new task of Christ to become "Lord of karma" by the end of the 20th century. After our death, we will then appear before Christ, who will be judge of our karma and ask us to judge our lives ourselves. He will also ensure that the good deeds with which we harmonize our negative karma will benefit as many people as possible.[4]

On September 20, 1924, in a lecture to the priests of the Christian Community on the theme of the Apocalypse, Steiner warned:

> Before the etheric Christ can be properly understood, humanity must first have vigorously and successfully endured the encounter with the Beast from the abyss, who rises in 1933.[5]

---

2. Ibid., 108–10.
3. Rudolf Steiner, "The Etherization of the Blood" (lecture of October 1, 1911), in *Esoteric Christianity* (CW 130); Gunnar Hillerdal and Berndt Gustafsson, *Sie erlebten Christus* [They Experienced Christ], Basel, 1979; Rolf Tschanz (ed.), *Vom Christus-Wirken der Gegenwart* [The Working of Christ in the Present Time], Dornach, 1991.
4. Rudolf Steiner, lecture of December 2, 1911, in *Esoteric Christianity* (CW 130).
5. Rudolf Steiner, lecture of September 20, 1924, in *The Book of Revelation and the Work of the Priest* (CW 346).

Rudolf Steiner and Peter Deunov

This beast, given the number 666 in the book of the Apocalypse of St. John, is the sun demon (the opponent of Christ, the Spirit of the Sun), whose activity is linked to black-magic impulses of the academy of Gondishapur in Iran, where, according to Steiner, the sun demon sought to manifest itself around the year 666. In the early 14th century (2 x 666), his intervention led to the destruction of the Order of the Knights Templar. In the darkening of the etheric world around 1933, we can recognize the return of this impulse. In the decades around 1998 (3 x 666), this impulse was present again.

Steiner also warned of the incarnation of Ahriman, the spirit of lies (or Satan), at the beginning of the 21st century. Modern man, in the cultural period that began after the Middle Ages, is confronted with the mystery of evil, which he must fathom before he can work to transform it. The archangel Michael precedes him in this struggle against the dragons—the fallen angels—who are kept under control by his lance.

Whereas Steiner placed the Second Coming of Christ in the context of the attack of the dark powers on humanity, for Peter Deunov the Second Coming was the beginning of a new activity of Christ, the beginning of the establishment of the Kingdom of God, which will unfold slowly. From 1910, he too spoke of the approach of the Second Coming, which had already been announced by the angel Elohil in his call, in 1898, to the Bulgarian people.

In October 1910, Deunov said to his circle of disciples in Sofia:

> Christ has already come. He has not, however, manifested himself in the way the churches have been expecting, but in a completely different way. Christ will come in 1914. A small revival will then begin. The present order must be destroyed and the forces that are now active must be rotted away.... The world has to be punished, and everyone will receive his or her due.... The Lord has begun to purify the world.... Archangel Michael will dispel all evil spirits.... People will suffer until they have settled their accounts with the Lord.... The world will be cleansed when humanity has purified its karma. The planet and its climate will also be purified as a result of this process.[6]

---

6. Beinsa Douno, *The Teacher*, vol. 1, 17–19.

The Second Coming of Christ

Sunday, March 22, 1914, was the day that, according to Deunov, marked the beginning of the End of Time, the beginning of the Apocalypse, which will end with the establishment of the Kingdom of God and the coming of the New Jerusalem. On this day, Deunov invited the spiritual circle of people (who had gathered for his lectures over a number of years) to a festive meal. After reading the final chapters of each of the four gospels, he spoke:

> Not many realize the importance of today's date. But for some it will be a day to remember, because today one epoch has ended and a new one is beginning. Today is a great spiritual day. There is a gathering up above, from where all our friends are sending you their greetings.... Today a new epoch is beginning in the invisible world.

The closing words of his speech were:

> Let us uplift ourselves and imagine the divine picture of today's celebration in heaven. The spirits will descend from heaven to make human beings satisfied with what they have, and Christ will come with them. Either they will come with a blessing, a renovation of the contemporary order, or, if it is seen that it cannot be renovated, they will come with a catastrophe that destroys everything from the foundations—after which the building will begin completely anew. We must not be afraid of this possibility.
>
> Christ is always above us and between us. Let us leave this meeting with Christ in our souls. Let us open our hearts and our souls so that Christ can enter them and bless us. Amen.[7]

According to Deunov, the return of Christ will take place in stages. The first wave that started in 1914 would last 45 years (1914–1959). After that would come a pause, then another wave. This process would repeat itself rhythmically.[8] In several talks in the year 1944, Deunov, like a prophet, explained the deeper background of Christ's return:

> Our solar system will depart from heavier matter and enter into a less dense medium. Because of this, there will exist conditions for

---

7. Ibid., 119–22.
8. Peter Deunov, *Harmonizing of the Human Soul*, 50.

the manifestation of a higher consciousness for humankind. The solar system departs from the so-called "13th sphere."[9] At the same time, the sun will enter the Age of Aquarius. Now is the end of the dark epoch, the Kali Yuga. Because the earth is entering a new realm, all the old forms will change. New forms will destroy the old ones. People will not notice how they will grow and become *new* people. Old forms will fall away as do the leaves in autumn. In the place of the "old" people, new ones will come with new ideas.[10]

Earlier he had said:

A new wave is coming from out of cosmic space, the wave of divine love. It is also called the *wave of fire*. This wave has powerful vibrations, which not every human being can endure. For this reason, it has been said that God is an all-consuming fire. For those who are ready to withstand the vibrations of this wave, and who receive it, this wave will become luminous. But for those who cannot bear the vibrations, it will be a fire that will either consume them or will cause them to pass through great suffering. This will prepare them to awaken, and to receive love. For this reason, this wave of love, which is coming, is also called *the divine fire*. Everything old and impure will be consumed in it. After humankind passes through this divine fire, the Kingdom of God will come to earth. I say: When the fire of love comes, some people will become luminous; but others will burn and pass through repentance.

Today we find yourselves in a great phase of life. Not too much time will pass before we find ourselves passing through the fire. This will be in our lifetime. This wave of fire will soon pass over the world and purify it. All human thoughts and desires will pass through this fire and become purified in the most perfect way. The great life will enter us and we will be transformed. As the smith places the iron in the fire in order to refine it, so will the great intelligent world bear us through the fire, so that we, too, can be purified and tempered.

---

9. About this thirteenth sphere, Deunov said that the entire solar system passed through this sphere over a period of thousands of years. Here, long ago, was another system—which has disappeared, but whose dust has remained, poisoning all beings in the solar system except a few in the sphere of the sun. See Beinsa Douno, *Sacred Words of the Master*, 215–16.

10. Boev and Nikolov (ed.), *The Wellspring of Good*, 292.

The Second Coming of Christ

The great destruction that occurs today is due to this great life, which is coming now. If people do not accept Christ voluntarily, modern culture will pass through fire seven times—but in the end, it will be purified and renewed.

The Lord is coming and he has already set his foot upon the earth. I can easily prove that he has set his foot upon the earth. How? The great suffering, which is constantly increasing, is the proof that the Lord is coming into this world. Do you know what his decision is? Everything impure is to burn. One has never before seen the dust that will be raised on earth. You have never suspected what great cleansing is coming before the Great Day! Nothing will remain of the European nations and of the planning of the European diplomats. Love will destroy everything old. After that, we will begin to build. This turbulence among societies, this unrest among those who are in distress, indicates that God permeates everything. All this is linked to the eradication of the karma of humankind, which has accumulated for thousands of years. Until all old concepts, thoughts, and feelings burn in the fire of suffering, human beings cannot enter into the new life, which is due to come now.

That these forces now turn against us is because, for thousands of years, we have been under the influence of negative forces. People have strayed from the right path, and all misfortunes are due to that. They have deviated from many things, and for this reason have remained behind in their development. The invisible world wants to help them so that they may develop properly. The invisible world is sending workers with their hammers to work on people's homes. These misfortunes are called "the unfavorable conditions of life."

The karma of the European nations is already ripe and creates suffering for the whole of humankind. These tribulations indicate that people need to change their way of life and apply the divine teaching.

Modern culture is in its leave-taking. The new culture is coming, and its application in life will begin. The invisible world has decided to teach modern civilized people a lesson, which they will remember for a thousand years.[11]

---

11. Ibid., 285–89.

Rudolf Steiner and Peter Deunov

Deunov regarded the suffering that various peoples went through in the first half of the 20th century as the repayment of their karma. He used for this purpose the word "liquidation." Karma was the result of negative actions of nations, as well as of communities and of individuals from the past. Deunov placed World War I and World War II also in such a context, and viewed them as opportunities for humanity to reach a higher level of consciousness. Of the liquidation of karma, he said in 1944:

> Today, most people's karma is eradicated through suffering.... One day, God will erase all human error. Karma will be erased and will remain only as a moving picture show. You will then see what you have been in the past, what you have been doing. The past will be erased as karma, but will remain as a film. We need to leave the realm of karma. There is no solution to the issues in it. It is a deviation from the Divine path. [12]

And further:

> Instead, we can do good for others, settle our negative karma, and reap the blessings of our good deeds. We then live from the power of love. By working for others, for God, through love, man can liquidate his karma. When we forgive those who have done us harm, the karmic connection is broken.[13]

Rudolf Steiner placed different emphases. He spoke of old karma that binds us to the past, and new karma that people create for the future. This can also be positive karma. He also expressed that we can take on some of the negative karma of others who have been overburdened by it. Within a community, one can help carry the heavily burdened karma of another individual.

An important feature of Deunov's teachings is the contraction of time. He speaks of developments that began in the 20th century and will continue for centuries to come. The coming of the Kingdom of God has entered a new phase with the return of Christ, but its realization is beyond our time horizon. This is apocalyptic thinking.

---

12. Ibid., 419–20.
13. Peter Deunov, *Harmonizing of the Human Soul*, 49.

The Second Coming of Christ

Thus he said, "At the end of the *vek*, all who had part in good and evil will be tried, and karma will be liquidated."[14] The Bulgarian word *vek* means not only "century," but also "era."

And so we have these two different temporal perspectives. Compared to Steiner, Deunov placed less emphasis on the appearance of the apocalyptic powers of evil at the time of Christ's return. He did talk about Lucifer and Satan[15] (Steiner referred to Satan as *Ahriman*), but he warned his students not to focus on evil, as it could then take possession of them. He said, "Man must not fight evil. He must escape it. He must, rather, set good against it.... The only being who can harness evil into work is God."[16]

On October 10, 1911, Deunov spoke of dramatic changes that would take place in the world, especially in 1914, changes that would lead to a manifestation of the Kingdom of God. These events would begin with a purification of the earth that would continue until 1927 or 1933. The chains binding evil and all negative orders would be broken. What would happen after that would depend on two currents (the good or the evil). He noted in this regard:

> When Christ was on the earth, Satan was in the astral world. Now it is the other way around: Satan is on the earth and Christ is acting in the astral world. The destructiveness of Satan will now be manifested in a much greater way than at any previous time. Satan will be incarnated here, in Europe, in a king's home, and he will attract all negative elements to himself.... Finally, however, he will be crucified.

In 1939 he said:

> The task of all people is to study the forces of evil in order to learn how to turn evil into good.... The only force that can defeat evil is divine love.[17]

The people of the future can transform evil. Deunov noted that we

---

14. Ibid., 246.
15. Both Lucifer and Satan (whose name means "accuser" in Hebrew) appear in the Old Testament.
16. Beinsa Douno, *The Master Speaks*, chapter on "The Good."
17. Peter Deunov, *The Language of Love*, Sofia, 2012, 119.

must let God, and *not* the fallen angels, work through us: the issue is the Second Coming of Christ, about which he noted:

> Christ comes now to visit our minds and hearts.... Christ is a manifestation of the love of God. And he will come as an inner light in our minds and hearts.... The opening of the mind and heart and the inner receiving of Christ will be Christ's return to earth. He will preach especially on the great science of love and the methods of applying it.... For some, Christ will come even today, for others tomorrow—and for still others after years. We will see him when we are ready. We must receive Christ in our hearts as a friend, and in our minds as a teacher.... He will teach us self-sacrifice and love. He brings love, wisdom, knowledge, freedom. The light of Christ penetrates everywhere.[18]

> Christ's return will be complete when people have opened their hearts to him. He constantly visits people, but they do not recognize him. Usually he visits those in need, those who are suffering, poor, sick, and abandoned. Christ knocks on everyone's door, and one day all will see him. They can find him when they purify their hearts, are meek and humble, and come into harmony with him. They can meet him not only in a mystical experience, but also in nature.[19]

---

18. Methodi Konstantinov and others, *Uchitelya* [The Teacher], Sofia, 2005, 394–96.

19. Svetla Baltova (ed.), *Peter Deunov za Christos i novoto chovechestvo* [Deunov for Christ and the New Humanity], Plovdiv, 2011, 138–62.

4

The Evolution of Consciousness

Through the death and resurrection of Christ, the process of involution is turned into a process of evolution. This is linked to the emergence of a new consciousness in humanity, in which we can connect with our higher Self. Rudolf Steiner has described the development of human consciousness from many perspectives. Modern man possesses an awake and thinking consciousness with which he can objectively perceive the world and himself. The development of this "consciousness soul" commenced at the end of the Middle Ages. Its preparation had already begun in Greek philosophy; and if we go back even further, its origin lay in the late period of Atlantis, in the solar oracle of Manu, who brought together people with the incipient faculty of thinking and with diminishing clairvoyance. At the time of Atlantis, people still had a consciousness with which they could perceive in the spiritual world by day and by night.

After World War I, Steiner spoke several times about humanity having unconsciously crossed the threshold of the spiritual world.[1] This process pertains to the age of the consciousness soul, which began in 1413. It is a process that has been taking place since Archangel Michael purified the atmosphere around the earth from the so-called "spirits of darkness" between 1841 and 1879. This unconscious passage across the threshold has great consequences. Namely,

---

1. Rudolf Steiner, lecture of April 11, 1919, in *Spiritual Emptiness and Social Life* (CW 190).

according to Steiner, it leads to a separation of the three soul forces of thinking, feeling, and willing, which were previously naturally connected. This separation also takes place at initiation. This process of separation forces modern man to bring his soul forces under the control of his I, and to consciously create harmony in his soul. Another consequence is that people, especially young people, have special spiritual experiences that they do not understand. These may include perceptions of (aspects of) their double—their negative aspects, or shadow. To deal with them, spiritual awareness is needed.

Peter Deunov highlighted the development of consciousness from a social perspective. In the earliest stages of history, people had an unconscious and dreaming collective consciousness, which they shared with the members of their group or tribe. This was based on blood relations. War was waged with other tribes. In Lemurian times, they could not yet experience themselves as individuals; instead, they felt themselves as being part of a larger context and nature. By the time of Atlantis, individual consciousness and intellectual abilities had begun to develop. People lived more in their inner world than they did in the outer world. In short, self-consciousness has been forming ever since. In this process of individualization, collective consciousness weakens; people experience their freedom, and they connect more strongly with the material world. In materialism, the awareness of an invisible world fades, and the old clairvoyance is largely lost. In the future, however, people will be again clairvoyant.

In the 20th century, according to Deunov, the development of individual consciousness reached its end point. It is now possible again to develop a new collective consciousness. If we continue along the path of involution, humanity will degenerate into more and more conflict and violence. Through the coming of Christ, and especially through his Second Coming, the path of evolution, of love and freedom, has been opened. Deunov said of this:

> From now on, humanity is moving into collective consciousness—that is, people are beginning to understand that we need each other. Until now, each person has lived only for himself, everyone has sought salvation for himself; but now, all humanity

The Evolution of Consciousness

internally experiences that the common lot must be improved. Indeed, the situation *must* be improved, not for one social class, but for all social classes, and intelligently. We must no longer think that we alone can improve our lives.[2]

This new, conscious, collective awareness will encompass all of humanity. Deunov sees in it the development of superconsciousness, which is the next step in the development of unconsciousness, consciousness, and self-consciousness. From the new, super-conscious, collective consciousness, he believes, will emerge the cosmic consciousness that will be connected to the entire universe through new brain centers and abilities. The initiated already possess this consciousness; in others it can sometimes be experienced. Deunov speaks here of the "new people." At an even higher level lies divine consciousness.

About the different levels of consciousness, Deunov said that some people live in their subconsciousness, others in their consciousness, self-consciousness, or superconsciousness. These levels have their center, respectively, in the human soul, heart, mind, and spirit.[3] These are the four basic principles in man's being.

According to Deunov, the emerging new collective consciousness enables us to live for "the whole." This new life encompasses several aspects.[4] Through the awakening of the power of love, human beings will experience themselves as a part of a greater whole. The new forces of consciousness will enable them to live accordingly. We can thus understand life as a unity in which all beings are connected—for the destiny of each being is connected to the destiny of others. The entire cosmos appears, then, as an all-encompassing organism.

Life for oneself, for society, and for the whole are summed up in life for God, who encompasses everything. In all beings, we can love God; and from this consciousness, every action can be an act of love. In this connection, Steiner spoke of encounters in which we will see in the other human being the image of God. Such encounters will

---

2. Quoted in Kovacheva, *Die Weisse Bruderschaft* [The White Brotherhood], 242.
3. David Lorimer (ed.), *Prophet for our Times*, London, 2015, 94.
4. Kovacheva, *Die Weisse Bruderschaft*, 244–49.

then be a sacrament. In a broader sense, he spoke of a future sacramentalism in which Christ will work through us in everything that we do for others out of love and service.

Deunov formulated a law that any action which does not correspond to the principle of unity will bring suffering; and conversely, that any action which does correspond to it will bring joy. When we correct our relationship to the whole, our conditions of life improve. Another consequence will be that all our dormant strengths, talents, and endowments will blossom. From the new consciousness, the strong and the more advanced will help the others. This principle of mutual help and cooperation also exists in intelligent nature. Following this principle brings man into harmony with its laws.

This principle also applies to relations between nations. Each nation has its own mission in the whole of humanity, and has developed its own qualities. Each nation is important to humanity. Living for the whole, according to Deunov, will produce a new culture—in which every person, every group and society, every nation, will consider themselves part of the great whole, and will contribute to the well-being of the whole organism. This new culture of love, according to Deunov, will dawn in the next cycle of culture—which, using a term from Theosophy, he called "the sixth race." We will call this *the people of the sixth cycle*. In the present cycle, the fifth, the human individual (with his intellect and personal freedom) has developed; in the next cycle, it will be about love and life *for the whole*. According to Steiner, this next cycle will not begin until around the year 7893. Both Steiner and Deunov believed that the main bearers of this new cycle will emerge from the coming Slavic culture period.

Deunov often spoke about the new culture of love. In conversations with his disciples in 1944, he gave the following description:

> People of the new epoch are present everywhere, in all nations. You can encounter an intelligent child, a young person with noble character, or an elderly person as being representative of that group.... In the Kingdom of God, all nations will be united. By "the Kingdom of God," one should understand the "people of love." They will live as brothers. All nations will be represented in one unity.... From the invisible world, advanced beings, people of the sublime love or the so-called forerunners of humankind, are

The Evolution of Consciousness

coming. These are workers who are coming from above. When they find souls ready to work, they will incarnate in them and act through them.[5]

The new human being expected to develop in the future has all the good qualities of the preceding stages. In this regard, he represents the essential synthesis of the human virtues.... The new epoch is one of justice and of the Kingdom of God. This epoch is already coming; and then the Kingdom of God, on a small scale, will be established on earth.

The sixth epoch brings positive beauty. The people of love will have very proportional features: they will be beautiful. They will be inspired by the high ideal within themselves, which will make them beautiful. They will be a much more beautiful people than you have seen until now.... The color of these people will be radiant, like someone illuminated by the sun. Light will emanate from their faces as if they were radiating. At night there will be no need for lamps. Wherever these people go, there will be light, because human beings will radiate light. Their eyes will see at a distance; they will see also in the dark.... With the coming of the new epoch, humankind will enter paradise and will depart from error....[6] In the future, one will remember one's past incarnations.... The human being of the new epoch will be musical. When he visits people who are not well, then—just by singing or playing an instrument to them—the sick will regain their health.

According to Steiner, the coming culture periods will not bring comprehensive world peace. He spoke of a confrontation between two groups of people: the good and the evil. In the seventh cultural period of the present cycle, there will be a great apocalyptic war of all against all, which he said is in preparation already in our time. The good people will form communities in which altruism is developed; the evil people will become trapped in their selfishness. Steiner called altruism the "life-stream of humanity." This social consciousness is beginning to form as we begin to feel a part of larger wholes.

As a result of humanity's unconscious passage across the threshold of the spiritual world, which Steiner described, great changes

---

5. Boev and Nikolov (ed.), *The Wellspring of Good*, 370–76.
6. Peter Deunov: "Paradise is the place where people love each other and one lives for the other."

are taking place in our personal consciousness. We are now in the spiritual world with an awakening consciousness, and with this are connected entirely new spiritual experiences. A century ago, people became anxious when they met the lesser guardian of the threshold and had a perception of their double. Nowadays, many people (and especially the young among us) are able to see themselves as they really are in their positive and negative characteristics. This happens frequently in reflecting on one's own behavior. In meeting the greater guardian, we are asked what we want to do for others. A century ago, many were included in closed communities. Many are now able to choose a positive purpose, beyond their ego, that is of significance to others, even to all humanity.

Because of these new experiences, a growing number of people are developing the awareness that:

> we have a higher Self to which we can connect;
>
> we are accompanied by angels and spirit guides;
>
> spiritual beings want to help us;
>
> Christ is healing, counseling, and comforting us;
>
> there is an afterlife;
>
> there are nature beings working in living nature;
>
> there are negative beings who abuse our weaknesses and influence our behavior.

5

The New Culture of Community

Rudolf Steiner was a keen observer of the society of his time. He had insight into social processes. Until his fortieth year, he wrote about them in a large number of newspaper and magazine articles. Then, as leader of the Theosophical Society in Germany, he faced the task of building a spiritual movement, which was also to be a social community. In this community the social life of a future culture was to be prepared, as it was also in the School of the White Brotherhood and in the settlement of Izgrev.

Steiner's lectures on social life contain numerous elements that can be considered components of an anthroposophical social impulse.[1] This impulse points the way to a community culture that has the following principles:

The community is inspired by a common vision.

The community serves the development of its members.

Greater well-being depends on the degree of separation of labor and income.

Members of the community create inner space to meet one another.

The community possesses a body of law, in accord with which the whole is ordered.

The members of the community harmonize their mutual karma.

In the community, there is conscious cooperation with spiritual beings.

---

1. Harrie Salman, *The Social World as Mystery Center: The Social Vision of Anthroposophy*, Mountlake Terrace, WA, 2020.

Rudolf Steiner and Peter Deunov

In social processes, we can help each other to develop individually. Steiner noted that, out of a deep interest in other people, we can ask each other questions of an awakening nature. We may then gain a new perspective on our own life, so that our consciousness grows. Steiner spoke here of "awakening to the soul and spirit of another human being," whose thoughts can exert a stimulating influence on us. We can also hold up a mirror to each other and thereby make unconscious aspects visible. Done lovingly, this can help make our behavior more conscious and even transform it. Developmental processes thus take on a social character. This is an example of new forms of guidance and encouragement that we can give each other, so we can become midwives of the I of our fellow human beings.

On December 17, 1912, in his lecture "Love and its Meaning in the World," Steiner placed these social processes in the context of love.[2] In this way, the power of love can become operative between us. Moreover, in our loving encounters with each other, Christ is present among us.

When we speak enthusiastically with each other about spiritual topics and look for solutions to problems that arise in life, our consciousness grows. According to Steiner, it is then possible for us to receive—in our higher consciousness—inspirations from spiritual beings. To perceive the presence of spiritual beings in this heightened state of consciousness requires wakefulness on the part of the participants in such conversation. In this situation of incipient communication with spiritual beings, the social world becomes a new mystery place. In the future, this form of communication with the spiritual world (which Steiner called a "reverse cult") will be an important addition to our ability to communicate individually with spiritual beings and to be inspired by them. Deceased beings and angels, according to Steiner, are ready to help us build a new spiritual culture together. They are waiting for this.

Based on these thoughts of a conscious social life and a restored communication with the spiritual world, we can imagine that Steiner described the next culture in terms of love and brotherhood

---

2. Rudolf Steiner, "Love and its Significance in the World," lecture of December 17, 1912 (CW 143).

The New Culture of Community

among human beings, and of cooperation with spiritual beings. He did not describe in depth the lineaments of this new culture, but he did describe the path to it. For his part, Peter Deunov elaborated both aspects in his own way, pointing out the role of the Slavic peoples and of the Bulgarian people in particular. The *Call to the Bulgarian People*, which he put forward in 1898, determined the direction of his future work.

Deunov then revealed the message of the Archangel of the Bulgarian people, who announced that the Kingdom of God would soon be established, and that it was the mission of the Bulgarian people to play an important role in it. Deunov's work aimed to prepare the Bulgarians for this. They had, according to him, three good qualities. From the Thracians, who used to live there in antiquity, they had the inclination toward the mystical and the spiritual. From the Slavic tribes, who settled there in the early Middle Ages, they had altruism and the willingness to sacrifice, and from the horsemen of the Bulgarian steppe (who conquered the country in 681), they had the quality of courage.

Bulgaria, according to Deunov, owed its spiritual development to the mountains, from which "a mighty divine stream" descends. From 1899 until 1944, when the Communists came to power, the country was in its golden age, and the conditions for fulfilling a spiritual mission were favorable. After a 45-year hiatus (i.e., from 1989), this mission could continue. For this mission, Bulgarians had to accept and spread throughout the world the new teachings taught in the School of the White Brotherhood. If they did not do so, they would have to wait at least two thousand years for favorable conditions for a new spiritual revival.[3]

In talks with his disciples, Deunov spoke of a new social order in which, through love, social problems could be solved in a world without private property, money, violence, and war:

> The future social order will be an order of love. Then, as an external manifestation of love, four qualities will be applied: honesty,

---

3. Boev and Nikolov (ed.), *The Wellspring of Good*, 362.

justice, purity, and selflessness.... This is an issue of the awakening of consciousness.[4]

Deunov predicted that, thanks to agricultural methods based on love, yields would increase tenfold. Fruit trees, he said, should be planted everywhere in Bulgaria. Bulgaria would thereby become a paradise. And in the future, European countries would unite in a federation.

In Deunov's vision (and in Steiner's), the Slavic peoples are the forerunners of the people of the new (sixth) cycle of cultures. They are the seeds of the new humanity, which will include representatives from all nations. In the present culture (the fifth of the fifth cycle), Western Europeans and Anglo-Saxon peoples have developed the logical mind. According to Deunov, in the next cultural era (the Slavic, the sixth of the fifth cycle), the heart will be developed and the peoples will fraternize. About the Slavic peoples, he said the following in 1944:

> The western nations have reached the height of their development. They have blossomed and have come to fruition. The Slavic people will blossom from now on and give fruit. It is wrong to think that the Slavic nations need to dominate, to command other nations. The opposite is true; they will be the sphere in which the positive features of other nations will manifest.
>
> The Slavic people will bring something new. They come now to create the new culture. In a sense, they are now the spiritual Israel.
>
> In general, western people have a developed intellect. In the Latin people, the feelings and heart are developed. The Slavic people now carry the power of the soul—love. They are the people of love for humankind. They carry the culture of brotherhood. Among all the Slavic nations, Bulgaria represents the will. Therefore, it is like a central point in which the two forces—mind and love—need to become balanced.
>
> God wants the Slavs to fulfill a mission. Through the Slavs, a sense of the new, of generosity, needs to be introduced. Generosity is a Slavic quality; no other people are as generous as the Slavs.
>
> One of the great characteristics of the Slavic nations is self-sac-

---

4. Peter Deunov, *Harmonizing of the Human Soul*, 342.

The New Culture of Community

rifice. Among the Slavs, the spirit of sacrifice is working. Therefore, the future is in the Slavic nations. The new culture will be born out of the Slavs. A beautiful quality of the Slavic nations is altruism.... The Slavic nations are the bearers of the Divine Idea. In the Slavic consciousness, there is something sublime: the love for God.

God is tempering the Slavs through fire. There are no other people in the world who have gone through such suffering as the Slavs. God says, "From you, something good must come." It is determined that the Slavs, as one great family, need to fulfill God's will. In this lies the greatness of their mission.

By the end of the 20th century, many advanced beings—the brothers of love and ancestors of humankind—will incarnate among the Slavic nations. They will bring a great spiritual uplifting. Yet they are not the vanguards only: they are the main forces.

The Slavic nations are a living tree onto which England, Germany, America, and France will be grafted. They are the four teachers of the Slavic nations. And the new, sixth cycle of cultures will be the fruit of this grafted tree. This fruit will combine all the positive features of these nations.

The Slavs will be united; they will be the bridge between Europe and Asia. All Slavic people need to unite into one. After the unification of the Slavs, the whole world will unite. The future people of love will unite all.... The Slavs will introduce a spiritual element into the world—that we may become as brothers. Their mission is the unification of all nations.[5]

---

5. Boev and Nikolov (ed.), *The Wellspring of Good*, 377–80.

6

The Connection of Head and Heart

During his philosophical period, Rudolf Steiner intensively studied the relationship between thought and reality. As a spiritual scientist, he further expanded this research with entirely new viewpoints that encompassed both the logic of the mind and the logic of the heart. Peter Deunov also studied the relationship between the head and the heart.

In our language, we distinguish between the mind and reason. By *mind* (or intellect) we understand logical thinking, which forms concepts and representations, connects concepts into judgments, and draws logical conclusions. These are faculties associated with the intellectual soul, as Steiner called it. By "reason" we understand an ability that connects the knowledge of details that the mind *analyzes*. This *synthetic* faculty is related to the consciousness soul, which can develop in later stages of the soul's development. According to Steiner, Lucifer's influence caused our mind to remain on the surface and no longer lead to deep insights.

The development of the mind began in Greek culture. Intellectual thinking—thinking in clearly defined concepts, brought into logical coherence—was practiced in Greek philosophy, especially that of Aristotle. In the late Middle Ages it was continued in the universities. Steiner has shown, in a surprising way, that thinking in concepts was preceded by a clairvoyant perception of thoughts that were spread out in the world. Words such as thinking, knowing, idea, intuition, vision, and theory were originally connected with seeing or perceiving. Steiner also described how people used to think not with their brains, but with their etheric body. This was a living, dreamlike, visual thinking.

The Connection of Head and Heart

It was not until the 15th century that more people began to think with their brains. Previously, their thoughts were living thoughts; but then, during the development of intellectual thinking in the Middle Ages, their thoughts became dead and abstract. According to Steiner, Ahriman was responsible for this. He killed thought by tying it more and more to the physical brain. In this way, man becomes a thinking machine and loses access to the world of the soul and spirit. This intellectual and matter-oriented thinking is not connected to man's sense of truth and moral consciousness. It cannot give moral impulses to the will. Moreover, it loses itself in illusions and thought-models.

According to Steiner, the forces by which we think are *etheric* forces. The thoughts that thinking produces are not of a material nature. The brain does not produce thoughts, but has a mirroring function. Brain-bound thinking brings into consciousness, as thoughts, only that which is mirrored in the nervous system in the brain. Steiner noted that such thinking is *passive*. In contrast to this stands an *active* thinking that detaches itself from the brain and is consciously produced by man. In a further development, thinking can become conscious of its thinking activity.[1] This is conscious mental perception, which is a basis for spiritual research—whereby we develop *contemplative* thinking. Passive thinking is sufficient to find our way in the sense world, but it has no access to the spiritual world beyond the world of the senses.

Before the development of the mind, people thought in an unconscious way with their hearts. In the cultures of antiquity, the heart was assigned the central role as the organ of knowledge. This is still the case today in cultures in which intellectual thinking has not yet become dominant. Thinking with the heart was connected with a sense of truth and led to an understanding of spiritual connections. Even the philosopher Aristotle, who laid the foundation for the logical thinking of the mind, still regarded the heart as the central organ of thought.

According to Steiner, modern man can develop a new and con-

---

1. Rudolf Steiner, lecture of May 18, 1913, in *Approaching the Mystery of Golgotha* (CW 152).

scious thinking with the heart that is connected to our sense of truth, and can again provide insight into the aforementioned spiritual connections. In the process, however, the faculties of the mind must not be lost. "The path to the heart goes through the head," Steiner already wrote in his book *Philosophy of Freedom*. In this connection, he spoke of a former, *unconscious* logic of the heart, which was succeeded by a logic of the mind. And this logic of the mind must now make room for the new, *conscious* logic of the heart.[2]

According to Steiner, the development of a new thinking with the heart is connected to the archangel Michael, who in earlier times was the "administrator of the cosmic intelligence."[3] The archangel Michael gradually transmitted this intelligence to human beings so that they could develop their own thought life and act morally out of insight and in freedom.[4] Ever since the end of the Middle Ages, Ahriman has striven to take possession of this intelligence. With the help of Michael, and by accessing the cosmic intelligence in their thinking, people must thwart this. Steiner called this the *spiritualization* of intelligence or thinking. In 1924, he described this as the joint task of the Aristotelian and Platonic currents in the anthroposophical movement.

Michaelic thinking means that our thinking becomes an organ of perception for this cosmic thinking. Thoughts based on this cosmic thinking can then flow through the human heart. For this, we must neutralize the luciferic and ahrimanic forces that threaten the spiritual, moral, flexible, and creative qualities of thought and its connection to the sense of truth. This requires the Christ-force that can be activated from the heart. With the dawn of the Michael Age in 1879, this I-conscious spiritual thinking became possible. Since then, Michael allows new life to flow through the etheric body and mind of man. Steiner spoke here of a turning point, which he described as follows:

---

2. Lecture of March 30, 1910, in *Macrocosm und Microcosm* (CW 119).

3. On the role of the archangel Michael in the development of thinking, see Harrie Salman, *Valentin Tomberg*, Brooklyn, 2022, 207–27.

4. According to Steiner, this was made possible by the Seraphim and Cherubim, who guided cosmic intelligence into the human brain in the late Middle Ages. Rudolf Steiner, lecture of July 28, 1924, in *Karmic Relationships*, vol. 3 (CW 237).

The Connection of Head and Heart

One who understands how to observe such things knows what a great change took place in the last third of the nineteenth century with respect to the life of human thought. Before that time, man could only feel how thoughts formed themselves in his own being; he is now able to raise himself above his own being, and can turn his mind to the spiritual. He there meets Michael, who proves his ancient kinship with everything connected with thought. He thereby liberates thought from the sphere of his head, clearing the way for it to his heart. Moreover, he enkindles enthusiasm in his feeling life, so that his mind can be filled with devotion for all that can be experienced in the light of thought.

The Age of Michael has dawned. Hearts are beginning to have thoughts; spiritual fervor is now proceeding, not merely from mystical obscurity, but from souls clarified by thought. To understand this means to receive Michael into one's heart. Thoughts that at the present time strive to grasp the spiritual must originate in hearts that beat for Michael as the fiery Prince of Thought in the Universe.[5]

In mind-thinking, we face the world and thereby strengthen our self-consciousness. In heart-thinking, we reconnect with the world of spirit, in which our higher I also has its home. Looking to the future, Steiner noted:

> In the future, man will be in a much more intimate relationship to the laws of the world than he is today. And the esoteric disciple anticipates this intimacy in development. The head with the brain is only a transitional organ of knowledge. The organ that will truly look deeply and at the same time powerfully into the world has its disposition in the present heart. Note that it is the *disposition* of this organ that is in the present heart. To become an organ of knowledge, the heart still needs to be transformed in a wide variety of ways. But this heart is the source of humanity's future stage of development. When the heart becomes the organ of knowledge, knowledge will be warm and intimate, as now only the feelings of love and pity are. But these feelings will penetrate, from the dull-

---

5. Rudolf Steiner, "At the Dawn of the Michael Age," in *Anthroposophical Leading Thoughts* (CW 26).

ness and darkness in which they now only grope, to the clarity that today only the finest logical notions of the head possess.[6]

Thinking with the heart is not based on the physical heart, but on the etheric heart—which *forms* the physical heart and constantly *regenerates* it. The etheric heart is situated on the right side of the physical heart. According to Steiner, the etheric heart has been separating from the physical heart since 1721. This process will be completed before 2100; moreover, it necessitates that through anthroposophically-oriented thought their previously *natural* connection be established *spiritually*.[7] This new thinking with the heart takes place in a spiritual organ *near* the heart. This is a kind of thinking organ that, according to Steiner, enables a completely different kind of thinking:

> Whether something is true or false, whether we should say this or that about a thing or a fact of the higher worlds, requires no such considerations as are necessary for this in ordinary thinking—but it is instead immediately apparent. As soon as you have the images before you, you know what to say about them to yourself and to others. This immediacy is the characteristic of heart-thinking.[8]

This new thinking, which makes such direct connections visible, unfolds in inwardly experienced images, in imaginations that are "sounded through" by inspirations. It thus becomes the source of renewed clairvoyance and spiritual research.

Steiner opened another perspective with the theme of the "etherization of the blood." Thinking with the heart does not function with natural etheric forces, but with new etheric forces of the heart, which are created by the activity of the Self radiating to the head. During the waking state, according to Steiner, very small amounts of the fine physical blood in the heart are constantly being converted into etheric substance. In this process, a stream of etherized

---

6. Rudolf Steiner, *Esoteric Lessons 1904–1909* (CW 266a), 100.

7. Rudolf Steiner, lecture of April 5, 1919, in *Spiritual Emptiness and Social Life* (CW 190).

8. Rudolf Steiner, lecture of March 29, 1910, in *Macrocosm and Microcosm* (CW 119).

The Connection of Head and Heart

blood rises from the heart to the head, where this blood flows around the pineal gland, illuminating and irradiating it. These etheric forces permeate the brain and radiate above the head. Through clairvoyant vision, this can be perceived in the aura as a halo (for example, in saints).

Only through these etheric forces are we able to form thoughts that are not completely tied to the egoistic needs of our organism. After Christ's blood flowed into the earth at his death, the etherized blood of Christ, which has been present in the earth-ether ever since, can connect with this ascending ether current from our hearts.[9] This happens only when man has a correct understanding of what the impulse of Christ entails, and realizes that Christ can now appear in his etheric form. Thereby we open ourselves to the perception of Christ.

According to Steiner, it can be clairvoyantly perceived that, in someone who is asleep, a current from the cosmos passes through the head to the heart. In people with high moral principles, this is a flow of a very different quality than it is in people with low moral powers. At the moments of falling asleep and awakening, the two streams meet at the pineal gland. These are the microcosmic stream (with intellectually colored light effects) from the heart, and the macrocosmic stream (of a moral-aesthetic nature) from the cosmos: the etherized Christ-blood. Steiner noted that these insights were the result of particularly careful spiritual research by individual true Rosicrucians from earlier times.

Through these insights, we can understand the heart as a secret mystery place where the microcosmic human self connects with the macrocosmic Christ-I. Only through this can human beings consciously ascend to their higher Self. In an esoteric lesson, Steiner used for this mystery place of the heart the image of the Holy of Holies, where the Holy Grail can be found:

In the temple of the human body there is the most sacred place. Many people inhabit this temple without knowing anything about

---

9. See Rudolf Steiner's lecture of August 25, 1911, in *Wonders of the World, Trials of the Soul, Revelations of the Spirit* (CW 129), and "The Etherization of the Human Blood" (lecture of October 1, 1911) in *Esoteric Christianity* (CW 130).

it. But those who suspect it thereby receive the power to so purify themselves that they may enter this most sacred place. There is the holy cup that has been prepared throughout the ages so that, when the time comes, this cup will be able to contain the blood of Christ, the life of Christ. When man has entered this temple, he has also found the way to the Holy of Holies in the great earth temple. Many live on earth without knowing anything about it, but when man has found the way to his inner sanctum, he may go in and find the Holy Grail. The cup will first show itself to him as if cut from wonderfully glittering crystals, forming symbols and letters, until he gradually becomes aware of the sacred contents, so that these contents shine before him in golden brilliance. When a man enters the mystery place of his own heart, a divine being emerges from it, and this unites with God beyond, with the Christ being. It lives in the spiritual light that shines into the cup and thereby sanctifies this cup.[10]

Peter Deunov also talked about the relationship between the mind and the heart in several lectures. Among other things, he said:

By "the heart and the mind" I mean the two principles that God has placed within us as intelligent forces. The heart must be full of the thoughts of the mind, and the mind must be full of the desires of the heart.

One of the great laws of development is the following: the Spirit of God descends into us only when the mind and the heart are working in the right way. When one principle does not cooperate, the Spirit does not descend. Let there be no doubt in the mind and no bitterness in the heart!

There must be a connection between the images of the mind and the aspirations of the heart. The mind always aspires downward, and the heart always aspires upward. Consequently, it is not the mind that influences the heart, but the heart that influences the mind. (The mind does influence the heart, but the heart's influence is stronger.) And "strong minds" are not those that have a powerful mind, but are those who have a strong heart. And there is intelligence in the heart itself.

---

10. Rudolf Steiner, *Zur Geschichte und aus den Inhalten etc., 1904–1914* [From the History and Contents of the First Section of the Esoteric School 1904–1914], GA 264], 418.

The Connection of Head and Heart

I will define what consciousness is. Consciousness is not a property of the human mind, nor does it have anything to do with the mind. Consciousness is only a principle of the heart. It carries light within it. Consciousness refers only to the human heart. And when we say that man leads a conscious life, we by no means mean an intelligent, learned life. Everything that consciousness carries within it is based on experience. In consciousness there is nothing that has not been experienced. Therefore consciousness is a base, a foundation, upon which the human mind can develop and grow. Just as light is necessary for the disciple to grow, so consciousness is necessary for the mind. The mind is the *outer* side of things, while consciousness is concerned with the *inner* side. A human being may not be very intelligent, but he can be a conscious human being. Therefore, consciousness is that which propels life to develop, and it is one of the great qualities of the soul. I say: consciousness is the first ray that the soul projects into the heart. I do not speak of the ordinary soul, but of the divine soul. The first ray is consciousness, and from this ray already manifests the human mind as the second [ray]. The forces of consciousness in turn awaken the centers and faculties of the mind.

And so all of you, under the present circumstances, must develop your consciousness. Be sure that your heart and mind will develop properly. Your thoughts, your will, and your desires will then develop properly. It is said: "Think with your heart." This applies only to conscious life. Do not say: "I think with my head," but "I think with my heart." This means that one is thinking with the ray that comes from his soul, and then manifests this ray.

The intelligent forces that formed the human heart are of a higher order than the forces that formed the mind. The human heart is formed by Cherubim and Seraphim, who are the highest [in the hierarchy of angels]. In human life, however, the mind occupies a higher place than the heart. Why? For the simple reason that the mind deals with matter objectively. The mind deals with the external side of life; and, because we pass through the material world, the beings who created it rule over matter. And so the mind—as a living force emanating from them—can better guide us under the present conditions of life.

Both the mind and the heart have a twofold influence on man: downward and upward. When the heart—as one force—is directly connected with your lower soul, it has one influence; and when it is connected with the higher beings, it has another influence on you. I call the first influence "descending," and the second "ascending." When our feelings are under the influence of the Cherubim, Seraphim, and other higher beings, we are in an ascending state. The mind also has a double influence on man.

Many of you are unbalanced in spirit, nervous only because you do not let the intelligent heart speak. When it begins to speak, you say to yourself: don't listen to your heart, listen to your mind. No, first man must listen to his intelligent heart, and then to his mind!

There is no fear in the actions of the intelligent heart. When the mind reasons, there is fear. There is no anger in the intelligent heart. In this heart, in the good habits, there is no envy; but in the mind, there is envy. All negative traits are due to our mind; but when we follow our good habits, everything is reasonable, everything is in harmony. Your intelligent heart will become the basis of your life—and from this basis, your mind will develop in a new direction.

Deunov gave this saying to his students:

> I want my heart to beat rhythmically, my heartbeat to merge with the pulse of the sun and to radiate its energy appropriately all over my organism—just as the Sun radiates its energy all over the world.[11]

According to Deunov, only with our will can we harmonize our mind and heart. We must be guided in spiritual matters by our intelligent heart and in material matters by our intellect. On April 2, 1924, he spoke of the intelligent heart.[12] This is the heart of man connected with God. The mind of God works in this heart. It is the inner voice of God; it contains our good habits. The problems in the world stem from man's objective mind. Therefore, in all situations we can turn to our intelligent heart to listen to what it has to say to us, what we can do. "The feelings of the heart are more true than the considerations of the mind. A right thought springs from a deep feeling of the heart," he said. When we open our intelligent heart,

---

11. Svetla Baltova (ed.), Peter Deunov, *Zdrave, sila i zjivot* [Health, Power, and Life], Plovdiv, 2010, 100–04.

12. Peter Deunov, *The Mindful Heart*, Sofia, 2003.

The Connection of Head and Heart

Christ will come to dwell in it. The Kingdom of God will come when we are ready to do the will of God. This, according to Deunov, is the path to man's rebirth.

Some further thoughts of Deunov on the heart are:

> In the heartbeat, the whole universe pulses. The heart is connected to cosmic energy. Each heartbeat spreads energy and regeneration to the whole body.... In fact, the heart as a physical organ does not have the power to push arterial blood through the body. The heartbeat is due to cosmic electricity and magnetism.... Blood circulation is due to electromagnetic currents.... A stream of light comes from everyone's heart and spreads throughout the body. This current indicates the level of development of feelings.... In addition to the heart in the physical body, we also have a heart in our spiritual and mental bodies. These hearts also send energy to the corresponding bodies to nourish all parts of the organism, material and spiritual. Through these three hearts, man is connected to three cosmic energies that determine the complete development of the organism.... What is a healthy heartbeat? It is a heartbeat that is musical and rhythmic.... Every heart is connected to the common cosmic heartbeat, to the cosmic heart.... Do not allow negative feelings into your heart.[13]

> In the Scriptures it is written: My son, give me your heart (Proverbs 23:26a). God does not want your mind, but your heart. When you give your heart to God, you will have life in abundance. It is said of the human body that it is the temple of God. The hearth of this temple is the heart, where the fire is constantly burning.[14]

---

13. Baltova (ed.), *Peter Deunov: Child of the Universe*, 38–42.
14. Lorimer (ed.), *Prophet for our Times*, 110.

7

The Paths of Schooling

A good starting point for comparing the schooling paths of Anthroposophy and the School of the White Brotherhood is to juxtapose the inner paths of Rudolf Steiner and Peter Deunov themselves.

During his years as editor of Goethe's natural scientific work, Steiner was intensely concerned with the development of conscious thought. In a November 13, 1909 lecture, he emphasized its importance.[1] He pointed out that the transformation of thought is the necessary condition for spiritual research. The training of logic and judgment must precede the development of modern clairvoyance. In many people, there are still remnants of old, innate forms of clairvoyance; in others a natural clairvoyance develops; and in a third group, the anthroposophical path leads to a schooled clairvoyance. Conscious thinking is necessary to arrive at a judgment about our clairvoyant perceptions, which can be chaotic and unreliable. Only then can we speak of a modern form of clairvoyance, the results of which can be judged by human reason, and, where possible, tested against facts.

The anthroposophical path of schooling begins with the development of thought. Here, Steiner's book *Philosophy of Freedom* can serve as an exercise manual for intuitive thinking that leads to insight, and for the formation of moral intuitions that can give direction to our actions.

In 1896 came a turn in the life of the 35-year-old Steiner, which

---

1. Rudolf Steiner, "Über das rechte Verhältnis zur Anthroposophie" [The Correct Relationship to Anthroposophy], lecture of November 13, 1909, in *Deeper Secrets of Human Evolution in Light of the Gospels* (CW 117).

The Paths of Schooling

led him to stand with greater awareness in the world of sense perception. He was able to take an example from Goethe's study of nature, which focused on discovering primal phenomena that manifested in the world of the senses. In practice, this can be prepared in practice in phenomenology, which helps us perceive purely, without concepts, prejudices, and emotions. Then these perceptions can resonate in our souls and open access to the transcendental forces at work in people and in nature. In a November 23, 1919 lecture, Steiner called this the "Michaelic" way of thinking.[2] The further extension of this path is that, in the transcendental world, we find the Christ-impulse of love.

In a lecture on November 30, 1919, Steiner opened a new perspective on our perceptions of the world. In earlier times, he said,

> just as it was customary to think of *air* as ensouled—so now must it become self-evident for us to think of *light* as ensouled; we must arouse this ability in us when we consider light the general representative of sense perception.[3]

We can connect with the world around us with both our souls and our senses in the perception of light, sounds, and warmth, and in the after-images and after-echoes of these perceptions; our senses then experience the sensory world *as well as* the spiritual element in outer nature. Steiner spoke of a "new yoga will" already expressed in Goethe's studies of nature. This search for the spirit and soul in matter is for Steiner the basis of the new Michael culture.[4]

The aforementioned turn in Steiner's life led to a Christ initiation that took place gradually between 1897 and 1903. He passed through a time of inner trial and reflection (1897 to c. 1899) during which he had an encounter with the lesser guardian of the threshold. This was followed by an encounter with the greater guardian of the threshold, which led to his *imitatio Christi*, his imitation of Jesus Christ. The experiences he then underwent were seeds that had to

---

2. Rudolf Steiner, lecture of November 23, 1919, in *Michael's Message* (CW 194).
3. Rudolf Steiner, lecture of November 30, 1919, in ibid. Steiner had already developed his view on the twelve senses.
4. See Bracker, *Grals-Initiation* [Grail Initiation], 237–46 and Yeshayahu Ben-Aharon, *Cognitive Yoga*, Forest Row, 2016.

Rudolf Steiner and Peter Deunov

ripen for several years. In this process (at the turn of the century, in 1900) he spiritually faced the mystery of Golgotha. At this time it is likely that he received an copy, and imprint, of the I of Jesus.

In accord with German anthroposophical researcher Klaus J. Bracker, we can speak here of a Grail initiation. From 1904, Steiner devoted many lectures to the path of the Grail, which is the path to inner rebirth. It is the path of Parzival and of modern man developing his consciousness soul. This path ultimately leads to receiving a copy of the I of Jesus. This I was formed from the part of the etheric body of Adam that was preserved in the spiritual world at the Fall. It is connected to the paradisal Tree of Life and provides for the rejuvenation of man. The Jesus child of Luke's Gospel was the first human being to take in this paradisal etheric body. This etheric body formed a provisional I, which was later supplemented by the I of the Jesus child of Matthew's Gospel. When we receive a copy of this provisional Self, it connects with our higher Self and becomes our higher I. We are then reborn and become a Grail initiate.[5]

The description of the anthroposophical path of schooling in the book *How to Know Higher Worlds*, written in 1904 and 1905, is an elaboration of the Grail initiation, although it does not make use of the symbolism of the Grail. This book is a modern version of the medieval Grail books for modern Parzivals. Ehrenfried Pfeiffer wrote about this Grail initiation:

> The highest fulfillment of the esoteric cult and the esoteric path is the experience that the body is the temple of the divine. On the altar of this temple—the heart—the person to be initiated himself offers the sacrificial bowl—the Grail. This he does by means of the purification of himself through the etherization of the blood, through the transformation of the earthly self into a divine being (the higher I), spirit self, etc. In this act, the I becomes God Himself, in the sense of "not I, but Christ in me."[6]

Until 1914, Rudolf Steiner discussed in his lectures and esoteric teachings a large number of themes from the path to the Grail. Such

---

5. Bracker, *Grals-Initiation*, 59–94.
6. Thomas Meyer (ed.), *Ein Leben für den Geist: Ehrenfried Pfeiffer* [Ehrenfried Pfeiffer: A Modern Quest for the Spirit], 187.

The Paths of Schooling

themes include the masters of esoteric Christianity, the Gospel of John, Sophia and the Holy Spirit, the Holy Grail, the two Jesus children, copies of the spiritual bodies of Jesus, the Nathanic Jesus, Vidar (the spirit of the North), the etheric return of Christ, the etherization of the blood, and the Fifth Gospel. In 1914, he closed the esoteric school because of the outbreak of World War I. This left unfinished the development of a mystery Christianity in the spirit of the evangelist John.[7]

This mystery Christianity forms the esoteric core of the anthroposophical path of schooling. It is about the encounter with the etheric Christ, about the rebirth of man (out of "water and spirit," according to the Gospel of John), about the birth of the new man (in the sense of the Apostle Paul), about entering the Grail sanctuary in the interior of our heart, and about the inner connection with the being Sophia, with the Nathanic Jesus, and with Vidar. According to Pfeiffer, Steiner wanted to form a Johannes Brotherhood—but even before 1914, actual esotericism was abandoned in the Society.[8]

These aspects of mystery Christianity will now be elaborated. What was essential for Steiner on his inner path also remains the necessary foundation for his students, for their own path of schooling. This concerns the development of conscious, intuitive thought and of perception of the sense world. Steiner pointed the way to the enlivening and spiritualizing of thinking as a prerequisite for the soul's connection with Christ in a Grail initiation. In the sense of the apostle Paul, Christ's disciples could thereby transform the "old man" in themselves into the "new man," who, through an initiation, is united with the powers of the original paradisal man. In an initiation, we connect with our higher Self—which lives in the spiritual world and brings inner renewal and rejuvenation.

Before 1914, Steiner had pointed out the inner transformation that takes place during an initiation. This is the beginning of a rebirth that reconnects us with the spiritual bodies of cosmic man that were not lost in the Fall, but were kept in the "Mother Lodge of humanity." The etheric aspect of cosmic man, of the "sister soul of

---

7. Von Beckerath, *Der Leidensweg Rudolf Steiners* [RS's Path of Suffering], 131.
8. Thomas Meyer (ed.), *Ein Leben für den Geist: Ehrenfried Pfeiffer*, 187–90, 230.

Adam," according to Steiner, manifested itself in Krishna and incarnated for the first time in a physical body in the Jesus child of the Luke gospel, the Nathanic Jesus child. After the resurrection of Christ, this etheric aspect is called the Nathanic soul or the angel Jesus. It can reconnect us with certain etheric powers of the original human being—powers which we cannot consciously dispose of and which are symbolized by the Tree of Life from paradise.

In the countries of the North, according to Steiner, Vidar is considered to be the bringer of rejuvenating forces from paradise, of spiritual childhood forces for an aging humanity.[9] In doing so, he is at the service of the Nathanic soul, which reconnects humanity with the Tree of Life. Awareness of its activity can lead to the development of a "Nathanic" Anthroposophy. Vidar and the Nathanic soul play a central role in the return of Christ, who appears in their etheric garb.

According to Steiner, with the birth of the Nathanic Jesus child and his connection with Christ, this pure childhood power from the Kingdom of God has come into every human being. It can be awakened if this seed is nurtured and ennobled by infusing us with what flows out from the Christ principle.[10] We can use the image of the Holy Grail here. In the previous chapter, a statement by Steiner was cited regarding the mystery place of one's own (etheric) heart, in which the Holy Grail is located. When we form a Grail chalice in our meditations in our etheric heart, the seed of the new human being in us can come to life in it.

The work on our soul begins with the transformation of our astral body into what in esoteric Christianity is called the "Lady Sophia," the purified soul. Through this *microcosmic* Sophia, we connect with the *macrocosmic* Sophia—the Divine Wisdom—in which the original soul forces of the cosmic paradisal man work. The inner Sophia, forming in us, can receive the Holy Spirit, who then individualizes within us.[11] In the cooperation between the

---

9. Rudolf Steiner, lecture of December 21, 1913, in *How the Physical World Projects into Physical Existence* (CW 150).
10. Rudolf Steiner, lecture of September 26, 1909, in *The Gospel of Luke* (CW 114).
11. Rudolf Steiner, lecture of May 1908, 31, in *The Gospel of John* (CW 103).

The Paths of Schooling

Sophia-in-us and the Holy Spirit, the beginning of our "spirit self"[12] forms, and the "birth" of the higher I can take place—which signifies the reception of a copy of the I of Jesus.

The inner Sophia can develop from the 20th century onwards under the guidance of the cosmic Sophia, who in our time has connected with humanity as Anthropo-Sophia, and mirrors to us our true being. In this process of development, which for many will only be possible in the distant future, we all may hope one day to receive a copy of the I of Jesus.

The creation of a mystery Christianity within the anthroposophical movement could have led to three interrelated aspects: a "Nathanic" Anthroposophy (from Northern and Central Europe, connected to the Nathanic soul and Vidar); a "Sophianic" Anthroposophy (from Eastern Europe, connected to the Sophia being); and a "Michaelic" Anthroposophy (from Western Europe, connected to the archangel Michael).

A systematic overview of the anthroposophical path of schooling was given by Rudolf Steiner in the articles published in 1904 and 1905 in the journal *Luzifer-Gnosis* and compiled in 1909 in the book *How to Know Higher Worlds*. As he wrote in the preface to the 1914 edition, this book was intended to be a first volume. According to a communication from him to Alexander Strakosch,[13] Steiner did not write a second volume because there were not enough people who had reached the steps of higher consciousness with the help of the first volume. Instead, he wrote some shorter texts.[14]

The aforementioned articles describe the path of schooling of the Rosicrucians, adapted to the conditions in which modern man lives. This is the anthroposophical path of schooling, aimed at the acquisition of higher knowledge in our imaginative, inspirative, and intuitive consciousness. It is the path of seven steps that Steiner described in his *Outline of Occult Science*, and that he himself traveled:

---

12. The spirit self is also called *manas* and develops through the spiritualization of the astral body.
13. Von Beckerath, *Rudolf Steiners Leidensweg*, 42–43.
14. Rudolf Steiner, *The Stages of Higher Knowledge* (CW 12), *A Road to Self-Knowledge* (CW 16), and *The Threshold of the Spiritual World*. See also Arthur Zajonc, *Meditation as Contemplative Inquiry*, Great Barrington, 2009.

1. Study of spiritual science, using the power of judgment developed in the sensory world

2. Acquisition of imaginative knowledge

3. Reading the hidden scripture (corresponding to inspiration)

4. Empathizing with the spiritual environment (corresponding to intuition)

5. Knowledge of the relationships between microcosm and macrocosm

6. Unification with the macrocosm

7. Experience of all the above as a fundamental soul mood.

According to Steiner, this path has some fundamental conditions: a mood of reverence towards truth and insight is needed, as well as an active inner life in which we let what we experience resonate. As practical rules, Steiner gives the creation of moments of inner peace in which we distinguish the essential from the non-essential. Everything we experience can then be perceived from a higher point of view. Thus we awaken in ourselves a higher being, who becomes the "inner ruler" of our lives.

A new intercourse with the spiritual world thereby arises: man then connects his thoughts with a living feeling and pays attention to the voices that sound in his inner being. This "life of the soul in thought" is what Steiner calls "meditation" (or "contemplative thinking"), which is a means of gaining transcendental insights. In conversations with his esoteric students, he also gave numerous personal meditations and aphorisms to help them along the way. He also gave meditations for general use, and meditative texts for developing virtues.

The book *How to Know Higher Worlds* covers the various stages and aspects of the path to initiation and gives more practical rules and conditions for occult training. These include the development of the chakras[15] and encounters with the lesser and greater guardians of the threshold to the spiritual world. We work on this path to transform our soul and restructure our etheric body.

---

15. These include the eight exercises of Buddha's eightfold path for the development of the throat chakra and exercises for the development of the heart chakra.

The Paths of Schooling

Steiner describes that, through meditation and concentration exercises, a provisional center for the currents of the etheric body is formed in the head. This center can then be moved to the larynx and then further to the area of the physical heart, where it becomes operative in an organ created within the heart—which must then be transformed to become an organ of knowledge. It is a spiritual organ of light in which a spiritual power of perception (the kundalini fire) can be awakened and then channeled through these currents and into the outside world. This organ is called the eight-petaled lotus flower. It is brought to maturity by our "love of inner freedom," according to Steiner. We can relate it to the Grail temple in our etheric heart.

It was not until 1924 that the path of schooling was further elaborated in the re-established esoteric school. At the Christmas Conference of 1923, Steiner became president of the Anthroposophical Society, after having been on the verge of leaving it. In cooperation with Ita Wegman, he wanted to establish new mysteries in which people could connect with the spiritual world in a conscious way. He spoke of a Foundation Stone, formed of the powers of God the Father, the Son, and the Holy Spirit (the powers of the heights, of the breadths, and of the depths), which the participants of this conference (and the absentees) could lay into their (etheric) hearts.

Their hearts had to be prepared to receive this Foundation Stone, which is sometimes called the new Grail Stone, for Steiner made the requirement that the members had to harmonize their mutual karma—i.e., meet each other with interest, get to know each other right down to their individual karma, and learn to cooperate with each other. At this conference, he described the soil in which the Foundation Stone was to be laid as: "our hearts in their harmonious cooperation, in their good will, imbued with love to carry the anthroposophical will through the world." He asked the members to go out into the world to collaborate on works that, together, would form the foundation stones of the *spiritual* Goetheanum. After all, the physical Goetheanum had at that time not yet existed anymore (as it had burned down a year earlier). Steiner gave members the Foundation Stone Meditation to support this joint work.

The members also had to learn to cooperate with spiritual beings, who wanted to help and inspire them.

February 1924 saw the First Class lessons, in which Steiner gave directions to the members of the First Class of the School of Spiritual Science on the path to initiation.[16] In these lessons, the meditator meets the lesser guardian of the threshold, considered to be the archangel Michael. This guardian, is thenceforth their admonishing and advising companion, stands on the boundary between the sensory and spiritual worlds and warns them of three beasts arising there from the abyss. These beasts are the enemies on the modern path to spiritual knowledge: fear of the spirit, mockery of spiritual knowledge, and laziness of thought. They live in the will, feeling, and thinking of people. Only with the courage of knowledge, the fire of knowledge, and the active production of insight can meditating human beings cross the abyss and enter through the gate into the hall of the spiritual temple. There, spiritual beings appear. To the extent of their inner development, the meditators can have an experience of these beings. Working with the mantras is a preparatory path to initiation proper, which may take place later.

We can identify five elements in this anthroposophical path of schooling, which build upon each other:

1. The schooling of thought and perception (including the development of the twelve senses).

2. Steiner's Grail Path, as described in the book *How to Know Higher Worlds*.

3. The anthroposophical way to insight: deepening into meditations (especially from the class lessons) for the development of higher consciousness, which is necessary for spiritual research.

4. Building an inner temple, which is our spiritual home in the spiritual world.

5. Building a social-etheric temple, in which people working together in the world are inspired by spiritual beings.[17]

---

16. This material has been published in English in two volumes: *The First Class Lessons: The Michael School Meditative Path in Nineteen Steps* and *The First Class of the Michael School: Recapitulation Lessons and Mantras*, Hudson, NY, 2017.

17. Harrie Salman, *The Social World as Mystery Center*.

The Paths of Schooling

This path of schooling has initiatory aspects. As a path of self-knowledge, it leads to an encounter with the lesser guardian of the threshold; and as a path of following Christ, it leads to an encounter with the greater guardian of the threshold. As a Grail path, it leads to the center of the heart, where the Holy Grail can be found. As a Sophia path, it leads to the transformation of the astral body into the "Lady Sophia" who opens to the Holy Spirit and our higher Self. As a Michael path to insight, it leads to a higher consciousness that can be placed in the service of Michael.

Peter Deunov's inner path differed from that of Rudolf Steiner. In 1884, Deunov went through a serious illness in which his ego "died." Thereafter, the Spirit of Truth lived in him. This was his first initiation. A next step came in 1897, when he received the mission to be a teacher for all humanity. And then, in 1912, the Spirit of Christ entered him.

Deunov described the "ascension of the human soul to God" in seven stages. He gave a first description of this on November 1, 1914. A more extensive account followed later.[18] The following is a summary.

    1. *God addresses man.* He draws man to himself "with the threads of his love." Deunov had turned to God in 1884, in a period of deep inner suffering, and thus began the awakening of his soul.

    2. *Repentance.* Deunov's response to God's call was to take stock of his life. In the process, the consciousness of a bright, pure life was born in him. He had a deep repentance for what he had done in his life up to that point.

    3. *Salvation.* Deunov experienced the spiritual wave that comes from God and leads to new conditions of life and to a new culture.

    4. *Regeneration.* "The divine manifests in man [now] to a greater extent. His consciousness increasingly broadens, as does his desire to serve God." Deunov decided to work for God and become a Methodist pastor.

---

18. Beinsa Douno, *The Teacher*, vol. 1, 282–83, and "Phases of the Ascension of the Human Soul," in Peter Deunov, *Harmonizing of the Human Soul*, 285–88.

5. *Rebirth.* This comes from God and is preceded by great suffering. It is the accelerated "liquidation" of karma. People must go through this to become free of their karma. Cosmic consciousness then awakens in them; they feel the unity of life and radiate love to all.

6. *Enlightenment.* After an even greater ordeal, comes enlightenment, in which consciousness expands further and new powers awaken. "Human beings begin to communicate with the advanced creatures: they enter their society, learn the sacred language of the perfect ones, gain great knowledge of the forces and laws of Nature." They also learn to work with them.

7. *Resurrection.* Now human beings go through a deep darkness, the final test, in which they feel entirely alone and abandoned by the invisible world. When they realize that God has not forsaken them, resurrection follows. They thereby complete their evolution on earth, and the divine in its completeness awakes in them. They can now show their brothers and sisters the path to liberation, the path to the light in which they live.

This inner path of the ascension of the soul to God stands in the mystical tradition of Christianity. The symbolism of the Holy Grail and the Rose Cross, as also that of the Christian path of initiation centered on the Passion of Christ, were unknown in Bulgarian culture. Deunov chose as the emblem of the human soul the grain of wheat. "This falls into the earth, dies and germinates, grows and brings forth fruit. The same thing happens to the human soul," he said on April 5, 1914. He also spoke of the blossoming of the soul and the awakening of the soul into a higher consciousness. One of his key words was the word *rabota* (work): we must constantly work on ourselves to put Christianity into practice in daily life.

The tradition of Methodism, in which Deunov had been educated, worked its way into the School of the White Brotherhood in praying, preaching, singing spiritual songs, and focusing on social life. From Bulgarian culture came music and circle-dance, and an awareness of the importance of healthy living. In the School, the mountains became places of spiritual experiences and of study of the world of nature beings. Here, Deunov's disciples held their summer camps together under difficult conditions, developing their social consciousness and absorbing new life forces.

The Paths of Schooling

The schooling path of the White Brotherhood was not presented, as in Anthroposophy, in a book of instruction or in lectures; instead, it developed out of the many methods of spiritual work given by Deunov. These methods support the transition from involution to evolution and the birth of the new man. They consist of engaging in activities that have positive effects on the health of the physical body, on the etheric body, on the purification of the heart, on the transformation of the soul, and on the development of spiritual powers. We will now describe these methods in more detail.

At the basis of this path of schooling is the healthy life that can be achieved by working with the forces of the four elements: fire (absorbing the sunlight), air (breathing correctly), water (drinking hot water), and earth (eating food correctly); and by doing daily physical exercises, by singing and playing music (or listening to music) daily, by going out into nature, and by dancing paneurythmy in the morning in spring and summer. These aspects involve absorbing the constructive forces of living nature and the positive vibrations generated by singing and music. Readings by Deunov, whose words radiated a creative energy in the experience of the audience, were always preceded by and concluded with a song.

The sacred circle dance of paneurythmy connects these aspects.[19] It unites movement, song, music, and spiritual ideas, harmonizing the forces of the sun and the earth in the human body. The natural movements of paneurythmy strengthen health. The three parts of paneurythmy summarize the path of schooling. The first 28 exercises symbolize the awakening of the soul in spring, and they harmonize human thinking, feeling, and willing. The second part, the Sunrays, symbolizes the birth of the human being as a free individual, as well as the absorption of the forces of the sun. By dancing the Sunrays, we prepare ourselves for the rising of the inner sun within our heart. The third part, the Pentagram, makes the dancers aware of the five most important qualities of the teaching, which they develop on their way to perfection. These are Love, Wisdom, Truth, Righteousness, and Goodness. The Pentagram given as a medita-

---

19. Kovacheva, *Die Weisse Bruderschaft* [The White Brotherhood], 125–50.

tion image by Peter Deunov in 1910 symbolizes the evolution of the human soul toward perfection. It is an image of cosmic man.

Deunov recommended that his disciples read the entire bible. John's gospel in particular, and especially its prologue, were to be studied meditatively. Many of his lectures opened with a bible text. Beginning in 1912, his disciples could turn to *The Testament of the Color Rays of Light*, which contains quotations from the bible as a meditation book. It can be used every day to acquire a virtue, overcome an illness, or solve a problem. In the introduction to one edition of the book, Deunov says of the light:

> Light is a divine power that reveals the inner qualities of things. Light is the essence of God, through which he reveals himself. When we examine and connect with light, we examine and connect with the Creator himself.

And:

> It is precisely the light that will awaken our sublime nature—through which we will know reality, the truth. If we consciously connect with it, the virtues corresponding to the color rays will develop in us, and thus we will be "in the image of God" and become loving beings. Therein lies the method of The Testament of the Color Rays of Light.

In his lectures, he gave many hundreds of exercises for the development of the soul and spirit, as well as musical exercises, breathing exercises, and physical exercises.[20] His student Vlad Pashov listed more than a thousand methods of work that can stimulate hidden forces of the human being to develop one's soul and spirit. Pashov's book also contains 150 formulas and short prayers by Deunov that can be spoken in certain situations.[21]

An essential part of this great exercise program is the acquisition of virtues. These are qualities such as faith, hope, love, humility, purity, mildness, unselfishness, gentleness, rationality, giving im-

---

20. Peter Deunov, *Okultni uprazhneniya* [Occult Exercises], Sofia, 2000.
21. Vlad Pashov (ed.), Beinsa Douno, *Imam dom nerukotvoren* [I Have a House Not Built by Hands], 2 volumes, Sofia, 2000, 2004. The already mentioned *Sacred Words*, dictated by Deunov, can be used for meditative contemplation.

The Paths of Schooling

portance to small things, punctuality, pliability, generosity, obedience, perseverance, patience, not putting anything off, independence, self-control, calmness, and courage.[22] According to Deunov, these qualities can also come from going through suffering.

Associated with the lectures in the classes of the esoteric school were assignments to be carried out during the following week. The disciples had to think about them, do research, acquire experience, and write something about them. In the general occult class, assignments were given such as: my greatest shortcoming, why children cry, the influence of music in life, the difference between human beings and animals, the difference between the heart and the mind. In the occult class for young people, assignments had to be completed on such topics as: the place of the will in life, the difference between soul and spirit, the origin of fire, and the difference between the philosophical views of Plato and Aristotle.

Sometimes the assignments had to be accomplished in everyday life. For example, one assignment read: If on the street a beggar comes up to you and begs for money, examine whether you feel a karmic connection with this person. If so, strike up a conversation with him or her, and give all the money you have with you. This is an exercise for developing karmic awareness. Another: If you see a pebble in your path on the street, pick it up and put it aside, and then pay attention to what thoughts occupied your mind at that moment. Through this exercise we can realize that, as we walk, we carry with us on our backs a bagful of old problems that occupy our thoughts and that we would do better to push these aside as pebbles in our path.

Another area of practice in the School of the White Brotherhood is creating a communal life. In the many meetings, in living together in Izgrev, during the excursions in the mountains and the summer camps, people got to know each other. Mutual help, friendship, and love could thus develop. If people wanted to form a picture of life in the communities of the Bogomils, Deunov referred to the social life in the school of brotherhood. For him, this social life was a workshop for the life of the next culture period. It should

22. *Harmonizing of the Human Soul*, 485–541.

Rudolf Steiner and Peter Deunov

be noted that people in Bulgaria were less individualistically inclined than people in Central Europe. Moreover, people from all social classes could meet in the school of White Brotherhood.

On the path of schooling that Deunov developed, living with the three principles of love, wisdom, and truth is of fundamental significance. Whoever takes up the work of divine science in the world finds himself on a battlefield, he said. We must then wear the shields of love, wisdom, and truth—which serve for our protection.[23]

> Love is the collective manifestation of all intelligent beings who have completed their evolution and become one with God.... Love is now established as a principle in the world.[24]

Love has its origin in God and is itself the source of life. The entire cosmos is the manifestation of divine love. Love rejuvenates man.

> The only real goal in the world is to know love. This is the only thing the soul strives for [...] Love must fulfill the human spirit. It must manifest itself completely, perfectly, and unlimitedly in the human soul. It must also dwell in the heart of man as its essence, and act in the mind of man as a loving force. There are four manifestations of love in man: love is the purposeful striving in the heart; love is the feeling in the soul; love is the power in the mind; love is the essential principle in the mind. That is the whole cycle of development from the beginning to the end. [...] The fire of love is now coming into the world like a great tidal wave. It will destroy everything that cannot endure the high intensity of love.[25]

Divine Wisdom, according to Deunov, brings light, knowledge, and harmony to the world:

> Wisdom is the world in which, from the beginning of time, all things are hidden that God and the higher beings have created and that humans have created on earth. Therefore, the world of wisdom is also open to us. True, essential knowledge comes from that world.... When wisdom shines in the human soul, everything in

---

23. *Sacred Words of the Master*, 188.
24. Kraleva, *The Master Peter Deunov*, 35.
25. *The Master Speaks*, chapter on "Love."

The Paths of Schooling

the human mind falls into place. All ideas become clear, distinct, and harmoniously ordered.[26]

The aspiration and desire of the human soul is to be free. This is a powerful driving force, not in the ordinary person, but in the one in whom higher consciousness is awakened.... Love constantly strives for truth.... When truth descends into you, it will enlighten your mind, bring peace to your heart, and give strength and health to your body.[27]

Deunov presented the following as "laws": love brings life; wisdom brings light and knowledge; truth brings freedom. Truth will make you free, the bible says. A summary formula reads:

Everything in the world is love. Love brings forth life. Life creates the circumstances.

Wisdom uses the favorable circumstances and brings insight.

Insight brings light. Light reveals truth. Truth sets free.

With these three forces, we can build three immortal bodies in our incarnations: the body of love, the body of wisdom, and the body of truth. In our time, we are laying the foundations of the body of love.

Those who live in the body of love have no enemies, for they bring life, peace, and the realization of every cherished wish. They bring gratification of all the needs to all beings. We then manifest love and actualize it in our lives. Love is eternal life and eternal rejuvenation, eternal knowledge of God, and eternal increase of freedom.[28]

For Deunov, prayer is the most powerful method for accomplishing the tasks of life and for spiritual growth. Through prayer, a person is constantly connected to the spiritual world.[29]

Prayer is a conversation with God.... During prayer, God teaches the human being.... During prayer, the human soul opens for the divine world, attunes with it, comes into a receptive state towards the energies from there, accepts the thought of God, and receives

---

26. Ibid., chapter on "Wisdom."
27. Ibid., chapter on "Truth."
28. Ibid., chapter on "The Body of Love."

from the life of God; new ideas burst into the human soul.... Prayer is a mystical, peculiar state of the soul. There is no better state than that, and it should never become a burden for the human being. It should not be unvaried, but varied. The human being has to pray for others as well. It is a privilege for the human being to pray.[30]

Praying to God is the breath of the soul.... Prayer purifies the mind and the heart.[31]

Deunov formulated a large number of prayers and formulas for different occasions: prayers and sayings for morning and night, meals, healing, the departed, thanksgiving, protection, and God's help on our path and on that of others.[32]

Prayers of Peter Deunov

Prayer for every day
Lord, enlighten my mind, bless my heart, strengthen my will, my memory, and my faith so as to justify my existence and fulfill the task for which I have come to earth.

Lord, please send your Spirit to bring into my heart, my mind, and my soul the fruit of love, the blessing of joy and peace—the foundation of your patience and mercy. Amen.

Morning prayers
I thank thee for making me a gift of another day of life, and for calling me to pursue my work on earth, healthy and restored.
Lord, I pray to you to give me living cosmic forces that will fill every cell of my body, bring life and health into it, and strengthen my spirit so that I can fulfill my task on earth. Amen.

---

29. Steiner also gave prayers and formulas to his disciples, for example the "Prayer of Surrender," in the lecture "The Nature of Prayer" of February 17, 1910 (CW 59). From Ita Wegman we know that he prayed his own version of the Our Father every day at 6 PM (Zeylmans van Emmichoven, *Die Erkraftung des Herzens* [Strengthening the Heart], 154). According to other sources, he prayed aloud the Our Father in Latin every day at noon.

30. Peter Deunov, *Harmonizing of the Human Soul*, 56, 62, 243.

31. Peter Deunov, lecture of December 5, 1913, in Beinsa Douno, *The Teacher*, vol. 1, 96.

32. *Prayers, Formulas, Devotional Songs*, Sofia 2017. https://ia600703.us.archive.org/3/items/PeterDeunov/Prayers-Formulas-Devotional-Songs.pdf.

The Paths of Schooling

> **Evening prayers**
> Thank you for the experiences of this day. Guide me through the coming night. May my soul attend your Divine School so that I may be guided and learn how to work effectively.
> Lord, when my body is resting tonight, surround me with your light and protect me. I am going above: to study, pray, and work.
>
> **Formula before and after meals**
> The love of God brings abundance and fullness of life. (3x)
>
> **Formula for healing**
> Lord, you are the source of life. Send us your life-giving strength, your Spirit, to heal us from all illness and suffering. (3x)
>
> **Formula for protection**
> God, protect me with your white light and surround me with your diamond wall. The Spirit of God, beloved of my soul, will do everything for me.

For the disciples who participated in the classes of his esoteric school, Deunov gave a picture of the disciple in his relationship to the teacher and gave recommendations for their development.[33] The disciple walks the path to perfection that leads to entering the Kingdom of God:

> When a person chooses this path, he adopts a different outlook and understanding of life. He seeks no external wealth, no compassion, no support, no reverence, no esteem. The disciple has passed through self-denial and is glad for the contradictions he encounters in life, viewing them as problems to solve. The disciple never criticizes nor moralizes. He is not interested in the mistakes of others. To him, these mistakes do not exist. The only thing that exists is the righteous life, the life of love. The disciple's ideals are love, light, peace, and joy. Once his mind is awakened, the life of a disciple is not a life of blessing, but of creative work. Grace is only in the aids he receives, but he is required to make efforts and do much work. The disciple is tested for a long time before being admitted to the Kingdom of God. Whether he will be allowed to

---

33. *Harmonizing of the Human Soul*, section "Master and Disciple," 351–47. Beinsa Douno, *Sacred Words of the Master*, sections "A Call to the Disciple" and "Recommendations to the Disciple," 9–200.

enter depends on the disciple's knowledge and wisdom, not on his love. One is not admitted in the Kingdom of God by grace.[34]

Elements of the Hindu tradition, Buddhism, and the Christian monastic tradition resonate in the relationship of the disciple to the teacher. The disciple who has found his teacher and has been lovingly accepted by him as a disciple obeys his teacher and acts as the teacher would act.[35]

Deunov offered himself as a mediator between the disciple and God, as a true teacher acting as a messenger of God, sent to earth with a mission. Thus his disciples accepted him as their teacher. The Theosophists in the West followed their masters from the East in this sense, but Steiner broke with this traditional form of mastership and appealed to the freedom of individuals who, from their free I, had to judge the teachings of their teacher on their value. In his vision, the teacher had to become increasingly a friend of his disciples.

In the patriarchal context of Bulgarian culture, a teacher like Deunov was given more spiritual authority over his disciples. His relationship to them was not about their obedience to his will, but about discovering the meaning of the rule of life, which he had given them: "In the fulfillment of the will of God lies the strength of the human soul." Deunov appealed to his disciples' own activity and gave them what they needed in terms of individual guidance. On October 9, 1921, in the lecture "Brothers and Sisters in Christ," he said:

> The one who wants to be a brother, sister, and mother of Christ must be a first-class hero in the world. A first-class hero, not just in the ordinary sense, but a hero in mind, soul, and spirit. He must have a heart as pure as crystal; in his mind there must be light like the sun; he must have a soul as lofty and noble and spacious as the whole universe; a spirit as strong as God and one with God![36]

He also gave the advice:

---

34. Kraleva, *The Master Peter Deunov*, 50.
35. Beinsa Douno, *Sacred Words of the Master*, 21, 25.
36. Sunday lecture of October 9, 1921.

The Paths of Schooling

Preserve the freedom of your soul, the strength of your spirit, the light of your mind, the goodness of your heart.

In the methods of the School of the White Brotherhood we can discover, in a similar way to Anthroposophy, a path of schooling with five interrelated elements. The emphases, however, are different. The schooling of thought received less attention. Steiner's Grail path, leading from the lesser to the greater guardian of the threshold, had the same goal as the path Deunov taught to his disciples within a religious context. Reaching a higher consciousness, which is the goal in Anthroposophy, was not a goal in the school of brotherhood, but a consequence of the path to rebirth. Deunov's disciples prayed, contemplated, and meditated in their "secret room"—but equally, building a living community was an essential goal of the School of the White Brotherhood.

1. An education of perceiving and thinking
2. A path to rebirth in Christ
3. The development of a higher consciousness
4. The creation of an inner sanctuary
5. The formation of a living community

Retrospective

The schooling path of Anthroposophy aims to develop higher forms of consciousness that are necessary for spiritual research. In the Anthroposophical Society, people could become acquainted with this path of schooling, which began in 1924 for members of the First Class of the new spiritual school. This was a limited group of members. In contrast, the White Brotherhood's path of schooling leads to the perfection that is necessary for entering the Kingdom of God. Peter Deunov had many thousands of followers, but the group of disciples who attended the classes of the esoteric school was also limited.

Against the background of the goals of the two spiritual schools, their teachings can be meaningfully compared. Steiner gave a comprehensive description of the development of the world, which Deunov did not address. Deunov spoke of the White Brotherhood in the invisible world and pointed to the intelligent beings operating in the world. The genesis of fallen humanity in the stage of involution, as well as its renewal in the stage of evolution, were described by Steiner and Deunov from complementary points of view. The death and resurrection of Christ, and his return, were presented by both teachers as the turning point in human history. Steiner highlighted Christ's Second Coming as a helper and comforter, while Deunov saw him knocking on the door of each person's heart, asking to be let in. These are complementary views. Both teachers worked to prepare the coming Slavic culture, which they described in identical terms of love and brotherhood.

In this new culture, the connection of head and heart is a necessity for spiritual intelligence and for the efficacy of love, which will be the two pillars of Slavic culture. The path of schooling of Anthroposophy is primarily focused on the knowledge or wisdom aspect; the path of schooling of the White Brotherhood is primarily focused on the love aspect. Thus they complement each other.

In the next section, we follow the further development of the two spiritual schools after the death of their teachers. This includes the significance of these schools and their future.

PART III

The Destiny of the Two Schools

If in our own work, individual human beings do not come together, Anthroposophy will not come about at all within humanity. Anthroposophy requires true human brotherhood to the deepest depths of the soul.... Anthroposophy grows only in the soil of brotherhood ... where one human being gives to another what they have and what they are capable of.[1]

—Rudolf Steiner, from a lecture of June 11, 1922

The future culture will be a culture of the human heart.[2]

—Peter Deunov, from a lecture of March 25, 1923

The heart must be full of love, the mind full of wisdom, the soul full of truth. That is the straight path.

—Peter Deunov

---

1. Rudolf Steiner, lecture of June 11, 1922, in *The Tension Between East and West* (CW 83).
2. Peter Deunov, "Awakening of the Human Soul," lecture of March 25, 1923, in *The Mindful Heart*, 63.

1

The Anthroposophical Movement after 1925

The founding of the new Anthroposophical Society at the Christmas Conference in 1923 was an attempt by Rudolf Steiner to continue his work with the members under his direct leadership. Only a month before, he had considered leaving the old Society and founding a kind of order with a dedicated group of disciples. Ita Wegman helped him make the choice to restart his work with all the members. Nine months later, in September 1924, he had to conclude that this attempt had failed and that the new impulses had not been taken up. The need for cooperation between the various groups, which required harmonization of karma, had not been understood.

And so, the Society met its provisional demise after Steiner's death in 1925. The already existing misunderstanding between Marie Steiner (and those associated with her) and Ita Wegman (and her circle) was growing. In 1935, Ita Wegman and Elisabeth Vreede were expelled from the board. At the same time, they—together with the members connected with them—were excluded from the Society. Also excluded were the Dutch and British Anthroposophical Societies. The work in the First Class of the esoteric school, which Steiner had partly entrusted to Wegman, had already ceased shortly after his death. Wegman wanted to continue the Class, but this was made impossible for her. The lack of cooperation in the board, which was rudderless without Steiner, was fatal to the Society. It fell apart in 1935. In the same year, the Anthroposophical Society was banned in Germany. Later, Marie Steiner was also cast aside by the remaining two board members.

Rudolf Steiner and Peter Deunov

In a lecture on August 22, 1938, Valentin Tomberg spoke in Rotterdam about Steiner's path of the cross, which had ended with his death. He was of the opinion that Steiner could only be revived by individual people connecting with him spiritually.[1] This was also the view of Ita Wegman and Ludwig Polzer-Hoditz in 1935. For them, the Dornach Society had no future. On February 22, 1935, Wegman wrote to Maria Röschl that individuals could form a "higher union" with each other that had its roots in the spiritual world.[2]

Some myths arose in the Society after Steiner's death that persisted into the 1990s, among them:

> Rudolf Steiner laid the Foundation Stone in the hearts of the attendees during the Christmas Conference (everyone must do that for themselves).
>
> The Christmas Conference succeeded (Rudolf Steiner spoke of failure in September 1924).
>
> The Michael movement in the spiritual world and the Anthroposophical Society are linked (that was so only from the end of 1923 until Rudolf Steiner's death in 1925).
>
> Rudolf Steiner is forever karmically linked to the Anthroposophical Society (he never said so himself).
>
> The board of the Anthroposophical Society is an esoteric board, that is, connected to the spiritual world (this was the case only with Rudolf Steiner there).
>
> The esoteric school of the Anthroposophical Society still functions (it lacks a spiritual leader).
>
> Only members of the Anthroposophical Society are anthroposophists.

Although the renewal impulse of the Christmas Conference of 1923 was not picked up at that time, it continued to work on. Willem Zeylmans van Emmichoven, the leader of the Dutch Anthroposophical Society (and from the circle around Ita Wegman), spoke after World War II about "the continuing impulse of the Christmas Conference." He wanted to keep this impulse alive, and worked to undo

---

1. Valentin Tomberg, *Inner Development*, Spring Valley, 1983, 81–97.
2. Von Beckerath, *Der Leidensweg Rudolf Steiners* [RS's Path of Suffering], 269.

The Anthroposophical Movement after 1925

the "great exclusion" of 1935. In 1960, the Dutch Society rejoined the Dornach Society, followed by the British Anthroposophical Society. This did not lead to the healing of the wounds, however; more time was needed for that. (Zeylmans died in 1961.)

The forces of spiritual renewal that had been in motion since 1900, but were blocked by the world wars, led to cultural changes appearing in the late 1960s. Large groups of people were striving for a more conscious way of life, and from this came an interest in a spiritual lifestyle, alternative education, healthy food, and awareness of one's own health. The anthroposophical movement, which until then had not been very outspoken, came into the spotlight because a subculture had developed in it with Waldorf education, biodynamic farms, holistic health care, and books on topics in which many people outside of Anthroposophy were interested.

As the anthroposophical movement began to grow, the number of initiatives increased and spread to all continents. In this sense, Anthroposophy became a cultural factor. A certain culmination was reached at the end of the 1980s and through the 1990s. But anthroposophical impulses were not strong enough to stop the decline of culture. Steiner had spoken of cooperation between the Aristotelian anthroposophists (who were on earth in his time and would return at the end of the 20th century) and the leading Platonists from the medieval school of Chartres. They would work together for the spiritualization of intelligence, that is, for the connection of the head and the heart in a new spiritual thinking. Steiner had made this cooperation dependent on the "dedicated care of Anthroposophy" by the Anthroposophical Society. But this did not adequately transpire after his death.

In a lecture given in Arnhem on July 19, 1924, Steiner said that at the end of the 20th century

> mankind will stand either at the grave of all civilization or at the beginning of that epoch in which, in the souls of those who in their hearts combine intelligence with spirituality, the battle of [the archangel] Michael will be fought in favor of the Michael impulse.[3]

3. Rudolf Steiner, lecture of July 19, 1924, in *Karmic Relationships*, vol. 6 (CW 240).

Rudolf Steiner and Peter Deunov

And indeed, the scenario of the downfall of civilization seems to have been unfolding since the end of the 20th century in the triumph of materialistic thinking and the increasing intrusion of technology into human life. Our multifaceted, creative, and moral intelligence is steadily being replaced by a unidirectional, logical, artificial intelligence. Instead of a threefold society of free people, we are experiencing the rise of new forms of totalitarianism.

The battle fought by the archangel Michael and his warriors is not over. The salvation of humanity is at stake. The path to Grail initiation must be kept open in a world increasingly controlled by consciousness-obscuring forces from the anti-Grail castle of the black magician Klingsor. People inspired by Michael are resisting the rise of the new forces of technocratic totalitarianism and transhumanism. Bred by these forces, the new technology-driven man will lack independent thinking, a connection to his soul and spirit, a natural immunity, a natural connection to life, and the ability to make meaningful products and provide meaningful services for others. The transhuman man will no longer live from love, wisdom, and truth. He will cease to be human.

The anthroposophical movement has thus far been unable to counteract technocratic totalitarianism and transhumanism with a sufficiently powerful "consciousness of our humanity"—which is the very meaning of the word Anthroposophy. It has largely lost its spiritual depth. But this is not the case in all anthroposophical circles. This loss began immediately after Steiner's death with the demise of the School of Spiritual Science, and was strengthened by the demise of the Anthroposophical Society in 1935. In his opening address at the 2000 Michael Conference, Manfred Schmidt-Brabant, then president of the General Anthroposophical Society, expressed his deep concern about the problems of the Anthroposophical Society. In doing so, he asked some completely unexpected questions:

> Is there not something like an occult imprisonment holding sway over Anthroposophy? Let us look at its outward effectiveness. In spite of all the institutions and endless work in lectures and courses, we remain stuck as in a ghetto. We do not get out, we do not get out to the extent to which, according to its significance, Anthroposophy should have long since become effective in the

The Anthroposophical Movement after 1925

world. And is there not also this same occult imprisonment within? [...] Is it not as if there were even walls erected between people? One looks at so many inquiring, industrious, creative, clever people [...] and yet it is not possible that they unite, that working communities arise.[4]

This situation is not solely a recent phenomenon. Already during Steiner's lifetime, cooperation among anthroposophists was a problem. Steiner was also fiercely attacked from outside, by the established order of society and materialistic science. The new, spiritual way of thinking posed a threat, and this is still the case today. Since the 1980s, the anthroposophical movement has been repeatedly put in the corner of racism by its opponents, although it is nonsensical to call Steiner a racist.

On the other hand, many hundreds of thousands of people have discovered the value of the anthroposophical vision of education, medicine, therapies, food production, and the meaning of Christ—and are living with this vision. That they are sometimes expressed in an intellectual and dogmatic way is not due to Anthroposophy itself, but to the people who have not yet fully absorbed it into their hearts. In the anthroposophical movement there is a growing awareness that in many cases Anthroposophy has become little more than a "method," and that more spiritual depth is needed.

The 100th anniversary of the Christmas Conference in 2023 may lead to a reflection on renewing the spiritual impulse of Anthroposophy. This has several aspects. People of great spiritual depth are necessary for this: people who examine with a spiritual perspective the forces at work in our time in culture, politics, and the economy; people who look for ways in which thinking can be spiritualized, and the power of the living Christ can become active; people working on themselves and trying to live from social impulses.

It is to be hoped that in the anthroposophical movement there will be a growing awareness of the apocalyptic character of our

---

4. Manfred Schmidt-Brabant, "Der Kampf um den ethischen Individualismus" [The Struggle for Ethical Individualism], in *Was in der Anthroposophischen Gesellschaft Vorgeht* [What's Happening in the Anthroposophical Society], nr. 39, September 23, 2001.

time, that is, of the return of Christ and of the activity of the sun demon and of Ahriman (with his fallen angels and his human initiates). Together with spiritually awakened young people, it is necessary to preserve for the future the seeds of a spiritual culture that Steiner sowed and that have blossomed in the course of the 20th century.

2

The School of the White Brotherhood after 1944

Peter Deunov said that the movement he launched was for all of humanity, not just for Bulgaria.[1] Bulgarians have the task of spreading this movement throughout the world. According to him, he had gathered his students in his school for three reasons:

> [First], to form a community of people who have great love towards each other, an environment of love, to send from here powerful waves of love over the world, reaching and awakening all the souls of humanity. Second, to prepare you to be preachers in future ages. You all, even the smallest, will be preachers in the future, ... to preach the ideas of the new culture.... Third, you do not yet belong to the White Brotherhood.... You are disciples of the White Brotherhood, and I am preparing you to become White Brothers.[2]

Unlike Rudolf Steiner, Peter Deunov was able to complete his spiritual work. It did not perish during Communism. The Communist regime that had established itself in Sofia more than three months before his death in 1944 did not initially take a negative view of the Brotherhood. Deunov's ideas about the spiritual role of Russia and the mission of the Slavic peoples, and about the significance of the Bogomils for European culture, had the sympathy of the Communist Party. There were even party members affiliated with the Brotherhood. The new Prime Minister, Georgi Dimitrov (1882–1949), had once been hidden by Deunov when he was wanted by the police. He allowed Deunov to be buried in Izgrev, where his grave

---

1. Peter Deunov, *Harmonizing the Human Soul*, 357.
2. Ibid., 385–86.

Rudolf Steiner and Peter Deunov

still lies. In 1948, the Brotherhood was recognized as a religious community, but the site of the central building in which Deunov lived was expropriated. In the 1980s, the Soviet Embassy was built here.

In 1945, after Deunov's death, Brotherhood leaders from dozens of Bulgarian towns and villages formed a Brotherhood Council of seven members, including Boyan Boev and Boris Nikolov. The people of the Brotherhood could meet to read lectures, dance paneurythmy, and hold their summer camps in the Rila Mountains. Stenograms of lectures were transcribed and texts prepared for printing. The Brotherhood's printing house printed Deunov's as yet unpublished lectures from 1945 to 1950.

In 1954, Todor Zhivkov became party leader. During the war, he was for several months in hiding in the Izgrev community,[3] but a few years later, the Brotherhood was nevertheless banned as a "sect." Books with Deunov's lectures were confiscated, to be destroyed or stored in the state archives. However, stenograms and many books could be hidden. In 1958, the Brotherhood's lands became state property. In 1959, Brotherhood leaders Boris Nikolov and Zhecho Panayotov were sentenced to 12 and 8 years in prison, respectively. They were released early on January 1, 1963, by amnesty. In 1970, the settlement of Izgrev was demolished by the government. The number of people associated with the Brotherhood declined steadily, and by the 1980s there were about 500 left.

As a result of the 1989 upheavals in Eastern Europe, the Brotherhood was able to re-emerge from its underground existence. On November 7, 1990, it was officially registered. It set itself the task of spreading the teaching developed by Peter Deunov in Bulgaria and abroad. Publishing houses and magazines were established, and local groups that had existed before the time of Communism were re-founded. Lectures, courses, concerts, large-scale meetings, and summer camps are again taking place in the Rila Mountains. Texts are being translated into other languages. The entire printed work of Peter Deunov (including lectures in the occult school) and trans-

---

3. According to Boris Nikolov, about twenty communists were hiding in 1944 in Izgrev. See Heinzel, *Weisse Bruderschaft und Delphische Idee* [The White Brotherhood and the Delphic Idea], 90.

The School of the White Brotherhood after 1944

lated texts have been posted on a website. Translated lectures are also published in other countries.

The White Brotherhood movement fulfills a great need for spirituality, which was suppressed in the Communist era. Many young people join it and ensure the growth of the movement. Several thousand people are affiliated with the local groups, and a larger number sympathize with the movement. People from other spiritual movements are also welcome to join paneurythmy. That does not mean there are no tensions and conflicts in the Brotherhood, as conflicts in the Council of the Brotherhood in 2021 showed. The Brotherhood, 100 years after the foundation of the Occult School in 1922, faces the task of consciously taking up, renewing, and carrying forward the spiritual impulses that led to this foundation.

Every August 19, the Brotherhood's main holiday, several thousand people gather on a large mountain meadow in the Rila Mountains to dance paneurythmy. For several years, Bulgarian national television sent a helicopter there to report on the event in the evening news; in recent years, the recordings are made with drones. People dancing paneurythmy are then shown on television. Deunov has again become the national figure he was in the 1920s and 1930s and even more famous than then, because books with his lectures are available in all bookstores in Bulgaria and his thoughts are propagated on the Internet. In 2007, he came in second place in a viewer survey by Bulgarian television of the most important Bulgarians in history. Instead of gymnastics, qualified elementary school teachers are allowed to do paneurythmy with the children.

The annual summer camp in the Rila Mountains has attracted numerous foreign participants since 1990. Many of them are connected with circles of the Brotherhood that have emerged in many countries through the work of emigré Bulgarians from the School of the White Brotherhood. Prominent among them is Michael Ivanov (Omraam Mikhael Aïvanhov), who went to France in 1937 to spread the teachings of the School of the White Brotherhood. His Universal White Brotherhood led to the worldwide fame of paneurythmy and the work of Peter Deunov.[4] Before his death in 1986, Aïvanhov was invited by a board member of the Anthroposophical Society to give a lecture at the Goetheanum in Dornach.

Rudolf Steiner and Peter Deunov

The Universal White Brotherhood

Michael Ivanov was born in 1900 in present-day North Macedonia. He spent his youth in Varna, in Bulgaria. After studying Hindu texts, from the age of 14 he practiced yoga, which led to intense spiritual experiences. When he was 15 he had a great mystical experience of divine grace. Two years later he met Peter Deunov, who became his spiritual teacher. At the instigation of Deunov, he studied different sciences. From 1932 until 1937, when Deunov suggested to him that he go to France, Ivanov worked as a school teacher. Deunov must have foreseen that the Brotherhood would be forbidden soon in Bulgaria and that from France it would be able to spread over the world.

Ivanov settled in Paris, where he received help from people who were connected with the Bulgarian School of the White Brotherhood. Already in 1938, before the beginning of the Second World War, he gave his first lecture in the French language. Until the end of his life, he gave thousands of lectures in France and in many other countries. He elaborated the teaching developed by Peter Deunov and deepened it with his own spiritual research. Deunov remained for him the "Master," while he called himself "Brother Michael."

Soon after the Second World War, Michael Ivanov established a spiritual center in Sèvres, near Paris, and in 1953 the center Le Bonfin, near Fréjus in the French Provence. He founded the Universal White Brotherhood in December 1947, which is currently active in more than 44 countries. His books have been translated into many languages. In 1959/60 he spent a year in India, where he met several spiritual teachers. From one of them he received the spiritual name "Omraam," which corresponds to the "solve et coagula" (dissolve and coagulate) of the alchemists. He changed his name, then, to "Omraam Mikhaël Aïvanhov." Moreover, after returning from India, his students addressed him as "Master."[5]

---

4. Today there is a good relationship between the Bulgarian and French Brotherhoods, but it has not always been so. In the 1990s, the leadership of the French Brotherhood was not so happy with its members visiting the summer camp in Bulgaria. The Bulgarian Brotherhood criticized Michael Ivanov for going his own way in France. As early as 1947, Ivanov complained that Bulgarians were spreading lies about his relationship with Peter Deunov. He later understood that Deunov had prepared him for his mission in France.

5. Omraam Mikhaël Aïvanhov, *A Living Book: Autobiographical Reflections* 1, Fréjus, 2011.

The School of the White Brotherhood after 1944

The teachings of the School of the White Brotherhood appeal to people who seek an authentic and pure life in harmony with the forces of nature, with the cosmos, and with the divine origin of man. As such, they appeal to the hearts and willpower of people.

3

The Significance of Rudolf Steiner and Peter Deunov

During Peter Deunov's time, Rudolf Steiner's work was studied in small circles in Bulgaria. Even under Communism, there were small groups of anthroposophists. In 2001, an Anthroposophical Society was founded in Bulgaria, with about 140 members. Bulgarian anthroposophists are mostly familiar with Deunov's lectures. There are also those who know and connect both Steiner's and Deunov's work. One of them is Dimiter Mangurov. He is committed to a synthesis of the work of both spiritual teachers. The need for cooperation between all currents working for the new spiritual culture and for the spiritualization of intelligence was emphasized by Steiner himself in 1924:

> Only by uniting such spirituality, as it wants to flow through the anthroposophical movement, with other spiritual currents, will Michael find those impulses which will unite him again with the intelligence that has become earthly and that actually belongs to him. My task now will be to show you by what ingenious means Ahriman intends to prevent this, in what a sharp struggle this 20th century finds itself. From all these things one can become aware of the seriousness of the times, of the courage necessary to integrate oneself properly into the spiritual currents.[1]

In Peter Deunov's school, the purification of the heart is central. It is the basis for love of God and our fellow man, and for the work of perfecting ourselves. Anthroposophy works more from the head, from the consciousness that wants to expand in order to gain

---

1. Rudolf Steiner, lecture of June 28, 1924, in *Karmic Relationships*, vol. 3 (CW 237).

The Significance of Rudolf Steiner and Peter Deunov

insights from the spiritual world. These insights must then be brought into the world from the heart. Deunov followed a religious-mystical path. This path results in an intimate connection with Christ, which anthroposophists often do not have.

In the anthroposophical movement, the application of methods developed in the fields of work of Anthroposophy usually takes the central place. Inner schooling, social consciousness, and Christ-consciousness, which belong to the core of Anthroposophy, receive less attention. Following Steiner, anthroposophists can enter upon their own Grail path to purify their personality, which is among the prerequisites for obtaining spiritual consciousness. In doing so, they can also fruitfully use the methods from Deunov's school, which are directed at the purification of the human heart and the development of moral qualities.

Steiner defined Anthroposophy in 1924 as a Michaelic path of insight, which seeks to lead the spiritual in the human being to the spiritual in the universe. At work in Anthroposophy is the being Anthropo-Sophia, the Divine Wisdom that has connected itself, first as Philo-Sophia, and in our time as Anthropo-Sophia, with human thinking. She, the Divine Wisdom, is the companion of individuals on their path to spiritual insight, holding up before them "the consciousness of our humanity" as in a mirror. This path leads to a new culture—one in which the higher self can connect with the human soul.

This new culture has two important aspects: that of knowledge or wisdom, and that of love. Anthroposophy emphasizes the knowledge aspect that can develop when insights become knowledge of the heart. The School of the White Brotherhood works primarily on the love aspect. Deunov described its teachings as the "science of divine love." The two schools are not exclusively focused on either wisdom or love, but work to varying degrees on both aspects. For Steiner, the Christ-impulse is the impulse of love, with which people in a spiritual culture can work on the urgent questions of our time. For his part, Deunov taught in his school the path to the origin of love in God, whom he called "the beloved of the human soul."

Two other aspects of the new culture are conscious community-building and the transformation of evil. This was prepared by other

Rudolf Steiner and Peter Deunov

spiritual currents, most notably by the movement of Mani (c. 216–276), the prophet of the Holy Spirit. Steiner pointed out that Mani had incarnated in the Grail current as Parzival in the ninth century and opened the way to the Grail for modern man. In a 1904 lecture on Manichaeism, Rudolf Steiner spoke of the new task of this movement to create the social forms for a future Christianity:

> But what has yet to be created is a form for the life of the sixth cycle of cultures. This must be created in advance, because it must be there so that the Christian life can pour itself out in it. This form must be prepared by people who will create such an organization, such a form, that the true Christian life of the sixth cycle of cultures can take place in it. And this outer form of society must come from the Mani intention, from the little troop that Mani is preparing. This must be the outward form of organization, the congregation, in which, first of all, the Christian spark can truly spill over.[2]

This preparation already began with the Bogomils (in Bulgaria, Macedonia, Bosnia, and Italy), in the resulting Cathar movement in southern France, and in the order of the Knights Templar. The Dutch anthroposophist Dieter Brüll considered the social impulse that Steiner associated with Anthroposophy to be a Manichean impulse—one that leads to a socially oriented Christianity that can actualize these new social forms.[3] In these social forms, evil can be overcome by mildness. This future form of Manichaeism cannot be separated from the incarnation of Mani in Parzival. Deunov brought to life the social impulses of the Bogomils in the community of the disciples of his school and spoke of the necessity of transforming evil through love. His school thus stands in the stream of a *future* Manichaeism and can be considered a metamorphosis of the Bogomil movement.

In his lectures, Steiner spoke of Sophia as a heavenly being who wants to connect, as Anthropo-Sophia, with individual human beings in our time. Deunov spoke of Divine Wisdom in connection

---

2. Rudolf Steiner, lecture of November 11, 1904, in *The Temple Legend* (CW 93).

3. Dieter Brüll, *The Mysteries of Social Encounters: The Anthroposophical Social Impulse*, Fair Oaks, 2002.

The Significance of Rudolf Steiner and Peter Deunov

with Divine Love and Divine Truth. By this he did not mean beings, but principles. Only exceptionally did he speak of Wisdom as a being:

> The Lord created the world through Wisdom and he put everything in its place. This is why he made Wisdom the adviser of the soul. Hear the voice of your adviser throughout the days of your sojourn on earth, so that you may be well and listen to the words of Wisdom.[4]

It has been noted before that Deunov's words can themselves be considered "wisdom literature." This is a tradition that originated in the Middle East and Egypt more than 3,000 years ago. His words can be considered wise counsel for the development of the soul. The path of schooling he offers has as its goal the transformation of the soul so that it can transform itself into "Lady Sophia," as it is called in Christian esotericism. On this basis, the methods developed by Deunov can be called "Sophianic." This is much less the case in Anthroposophy, which aims to be primarily a spiritual science, but does have the same transformation of the soul as a prerequisite.

Steiner spoke of four archangelic forces and connected them with the seasons. The Michael impulse of free thinking is associated with autumn. The Gabriel impulse with its artistic forms belongs to winter. The Raphael impulse of healing we can place in spring. And the Uriel impulse of community-building and religious consciousness lives in summer. The anthroposophical movement is primarily a Michaelic movement, with Ita Wegman in the Raphael current, and Marie Steiner in the Gabriel current. The White Brotherhood school, with its religious and social impulses, is, as a Slavic, Eastern European school, primarily a Uriel current.

Both Steiner and Deunov made visible the spiritual missions of the countries in which they worked. Steiner spoke of Central European culture and its pursuit of the I. Its mission is to bring people to a spiritual awakening and to create a Michaelic culture that develops healing impulses between East and West. Deunov spoke of the task of Bulgarians to make their contributions to a new culture of

---

4. Beinsa Douno, *Sacred Words of the Master*, 271.

Rudolf Steiner and Peter Deunov

love and brotherhood, which can develop from the forces of the Slavic soul.

The two great teachers Rudolf Steiner and Peter Deunov are the preparers of a new Christianity that finds its application in practical life, in service to fellow human beings, and in response to the needs of humanity and of suffering nature. Steiner spoke in this context of a new sacramentalism, in which everything people do takes on a sacred character. When they act from love, Christ can work through them. They then care about the destiny of their fellow men and of nature; and in their dealings with them, they work from the impulse of love and service.[5] This was prepared in the circles of the Bogomils and Cathars, and it lives on in the School of the White Brotherhood. Deunov spoke several times of "people of love." Such people of selfless love are already living in the new culture.

The people in this school are not members of a society, but are brothers and sisters in a growing family of humanity, in which we regard each other as family members and address each other as brother and sister, as happens in the School of the White Brotherhood. In the anthroposophical movement, such a loving sense of brotherhood and sisterhood could bring people closer together.

According to Steiner, this new, esoteric Christianity, will become the new world religion, uniting the esoteric currents of all world religions. Buddhism, according to him, will be the first to connect with esoteric Christianity. "One day all religions of the world will work together to gradually understand that which is hidden in the Mystery of Golgotha and make it accessible to people as an impulse," he said.[6] Deunov spoke of a "mystical Christianity" that will be the future religion of humanity, in which Christ is at the center of the new culture.[7]

From the spiritual world, countless beings inspire humanity on this path to universal Christ-consciousness. Steiner pointed to the appearance of Christ in the etheric world. Deunov said that Christ, in his Second Coming, visits all people and knocks on the door of

---

5. Dieter Brüll, *Creating Social Sacraments*, Wilton, NH, 2019.
6. Rudolf Steiner, lecture of September 24, 1912, in *The Gospel of Mark* (CW 139).
7. Kovacheva, *Die Weisse Bruderschaft* [The White Brotherhood], 264.

The Significance of Rudolf Steiner and Peter Deunov

their hearts, asking if he may come in and dwell in them. Steiner spoke in addition about the work of the archangel Michael, about Sophia, Vidar, the Nathanic soul, Buddha, and the Maitreya Bodhisattva, as well as Christian Rosenkreutz and Master Jesus, and the masters of the East. However, we do not know the whole picture of their activity.

The 20th century saw the beginning of a "Michaelic" Anthroposophy, especially in Western Europe and on other continents. In Russia, a "Sophianic" Anthroposophy could have developed in connection with the Russian Sophia teaching. These two could have been connected in Central European Anthroposophy, but this latter was not cared for with the required dedication after Steiner's death in 1925. It was therefore unable to act as a mediating center to bring together "Michaelic" and "Sophianic" Anthroposophy. For this, it lacked the Christ-consciousness, but also the consciousness for the activity of the Nathanic soul—which could have led to a "Nathanic" Anthroposophy. In 1933, the return of Christ in the etheric was perceived only to a limited extent. Nazism obscured the etheric and astral world at this time. Therefore, no all-encompassing access to the "Michael-Sophia-Christ mystery," as Mario Betti has called it, emerged in the anthroposophical movement.[8]

This is where Deunov's work becomes highly relevant. He points the way to the rebirth of man and the rejuvenation of humanity, which have fallen out of sight in the anthroposophical movement. The old human being—by going the way of Jesus Christ, the new Adam—can transform himself into a new human being, who will again possess the powers of the cosmic man of paradise.

On his Grail path to the cross at Calvary (prior to developing a spiritual science), Steiner received a copy, an imprint, of the I of Jesus Christ. This is the active path of the inquiring and searching Parzival, which fits the current culture of the consciousness soul. He leads to a culture in which people take initiatives and apply their insights concretely.

Deunov's way is a way of the heart, a path of love that we can call a Sophianic way. It fits more with Slavic culture, in which the soul

---

8. Mario Betti, *Platonismus-Aristotelismus*, Stuttgart, 2003, 153–60.

purifies itself and becomes "Lady Sophia." It leads to a new social life that people build with each other in humility and gentleness, in love and compassion, singing, dancing, and praying in a culture of the heart. In this school of love, the disciples must work on themselves with great willpower. It is therefore also a school of the will, in which the teachings must be applied in practice.

These paths cannot be separated as Central European and Slavic paths, as "male" and "female" paths, as paths of consciousness and heart, of insight and love. They belong together, just as Christian Rosenkreutz and Master Jesus together inspire the development of esoteric Christianity. The anthroposophical movement and the White Brotherhood can therefore mirror each other and learn from each other. The new man of whom they speak needs a healthy body, an etheric body that is energetically balanced, a pure soul, and a strong spirit. To this, both movements can contribute in their own way.

Conclusion:
The Cooperation of Head and Heart

The path of the White Brotherhood begins with the religious conversion of the soul and ends with the spiritual insights that come to the new human being. This path goes from the heart to the head. Anthroposophy goes the opposite way, from the head to the heart—a path that leads from science, through art, to religious deepening. Rudolf Steiner said of this that Anthroposophy everywhere

> begins with science, enlivens its ideas artistically, and ends with religious deepening; it begins with what the head can grasp, continues with what the word can form in the widest sense, and ends with what penetrates the heart with warmth and secures the heart, so that the soul of man may find itself at all times in its proper home, in the realm of spiritual beings. Thus, on the path of Anthroposophy we shall learn to begin with knowledge, raise ourselves to art, and end in religious intimacy.[1]

On both paths, we connect our head and heart. In ancient times, there was no need for this. People then could clairvoyantly perceive thoughts. In ancient Egypt, when the pharaoh's body was embalmed, the brain was removed. After his death, he did not need it. Pharaoh thought with his *heart*—and therefore the heart was preserved separately. This thinking, according to Steiner, occurred in an unconscious way.

As for thinking with the *mind*, this had a long preparatory period that began as early as the end of the Atlantic culture. People who had the aptitude for this thinking were brought together for its further development in the solar oracle in the north of Atlantis. Before

---

1. Rudolf Steiner, lecture of January 30, 1923, in *Awakening to Community* (CW 257).

the demise of this continent, according to Rudolf Steiner, such people as these left for Central Asia under the leadership of Manu. From there, groups were sent out in different waves to give impulses to the cultures of antiquity.

At the beginning of the Greco-Roman cultural period (about 750 BC, according to Steiner), the development of the *intellectual soul* began. This is a "male" function of the soul that allows us to understand what we perceive in the outer world and in our inner world. Our intellect works in an analyzing way and follows logical rules of reasoning; while the soul, in a "female" function, can also internalize from the heart what we want to understand in a non-abstract, living way. From the history of philosophy we can see the development of the intellect, which gives us the possibility of freedom and enables us to make our own decisions. It is the basis of our free personality.

But on the other hand, the mind thereby loses its connection with the spiritual world. The cosmic thoughts that man used to receive have become human, intellectual thoughts. They are dead thoughts. This process of the dying of thought accompanied the development of the intellectual soul, which was concluded at the end of the Middle Ages. At that time, this dead thinking became accessible to anyone who received training in this way of thinking through intellectual education. This process has accelerated in the Western world. We are now developing new faculties in our *consciousness soul*, in which we position ourselves in our scientific consciousness as subjects over against the world of objects. Materialism has become the prevailing worldview.

Anthroposophy is an answer to modern intellectual, materialistic thinking. It opens new paths to the spiritual world and connects thinking with the forces of the heart, so that a living, etheric, flexible, moral, and creative thinking can emerge. This is a new thinking with the heart, which, unlike in the past, is consciously accomplished through the power of the human Self. We are then no longer spectators of world events, but participants who feel connected to them. In Peter Deunov's Bulgaria, people's thinking had not yet become as intellectual as in the West. Only in his youth were schools opened in Bulgaria. Thinking was still strongly connected to the

Conclusion: The Cooperation of Head and Heart

heart forces. Deunov was therefore able to school the Bulgarians in a spiritual way of thinking based on these forces of the heart. We could say that the path of soul development for most Bulgarians runs through the heart, while for most anthroposophists it runs through the brain.

The new spiritual thinking that arises from the cooperation of the human heart and head is a new phase in the development of thinking, a phase that is also being discovered in many areas of science, such as in the investigation of the functions of the heart. For example, the research of the already mentioned American Heart-Math Institute, founded in 1991, speaks about the intelligence of the heart.[2]

In the new view of the heart, this organ is no longer considered a pump, as Steiner and Deunov already knew. The heart does not pump, but "sucks" the blood. About 60% of the cells of the heart are not muscle cells, but nerve cells that are connected to all parts of the body. Through these cells, and using other sensors, the heart receives information to which it responds by releasing hormones and sending messages to the brain in the head. This flow of messages is greater than in the opposite direction. In fact, the heart is a complex center where information is processed. It has its own functional brain, the "brain in the heart."

The heart is surrounded by a pulsating electromagnetic field with a diameter of several meters—a field that is many times stronger than that of the brain. This field envelops all the cells of our body and communicates with the fields of other people around us. This energetic communication between people can affect their brain rhythms and make them more sensitive to each other.

The dominance of our mind, which is only a few centuries old, has brought with it great problems. The essential problems in our lives and in society cannot be solved by our mind. The wisdom of the heart is needed—the mind needs the guidance of the intelli-

---

2. Doc Childre, *Heart Intelligence: Connecting with the Intuitive Guidance of the Heart*, Boulder Creek, 2016. Joseph Chilton Pearce, *The Heart-Mind Matrix: How the Heart Can Teach the Mind New Ways to Think*, Rochester, 2012. See also https://www.heartmath.com/.

gence of our heart. Our heart can make clear to us things that the head does not understand. We make the most important decisions in our lives by listening to our heart in a state of inner balance and harmony. This turning to the intelligence of our heart requires a process of purification; this is because fears and negative feelings also live in our hearts. Before an inner sun can shine from our heart, a deep inner transformation is needed. To this end, Rudolf Steiner elaborated the modern Grail path to enter the Grail temple of our heart before we can do spiritual research, and Peter Deunov pointed out the path to the purification of the heart that is necessary before Christ can live in our hearts.

From the cooperation of head and heart emerges the new human being who creates a new world from spiritual impulses. At the end of his Foundation Stone Meditation, Rudolf Steiner gave a prayer that can accompany this process of creation:

> Godly Light, Christ-Sun,
> Warm our hearts,
> Enlighten our heads,
> That good may become
> What from our hearts we found,
> What from our heads we direct with single will.

Translated Texts and Lectures of Peter Deunov

Translated texts from the years 1895–1944 can be read in English translation at https://powerandlife.com/txt_en/. English translations can also be found at https://arch ive.org/details/PeterDeunov.

English books, which can be ordered from the White Brotherhood Publishing Company in Sofia (izdatelstvo.bratstvo@gmail.com):

Child of the Universe (on health and illness), 2013
Health and Sickness, 2002
Harmonizing of the Human Soul, 2013
Life After the Death of the Physical Body, 2009
Methods for Self-Improvement, 2014
Paneurythmy (course book), 2004
Peter Deunov, Prophet of the New Age, 2014
Prayers, Formulas, Devotional Songs, 2017
The Beauty of Life, 2005
The Language of Love, 2012
The Mindful Heart, 2003
The Salt, 2003
The Blossoming of the Human Soul, 2012
The Wellspring of Good, 2015
The World of Great Souls, 2016
Woman—the Source of Love and Life, 2001

In the United States these books can be ordered from: https://www.everabooks.com/

Books of other publishers:

Beinsa Douno, *The Teacher*, vol. 1, *The Dawning Epoch*, London, 2016
The Sunday Lectures, volumes 1, 2, and 3, Eagle Rock, 2020–2021
David Lorimer, *Prophet for our Times—The Life and Teachings of Peter Deunov*, 2015

www.ingramcontent.com/pod-product-compliance
Lightning Source LLC
Chambersburg PA
CBHW020328170426
43200CB00006B/308